CONVENTS, JAILS AND OTHER TALES

An Overview of the Mystics and Why They Matter

SISTER BARBARA JEAN BROWN, AF

Published in 2015 by Whelkum Books, an imprint of Whelkum Productions.
Copyright © Whelkum 2015

Words of Celebration for Sister B. J. Brown

Don't let the incredible scope of this book scare you off! It is a resource that may prove essential to every person genuinely interested in the spiritual life. Sr. B. J. Brown wisely but simply summarizes centuries of human contact with the divine in a style that will be helpful for the novice to the spiritually adept. She writes both from her considerable scholarship and from her personal experience of "knowing as a form of loving," the mystic way open to all.

—Norvene Vest is a spiritual director and author of What is Your Practice? Lifelong Growth in the Spirit *(Morehouse)*

Concisely written, eminently readable but chock-full of information that will serve any student, any cleric, any would-be mystic or anybody who's ever wondered what on earth the religious life is all about, this is a tremendous historical resource. Sister Barbara Jean's wonderful work reminds me that we relied for centuries solely on the minds and pens of men and women in religious orders for the recording and preservation of human learning, and it is nice to see the tradition of monastic scholarship alive and well in her. This book belongs in parish libraries, in seminary libraries, in monastic libraries and in the libraries of ordinary Christians who love learning about our tradition.

—Barbara Crafton is an Episcopal priest, spiritual director, award-winning author and head of the online institute The Geranium Farm

Dedication

I would like to dedicate this book to all the holy women who have graced my life with their friendship, love, wisdom, guidance, and joy: especially Sharon Vander Zyl, who caused me to begin this book in the first place; Valerie Burg and Michele Whitford, who are my spiritual family; Sister Miriam Therese Putzer, CSA, my amazing spiritual director who taught me more about God with her gentle smile than I would ever learn in books; Sister Julian Wilson, my partner and co-founder of Anamchara Fellowship; The Rev. Emily Schwenker, my dear friend and mentor. And so many others, too many to be named.

Also, I want to thank The Sisterhood of the Holy Nativity who formed me in the Religious Life and nurtured me for so many years...The Anamchara Fellowship, who are my current monastic family, supporting me through their encouragement and love...and also I am so greatly appreciative of and thankful for Dan Somerset, my editor, without whom this book would never have completely come to birth.

CONVENTS, JAILS, AND OTHER TALES
an overview of the mystics and why they matter

Foreword

"How different it is with the man who devotes himself
to studying the law of the Most High, who investigates all the
wisdom of the past, and spends his time studying the prophe-
sies! He preserves the sayings of famous men and penetrates
the intricacies of parables. He investigates the hidden mean of
proverbs and knows his way among riddles. The great avail
themselves of his services, and he is seen in the presence of
rulers. He travels in foreign countries and learns at first hand
the good or evil of man's lot. He makes a point of rising early
to pray to the Lord, his Maker, and prays aloud to the Most
High, asking pardon for his sins. If it is the will of the great
Lord, he will be filled with a spirit of intelligence; then he will
pour forth wise sayings of his own and give thanks to the Lord
in prayer. He will have sound advise and knowledge to offer,
and his thoughts will dwell on the mysteries he has studied. He
will disclose what he has learned from his own education, and
will take pride in the law of the Lord's covenant. Many will praise
his intelligence; it will never sink into oblivion. The memory of
him will not die but will live on from generation to generation;
the nations will talk of his wisdom, and his praises will be sung
in the assembly. If he lives long, he will leave a name in a
thousand, and if he goes to his rest, his reputation is secure."
(Ecclesiasticus 39: 1–11   NEB)

Early in my life as a spiritual mentor, a woman
came to me and complained that she felt that she was
not capable of being a "good Christian". When I questioned her about this, she confided in me that a dear
friend had very enthusiastically given her the book
Dark Night of the Soul by John of the Cross, and it had

i

left her depressed and unsure of her own commitment to Christ. As we talked further, I discovered that she was fairly new to the Episcopal Church, having been raised in the Dutch Reformed tradition. My new friend and I sat for some hours discussing her predicament, and I began to realize that all of the wonderful writings of the "mystics" need to be chosen for spiritual reading with great discernment. Not every book is helpful to every soul at every time. Particularly those new to catholic spirituality need to have more background in the language and concepts of a sacramental or liturgical tradition. I believe it is also imperative to be familiar with the life and times of the chosen author, in order to have a fuller context of the writings. It is with these things in mind that I set out to write a book about the many authors of the Christian mystical tradition.

There is a meaning to life and a way of loving of which many of us are oblivious. We live from day to day, experience to experience, simply doing the things that happen to present themselves. We seldom stop to ponder the greater picture, the grandeur of the world and our place or purpose in the scheme of things. While our daily concerns center around feeding the family and paying the mortgage, our deep, inner concerns focus on war and famine, environmental pollution and a generation gone crazy on drugs. Still we may come to find that we are in the "golden age" of spiritual reawakening. Many seem to have a burning desire to understand the meaning of life and a hunger to make sense out of the contradiction between their Faith traditions and a 21st-Century perspective of the universe. Though we have made rapid advances in science and technology, there is a growing frustration that we are losing our identities, our souls, to progress.

This frustration has led, in recent years, to a new interest in the metaphysical realm of religion and philosophy. While "mainline" churches have experienced a decline in membership, new religious groups, denominations and para-religious cults have become extremely popular. Growing interest in various forms of spirituality, particularly from Eastern or Nature-based traditions, has also had an impact on current American culture to such a degree that many Christians are becoming confused and anxious.

With this search for "inner" truth, there has come a persistent inquiry into mysticism. The last few decades of the 20th Century played host to a rise in the exploration of ancient oriental mysticism by the popularization and even some vulgarization of those traditions. The cults of gurus, swamis and other teachers of meditation styles such as Zen and Transcendental Meditation grew with the interests of people for a deeper meaning to life. Even the use of psychedelic drugs offered one more avenue for the experience with "another dimension of consciousness."

The Christian Mystical Tradition is a rich resource out of our own Western experience and has a history and a significance that reaches back into the Ancient Hebrew experience of Yahweh and moves on through the establishment of the Church into our present experience. This Judeo-Christian expression of the Mystical life, a vast arena of revelation and intimacy spanning centuries and cultures, is therefore the focus of this present work. It is imperative that we learn to understand just what we are dealing with in the exploration of the Mystic Tradition. We need to recognize the common stamp which appears on the diverse coins from the mint of the mystic tradition. That commonality shows itself as a sense of "otherness", a sense of unreality or hiddenness, whether it is in the Judeo-Christian tradition or a tradition of the East. Somehow, somewhere, the mystic establishes a relationship of personal response toward something completely outside the temporal world which he/she regards as ultimately greater than him/herself. However, the "way" of the mystic is not always clear and can, in fact, be dangerous to our spiritual health if we are not willing to proceed with careful consideration of the subject.[1]

The increased popularity of literature pertaining to the inner search and the re-publication of the spiritual classics causes a need to develop a discerning eye before we plunge headlong into the mystic's world. We need to be cautious when picking up and reading any book by a Mystic and expecting it to have all the answers for our spiritual edification. We need to know where our own spirituality lies, and we need to know something about the Mystic of our choice. That is the main purpose behind this study. I hope to provide some basic understanding and discernment of the mystical journey.

In order to take a "mystical journey" to places seldom if ever explored, we will need a map. Maps are among the most indispensable tools for an explorer. They are helpful because they provide a means of locating where something is in relation to something else. They reveal patterns and connections that may otherwise remain obscured. Never totally accurate, a

---

[1] This could be considered analogous to the process of learning to swim. Not often does one begin that process by jumping into the deep end of a pool, but rather by getting used to the waters at the shallow end.

map simply stands as a symbol, giving a point of reference to the subject in question.[2]

So this journey endeavors to take the reader through several centuries of human encounter with the Divine, and begins by defining the term Mysticism. For my purposes here I defer to Evelyn Underhill, herself a 20th-Century spiritual writer and mystic, who describes mysticism as an intense loving between the human spirit and God. She would say that a Mystic is one who has fallen deeply in love with God. There are certainly other and more technical definitions of the term. However, I desire to emphasize that mysticism, in this context, is more a way of life than an isolated event and is ordinary in the life of the Church rather than extraordinary. Within the mystical life there may be moments of the ecstatic or the visionary, but these are not viewed as primary. Initial to the mystical process is its continuity throughout the entire experience of the spiritual devotee. We would do well, then, to dispel the image of the man or women hovering in ecstasy three feet above the prayer desk, even though some mystics did indeed experience such phenomena. Mysticism points to a special way of knowledge. Yet more than discursive reason, being an acquisition and processing of experiential information, mystical knowledge leads to a sense of the "something more". It contains an element of reason but couples with it the elements of intuition or faith. Whereas both discursive reasoning and mysticism lead to a transformation of an individual, mysticism works from the inside out rather than from the outside in. We can turn to the

---

[2] At the end of the present volume are several "Appendixes" which act as kinds of maps in this regard.

example of personal human relationships. In the relationship between two people most of the development happens through experiential interchange. A sense of the mystical is reached when those two persons begin to relate to each other with a more intuitive knowing. It is life-changing, life-enhancing, and life-illuminating. Mystical knowledge is not something that we in our human effort seek to accomplish; rather such an intimate encounter happens in and to us. Religiously speaking, it presupposes a God who desires this sort of familiar relationship with humanity. Christian mystical tradition is based upon the twin premises of "the unknowability of God" on the one hand, and "God's accessibility to love" on the other. It is impossible to find any Christian theology of mysticism which does not give LOVE a crucial role in the process of seeking union with God. In one way or another, each of the Mystic's writings will reveal that the road to union with God is paved by a perfecting of love in the soul. Some of them even go so far as to use sensual language to describe this encounter.

Sister B. J. Brown

*P*assaces

Sr. Miriam Therese Putzer, CSA

Young friend
when you have reached the needle's eye
 you'll stand quite self-assured measure it for size
  and stooping find its archway low – comfort-wise
   – but not impassable.
"Just the pack, the problem, and to lighten it no problem,
really,"

so you'll say...
  but then, in the decisions know the maddening delay of
tossing out retrieving fondling, letting do and
  snatching back again until at last, when
only water and a crust of bread have duped you to a sense of
readiness
   you'll clutch a friendly hand and cry, "Let's go!"
    You'll still not know there isn't room for two
         even in

single

file!
But, if before this searing truth you manage, yet, a stricken
smile
  and acquiesce I cringe against that later day
when I <u>must</u> hear you scream
     for Solomon
        or Socrates
         or Jesus
  to explain away
      the cheat – the optical illusion – when
       with back bent far beyond your will
        and threadbare sack quite empty;
         with gnarled hand pressed tightly
          to a bony thigh you find you still
           don't fit the measure
               of
               the
             needle's
              eye!

TABLE OF CONTENTS

the classical age of mysticism

APPENDIXES

A. Timeline of the Mystics and their Environment
B. Annotated Bibliography of the Mystics' Writings
C. General Bibliography of Works used for this Study
D. Glossary of Terms Concerning Mysticism
   Index

Chapter 1
the Growth and development of Spirituality

I

Christian spirituality came to birth out of a rich heritage of Jewish mystical tradition. I was helped to see these roots as I read a wonderful article on the development of Jewish spirituality, outlined by Rabbi Lawrence Kushner, in an issue of the Carmelite periodical, *Spiritual Life*. It helped me to outline the varied phases each person and institution might enter in the pursuit of a relationship with God. I could very easily see myself in Kushner's description.

The first phase or stage can be described as the *MIDBAR*. This is the stage of pristine freshness, in which the experience of God is unpredictable. Holiness breaks in upon humanity spontaneously, regardless of place or time and is symbolized by such events as the "Burning Bush," the "Pillar of Fire and Cloud", or the appearances of Angels. The Holy God can be encountered by anyone and the initiative is always His.

The next phase comes as a result of the unpredictability of God. Humanity needs order and a sense of management. Thus the era of MISHKAN inaugurates the beginnings of religious institution. Prayers begin to be said at set times and the "Tent" becomes the meeting place between the temporal and the divine. Hope remains that these requisites coincide with the holy event. Yet, as constraining as "tent worship" may be, it is also mobile. God may be worshiped and adored anywhere the "Tent of Meeting" or "Ark of the Covenant" resides.

The normal progression of the institution slowly permeated the spiritual mindset of Hebrew culture, leading to the next stage in its development. The focus of attention, once placed upon the ubiquity of holiness, shifted to the performance of "Solemn High Ritual." The *MIKDASH*, the age of the Temple, usurped the wild spontaneity that once held each person naked before God. No more was the sacred perceived in the wild; rather its solemnity was recalled and performed in strict adherence to ritual, thus establishing a holiness of its own.

The age of the Prophets and Mystics of the Old Testament struggled for a reintroduction of the primacy of personal relationship with Yahweh. Theirs was the age of AWE. They brought a new, symbolic language to their religion and sternly rebuked the "pharisaic" observance of ritual only. Prophetic utterance stirred to remembrance the spontaneous relationship with Yahweh that each person shared. Poignant is the love as displayed in the imagery of Hosea and Deutero-Isaiah.

As the people of Israel listened to these love songs, a final development emerged in their spirituality. A new beginning unfolded as MAKOM—the Place. This word began to be seen as synonymous with other names for God. Rather than venerating Him in a specified place, Yahweh was identified as Himself the place. One is reminded of the story in Scripture of Jacob's dream of the angels ascending and descending the ladder, with his resulting comment, "Truly God was in THIS PLACE and I didn't know it". Could the comment not be restated as correctly, "Surely God is GOD and I didn't know it."?[3]

Journeying through the Judaic experience helps us get a firmer footing upon our own awareness of the stages we have gone through personally and collectively. Though our cultures may differ, the basic religious formation of humanity seems to follow a common course. Whether it runs in cycles or as a continuous process matters not so much as the simple consideration of its influence upon our ability to discern how and where God is communicating His presence to us.

II

In the Christian tradition, mysticism is synonymous with being in touch with the "really real." But for those who have not experienced the ineffable otherness, it seems to be more an unreality. For the spiritual person, reality abides not only in the given, temporal density of earth, but also in that unfathomable abyss where God speaks silently at the depth of the human heart. Mysticism is a living experience of the Divine, not only as an object outside or other and therefore distinctly different from us, but as an encompassing power of love that, as St. Augustine of Hippo said, "is more intimate to us than we are to ourselves."

The goal of the mystic is to establish a conscious union with that Holy and Transcendent Other.

---

[3] The spontaneity of adoration and praise regained an aspect of the Wild, although there has never been a complete circle made to the worship of the MIDBAR.

Each has had a particular and sometimes peculiar way to approach this; but we must bear in mind that those ways proved inspirational for them, and they have much to teach us. The mystic's desire to KNOW in order that they might LOVE can become our desire.

Mysticism poses certain assumptions upon which it builds its framework of operation. First, it maintains that the human soul can see and perceive, as part of its intuitive nature, what lies beyond its normal experiential insight. This means that we have an ability to go "beyond" the physical sense of truth to its meaning or purpose or value. It gives us the power to comprehend as true and valid things that otherwise appear absurd. Second, it claims a human participation in the Divine nature. Because we are created in the "Divine Image", we share in some way, that nature, just as a work of art shares in the nature of the artist. Third, it requires purification of the self in order to attain to the knowledge of God. The purification process is the means by which a person gets rid of all that separates him/her from the true image he/she was meant to manifest. It's a coming to the truth of self. Fourth and most important, mysticism assumes that LOVE will be the guide on the path to union.

The classic or traditional way these assumptions get played out is in the three-fold stages of the Mystic Way. Those stages are generally referred to as Purgation, Illumination and Union. This pattern holds fairly true for all of the major forms of mystical tradition, though they may be expressed in different ways—and the pattern is simply a descriptive sort of "map" which shows the route over which the person passes in the journey toward God.

Let me explain, here, what the stages mean. When one begins the spiritual quest, perhaps in a novitiate type of training, he/she tends to focus on the purging of the negative elements within his/her life, such as sins or bad habits. There is a concentration on removing those evil tendencies or personality flaws which stand as obstacles to one's progress in the spiritual life. People who have attended a Cursillo weekend[4] may be able to identify this with the recognition of our Apostolic failures. As one grows in this knowledge and begins the maturation process, the focus of attention begins to shift from the negative elements within his/her life to those positive ones. This is a movement from purgation to illumination. A positive perception of spiritual values within the person replaces the concentration on removing obstacles. This second stage is more contemplative, a quiet sort of understanding, whereas the first was more active and severe. Finally, if the person continues to progress in the spiritual life and is given abundant graces by God, he/she may enter the final stage of union— habitual intimacy with God, as the climax of the spiritual journey.

The mystic way is a way open to all people, but few have chosen to pursue this way. It is arduous, time consuming and as demanding as any pursuit for excellence. And, for the most part, the mystic way has never fit cultural norms, leaving people hesitant to go the distance out of fear of reprisal or estrangement from what is familiar. I want to stress that the state of Union with God is not so much a "having arrived" as it is a continuous process of "becoming."

---

[4] a short course in Christianity

Psychologists use the term "actualization"; but for the Mystic it is a matter of being "self-in-God actualized" rather than merely "self-actualized." And the movement is ongoing, through life, into Eternity.

A difficulty arises in listening to the voice of the Mystic because many are unaware of several important factors: the historical background of the Mystic, his/her spirituality, and the context out of which the Mystic writes. It is critical to the reader's understanding of a text to know something of the historical setting in which an author lived, whether it be the blood baths of 2nd-Century persecutions, the devastation of the Black Plague, or the fear of nuclear holocaust. Equally important is an understanding of a Mystic's spiritual expression. Is he/she Apophatic or Kataphatic? Speculative or Affective? Finally, a reader must acknowledge the context out of which came a particular piece of mystical literature. Was the author a monastic or a lay theologian? Writing as a solitary or in community? In prison under persecution or at leisure within the comforts of a peaceful environment?

Let me now go back to some words that may have given the beginner in this pilgrimage some pause for concern. I said that a Mystic might be Apophatic or Kataphatic. Apophatic is a word that speaks of the spiritual tradition in which one only knows God by "not knowing." It is called the way of "negation" or the *via negativa* and proposes that anything we can say that we know cannot possibly be God because He is so much greater than our capacity to know. The Apophatic tradition says not that our knowledge of God is false, but simply inadequate, and so prefers to remove all human names and symbols in its pursuit toward union. The Kataphatic tradition, on the other hand, speaks of union with God through the experiences of life, using all that is human in sign and symbol to describe the process. Those Mystics who portray this type of spirituality use many images and allegories to describe holy things. To them, God becomes self-revealing through the experiences of this world.

Mystics might also be speculative or affective in their understanding and articulation of divine truths. Speculative Mystics depend primarily upon the mental processes of discursive reason. These tend to find God in the intellect, in the process of mental activity. The Mystics who lean more toward an affective experience of God do so by way of the emotions or affections rather than the intellect. Neither way is better than the other or more direct a path than the other. Each has its place in the development of religious devotion.

III

Just as we recognize the development of Judaic spirituality as a useful tool for discerning the encounter with a Reality beyond our reality, it might also be helpful to distinguish the development of the spiritual language in which the Mystics write. The fact of a specific or special jargon should not surprise us. In trying to communicate the ineffable, mystics have had to utilize the symbols and metaphors available to their own time and culture. As one reads a treatise of the 3rd Century one can grasp that the tenor in which it was written. As one reads a treatise of the 3rd Century one can grasp that the tenor in which it was written. From my reading of the history of Christian spirituality I believe that there have been five basic languages spoken in the course of the Christian Centuries.

Not long after the smoke settled from the Fire of Pentecost, disputes concerning the true natures of God and Man arose. The apologies and the true natures of God and Man arose. The apologies and treatises that form our foundational doctrines were expressed in ONTOLOGICAL language.[5] Some of this type of writing can be tedious and confusing to those who have never encountered it, and yet it is a very important and fundamental stage in the development of our understanding of the Divine and human encounter.

As Christianity became fashionable, causing the strictly devout to flee to the desert, a new language emerged. This was the language of the ASCETIC. The writings shifted from a defense of the Faith to guidance through "Spiritual Combat." The demons cloaked their identity as the passions and temptation of the human soul, and the Desert Fathers

---

[5] Ontology has to do with the nature of being, which discusses such concerns as whether Jesus IS or IS LIKE God, that He has ONE NATURE or TWO.

gave warning via their own experiences and discernment of them. The internal threat of spiritual dissipation held as much cause for alarm as did the external intimidation of the heretics. Once the Institution of the Church became a dominating force in society, politically, economically as well as spiritually, another language dominated, namely INSTITUTIONAL. This vocabulary resonates very much of "systemic control," which desires order and specific results through devotion. One is reminded of the era of *MIKDASH*, Temple Worship of the Hebrew heritage when rituals and formulas took the place of direct confrontation with the Divine. For "so many" prayers God will grant "so many" favors. As the age of science and Renaissance dawned, the religious language moved in the direction of

Apophatic Affective

John Cassian
Bernard of
Clairvaux
Adam of St. Victor
Hugh of St. Victor
Richard of St.
Victor
Julian of Norwich
the "Cloud"
Author
John of the Cross
Jane Frances de
Chantal
Madame Guyon
François Fénelon
Charles de
Foucauld

The mystics on these sidebars are listed in these various categories as I personally see them.
I believe there is room for debate and would entertain differing points of view. This is simply my way of painting a picture of the spiritual masters.

subjective idealism. This was a ROMANTIC age,[6] an age of flowery love songs and chivalrous declarations. The Protestant revolt helped break the absolute power of the Church and gave back to the people the courage to express their own understanding of God. The individual characterization of piety came through as a type of disincarnated interiority that led to the Quietist movement of the 17th Century.[7] To counter that extreme, piety also took the form of intense exercises which used the concrete mediations of Christianity's flesh and blood reality. This can be characterized as an extreme dependence upon rites and rituals, traditions and customs, leaving no room for the spontaneous inspiration of the Holy Spirit.

The last stage of development in spirituality's language, thus far, began to take shape in the exploration of human psychology. From Freud and Jung we have moved into the realm of the

[6] distinct from the specific period of the 19th Century
[7] The fundamental principle of Quietism was a condemnation of all human effort in relation to God, sort of the ultimate in passivism.

PSYCHOLOGICAL. The language is still subjective but has shifted from "idealism" to "behaviouralism." Many spiritual authors within the last hundred years have placed a greater emphasis on an individual's formation factors, be they environmental, cultural, or even parental. In taking the journey inward, toward the center of the soul, our present expressions of faith sometimes look more like religious navel-gazing contemplation.

So recognition must be made of the style or "language" in which a Mystic wrote of his or her experiences of God. None of this should put us off but rather help to enlighten us as to the true depth of the message contained within a work. Just because a piece of Mystic literature is written in quite a different style from what we are used to, discouragement need not arise as regards its relevance and ability to nurture us personally.

IV

By no means am I trying to imply that one must become a scholar before reading

Kataphatic
Speculative
dietRich
Bonhoeffer
Simone Weil
matthew fox
William Johnston
GeoRge maloney

and benefiting from the works of these spiritual masters. However, I am stressing the importance of spending some time learning the background and biography of the Holy person. Such knowledge helps that person become like a companion on the journey through the Mystic's spiritual experience. Often this can be easily accomplished by a thorough reading of the preface or introduction from an edition of one of these classics. Too often we skip over these because we are anxious to get to the heart of the matter.

Along with an understanding of the Mystic's spirituality is a need to begin a discovery of our own. As we begin to make this discernment, it will become clearer why certain Mystics really speak to our hearts and why others leave us completely baffled. In the process of disclosure, whether we are more "thinkers" than "feelers" or whether we prefer the use of imagery or not, we can begin to find those spiritual authors who elicit a response of understanding and solidarity in us. Then we will come to know them as spiritual mentors and realize just how timeless the Communion of Saints really is. Understanding that a Mystic—like Meister Eckhart of 14th-Century Germany—speaks from an Apophatic/Speculative tradition[8] will help one who prefers a more affective and image-centered spirituality to cope with what he/she is reading. It also gives an opportunity to the reader to experience an author of an opposite spirituality without feeling so intimidated. There are a multitude of mystical writers who are important to our Christian heritage. Some are well known and their works have been continually republished and read by generation after generation. Some, however, are little known, but are being rediscovered by the enthusiastic search for spiritual advancement.

This may still seem pretty cerebral or academic. Why should we want to know about this side of the Christian experience? Most of us are not called or inclined to the mystical way of life. At least we are not called

Kataphatic Affective
Henri Nuvelm
Baron Friedrich von hügel
Evelyn Underhill
Thérèse of Lisieux
Elizabeth of the Trinity
Thomas Merton
Mother Teresa of Calcutta
Henri J.M. Nouwen
Richard J. Foster
Madeleine L'engle
Desmond Tutu
William McNamara
Basil Pennington
Richard Rohr

---

[8] i.e., of the intellect and without images

in the same way as Moses, Augustine, or Julian. However, I believe that most of us have had, at one time or another, an experience in which we were touched deeply; moved to the point of tears or awe by some indescribable revelation—and it changed us—even if only for that moment. Or there is within us that gnawing desire to know more, to go deeper into our Christian experience. The Mystics help us make some sense out of all of this.

We touch on some rather heavy theological ideas as we look at the Mystics, but not all mysticism or mystical experiences are heavy. They may be nothing stronger than an intuitive "A-ha" experience or the "rush" caused by an exquisite experience of beauty. But these moments are periods of transcendent, transforming encounter with Something or Someone beyond our normal sphere of reality.

The Mystics are people who live their whole lives in communion or relationship with this Someone. All that most of us can hope for is the momentary glimpse "beyond the veil". St. Paul tells us that, "now we see through a glass dimly, but then we shall see face to face." The Mystics are those who have transcended the normal processes of time by anticipating in their lives what we all hope for in the age to come. They have basked in the Beatific Vision here and now; and this is why we look to them—even envy them—for they have been to "the other side" and share with us, through their writings, what it is like.

What follows is a somewhat chronological view of the Mystics and their times. Hopefully, this will give an introduction to the saints that are not commonly known as well as a reintroduction to the giants of the Mystic Way. My hope is that this will generate a desire in the reader to pursue a deeper understanding of his/her own spiritual journey and an interest to find out what contributions these Mystics have made to the Mystical Tradition and our own Christian heritage.

Chapter 2

The Early Mystics

would like to begin this tour of the Mystic Tradition with a story I was told while on a retreat, some years ago. It seems that a young man interested in the holy life went to seek advice from an ancient and venerable hermit. He found the old ascetic seated at the entrance to his cave, his faithful dog at his side. The young man presented his question thus: "Abba, why is it that some who seek The Way of Eternal Salvation leave it after a year or two of zealous prayer and pious devotion, yet others, such as yourself, are able to continue in their pilgrimage for a whole lifetime?"

The holy hermit, stroked his long beard and after a few moments said, "Let me answer your question with a story. One day my dog and I were sitting here, much as we are now, when the biggest rabbit I had ever seen came racing past us. Naturally, my dog, as old as she is, took out after the rabbit, howling at the top of her voice. She caused such a fuss that soon other dogs joined in the chase. They went up over hills, through streams, and into the briars and thorns of the underbrush. After a while the other dogs fell back, some to scratch a flea, some because they had been distracted by another scent, until only my dog remained in undistracted pursuit of the rabbit. In this story is the answer to your question."

The young man sat puzzled for several minutes and then found the courage to admit that he did not understand what the story of the rabbit chase had to do with his question. The wise hermit replied, "You do not understand the connection because you fail to ask the proper question. Why was it that the other dogs stopped the chase? They stopped because they had not actually seen the rabbit. Their interest was only in the excitement caused by my dog, who had seen it, and who kept after it until it was caught. Unless you see what it is that you are pursuing, the course is just too difficult to maintain. So it is with the pursuit of holiness. Unless you have seen the Lord for yourself, you will soon lose heart, or lose interest." As much as this story applies to each of us on our spiritual journey, we will see how truly it exemplifies the lives of the Mystics. These people committed themselves to the chase and were able to persevere vibrantly, though not without hardship, throughout their varied lives of holiness. They had seen the rabbit. They had seen Jesus. And they never allowed themselves to lose sight of Him, even in their darkest nights.

The Early Church, as I define it, is the period from the feast of Pentecost to approximately the 8th Century, was marked by persecutions and heresy. This was also the age of the Roman Empire and its subsequent fall to the barbarians from the North. It was a critical age when the foundations of our doctrines were defined. We might well call it the Great Age of Doctrine, for it was the time when the Creeds were formulated and the Church was forced to define and defend its belief in such a way as to leave no doubt as to its unique place in history.

I want to add a footnote here about the study of any aspect of our Faith. We must be willing to look at the environment in which the expression of the Faith lived: social, economic, political and religious. Most often these influences have had a great impact upon our tradition and understanding, yet we have allowed our historical ignorance to keep us blinded to their importance.

Paul of Tarsus
c. 5 – c. 67
KATAPHATIC
SPECULATIVE

The first Mystic we meet on our journey is Paul of Tarsus. Of all the Mystics, he is probably the most familiar to us; yet we possibly have not considered him in this category.

Paul possessed a temperament susceptible to his environment. An ardent Jew of the Pharisaic party, he also was influenced by the Hellenistic culture in which he lived. His familiarity with Greek philosophy is evident in many passages of his Epistles. He was eloquent and yet possessed of an earthiness that had an appeal to the several levels of society. Paul's natural appeal was toward religion. To him God was the Holy, Omnipotent Lord, with whom he craved total intimacy. The Mystic process and Mystic's goal exude from his spirituality.

The experience on the road to Damascus is probably the most celebrated of all mystical phenomena, but notice that it is not the "experience" alone that commands our attention; rather, it is Paul's transformed life. From the moment of his blinding conversion, throughout his tempestuous journeys and ultimately to his death at Rome, we find a man whose every breath and movement were calculated in accordance with his commitment to running the race set before him.

He speaks this way in several passages of his epistles, and he uses language that reminds us of those three classical stages in the pursuit of holiness: The Purgative Stage (Ephesians 4:22): "Put off your old nature which belongs to your former manner of life." The rest of chapter 4 deals with the specifics of how to do just that. The Illuminative Stage can be seen in a passage such as Galatians 6:14: "But far be it from me to glory except in the Cross of our Lord Jesus Christ, by which the world has been crucified to me and I to the world". Finally, in the Unitive Stage—of which Paul's letter to the Philippians is an example—he speaks with the imagery of the unitive life (3:8): "I count everything as loss because of the surpassing worth of knowing Christ Jesus my Lord."

He exhorts his hearers to pray constantly and in the most famous and beloved passage, I Corinthians 13, we become aware that he uses expressly poetic imagery to bring a soul to the knowledge of divine love. Paul shows us plainly throughout his letters that he is convinced of man's participation in the Divine nature, a conviction that is at the heart of all mysticism. It is this affinity that makes the finite human capable of being filled with Divine Love.

Paul not only was a Mystic, but also he was a teacher of mystical doctrine. He may have based his teaching on his own radical experience, but his methods were influenced by the educational model of his day, Hellenism.

ORIGEN
185 - 254
KATAPHATIC
SPECULATIVE

It is this model I want to explore next, in one of the most dynamic figures of the early 3rd Century: Origen of Alexandria. Origen's life story is preserved primarily through an early book on Church history by Eusebius of Caesarea. One advantage we have in reading of Origen there is that it was written when the teaching and memory of Origen was still fresh. Written about 300 A.D., it gives us a rare glimpse into an era of the birth pangs of our own Christian heritage.

Origen was born in the years of the persecution by Septimius Severus. His own father was killed in this persecution about the year 202 A.D., when Origen was seventeen years old. It is of significance that Origen was born into a Christian family and had a Christian upbringing. Many other great teachers and saints of this period were converts from other religions or from schools of philosophy, so it holds some interest to us that Origen begins his life in a Christian household, being taught at an early age by his father the Faith that he cherished.

Origen was anxious to follow the example of his father and claim the crown of martyrdom but was thwarted in this pursuit by his mother.[9] Though he did not die with his father, this event in Origen's life began within him a profound "martyr mentality", to be faithful even to death. In Origen's view, the body wholly surrendered to the task of signifying a commitment to God's call. This was a perspective to which he clung for the rest of his life. For him, martyrdom brought a soul to the reality of the Resurrected

---

[9] hiding his clothes so that he could not get out of the house

life. Martyrdom became a kind of continuation of the work of redemption. Even the people who came to Origen for instruction in subsequent years were running the risk of martyrdom, so his teaching of the Faith and the preparation for martyrdom were essentially one and the same. Origen taught by example as well as by word, for he made it a practice to visit those who were condemned. He saw to their physical and emotional needs even as they were being led to their deaths. Oddly enough, Origen's own persecution came not from the State, but from the Church he dearly loved. Demetrius, the Bishop of his home diocese of Alexandria, was much opposed to Origen and jealous of his intellectual abilities. He first forbade Origen to preach in Alexandria and then proceeded to depose him from the priesthood altogether. Origen's exile took him to Caesarea, where he spent the next twenty-two years writing and building up his phenomenal library.

The study of Holy Scripture was Origen's burning passion. In his lifetime he was able to complete a commentary or sermon on almost every passage of the Old and New Testaments. As he progressed in his catechetical teaching, the scientific[10] exploration of each and every passage became foremost. Even from his earliest childhood we read of his interest in the inner meaning of Scripture, and as he matured he blended the cosmology[11] and anthropology[12] of his day with his interpretation of Scripture.

The times of early doctrinal development and practical survival mark the era of Origen's influence

---

[10] as science was conceived in his day
[11] view of how the world operates
[12] how humans operate

on the Church and on its spirituality. Christianity arose on Jewish soil and was firmly rooted in the theology of the Old Testament, but relatively soon, as noted with Paul, this religion spread into the Hellenistic world. Origen played a very large role in the wedding of two distinct religious cultures, Judaic and Greek, into one homogeneous entity. Once he melded the two minds, the road was paved for Christianity to become a religion of Europeans, or Western dialectics.[13] It was thus of prime significance that the Alexandrian school of theology blended both the religious and philosophical elements of knowledge into teaching that held doctrinal and ecclesial authority. In the East, Christian thought was not so sharply defined nor rigidly regimented, making various approaches to theology more open to variety and shift. In the West, the eclectic approach to theology was viewed with grave suspicion. The Church, under Tertullian's influence, became much more institutionalized and theology developed along a narrower scheme. It was from the West that Origen met with his most ardent detractors, primarily Jerome, two centuries after his death. They seemed to ignore the fact that Origen himself made their rebuttal possible.

Origen's background in grammatical (secular) education and his insistence that his students learn all they could in these fields show this trend toward cooperative intermingling between faith and reason, philosophy and Gospel. It becomes evident as one reads his work that by combining several different activities—Biblical allegory, Greek philosophy, and Judaic revelation—he, more than any other theologian

---

[13] this being a dialogue of reasoning about a subject or thesis

until Thomas Aquinas, tries to unite the world as one entity. However, in comparing him to Thomas one must be aware that Thomas' theology was built upon a grand systematic structure, whereas Origen's was built upon a structure that was still in infant stages of development.

One piece of Origen's which has come down to us and which is illustrative of his place among the early mystics is his commentary on the *Song of Songs*. In it we find his thesis of the human potential for union with God. He submits that we were created in God's image in order to bring forth a capacity for knowledge and fellowship with Him, which other creatures do not possess. Our striving for a union of love with God is actually a completion of our true nature. Yet, as great a burden as this is, it is only a potential, for God alone holds the power to cause this unity. Here we find an early proposition of God's ability and humanity's "response-ability," which leads to Divine Union.

Cappadocian fathers
e.g., Gregory of Nyssa
330 - 395
APOPHATIC
SPECULATIVE

It may be argued that Origen belongs to the category of early Scholastics rather than Mystics, for so much of his work sets up the beginnings of systematic theology. However, by broadening the definition of Mysticism to include all who are possessed by a love affair with God, he most certainly fits within the roles of mystical culture. In fact his contribution has been invaluable to it. Origen closed the gap once and for all between Christianity and the philosophical world. He brought intellectual competence into evangelical witness and made it possible for Christianity to gain respect. He, along with the rest of the Alexandrian school, helped to transform a heathen empire into a Christian one by converting Hellenistic philosophy into ecclesiastical philosophy. He established the principle that Christianity is an intelligent religion as well as an intuitive one. By bringing the vigor of Greek philosophical insight to bear on the light of Hebrew tradition and Christian devotion, Origen made possible an expanded articulation of the mystic's experience. He paved the way for Gregory of Nyssa (330–395), who is the next beacon on our pilgrimage. Gregory was the younger brother of Basil the Great and a good friend of Gregory of Nazianzus. He was made bishop of Nyssa, a small See, under the greater jurisdiction of Basil. He hated the position and always felt diminished by the dynamism of Basil. Of these three Cappadocian Fathers, Gregory of Nyssa is the one to whom we can best relate. He is the least proud and possibly the most subtle of them. His commitment to the magnificence of humanity comes through his two great mystical works, *The Life of Moses* and *On the Creation of Man*.

In the Eastern tradition, mysticism primarily applies to the forms of perception related to the Christian mysteries rather than a pursuit of the will toward a defined goal. What this means is that within Eastern spirituality there is an innate sense of the holy which dwells within creation. The West systematizes spirituality into a more or less dualistic pattern of striving after a holiness which was lost at the Fall.

Western Christians tend more to explain and justify the great realities of life instead of simply reveling in them. It is, for someone like Gregory, more important to simply stand in the presence of mystery, gazing intently, than to come to some responsive conclusion about it.

To be sure, holiness does not just happen to the soul who desires it, according to Gregory. Holiness is the result of a life of virtue in the one who deliberately seeks training and illumination, as Moses did. The reward for this diligence is an even greater desire, a yearning for the hidden life of God, and because God is without limit, in Gregory's theological concept, the soul's journey toward Him is just as limitless.

In all of the awe we might develop for a spiritual visionary such as the Bishop of Nyssa, it is enjoyable to note how very down-to-earth he actually was. An illustration of this comes by way of a story about him. It seems that Basil was having a quarrel with his and Gregory's uncle, also a bishop under Basil's jurisdiction. Gregory was sensitive to this family rift and sought to help heal the feud by forging a letter of apology from his uncle to Basil. We are told that Basil became aware of the fraud and scolded Gregory for his un-episcopal and immature action. However, it seems that the reconciliation desired by Gregory held.

The works of Gregory contributed to the great stream of English mysticism of the 14th Century, for he clearly influenced Pseudo-Dionysius who, in turn, influenced several Medieval Mystics. It is Gregory who was first to speak of "the dark night of the soul" and first to describe in any detail the complexities of the mystical consciousness. We are indebted to him and the rest of his Cappadocian brethren for articulating the Faith in such a way as to root us deeply in the orthodoxy of our heritage. We need always to recall that to be "orthodox" is to pursue the Truth in all its integrity. Every age is afflicted with a tendency to wander off in myriad directions, following the whims and fancies of popular opinion. Anglicanism, particularly, has continually sought guidance from these early "Fathers of the Church" for this very reason.

Evagrius Ponticus
346 - 399
APOPHATIC
SPECULATIVE

Around the same time, another figure was emerging in the fertile pastures of the Middle East. Evagrius Ponticus, deeply influenced by Gregory and Origen, was able to maintain his own distinctive character, and in turn influenced others. I suppose that technically I should place my discussion of him in the chapter on Monasticism, but it is important to discuss him here in that he acts very much as a bridge between the dogmatic fathers and monastic fathers of the Early Church.

Evagrius was the son of a "choirbishop".[14] Evagrius was ordained Deacon and in the early period of his ministry was quite ambitious. The prestige and pleasures of the world worked their wiles on him; but after a traumatic experience in romance with a married woman, he chose to escape the clutches of licentious living. He began a pursuit of austerity

---

[14] one who has all the essential powers of the episcopal order but is limited in function and is usually under the jurisdiction of a Metropolitan

through desert monasticism and became known as one of the founders of this distinctive spirituality.

It was not long before Evagrius' pursuit of holiness was noted throughout Egypt and Palestine. His piety and articulate wisdom began to filter out from his place of solitude to the Church at large. The Patriarch of Egypt was impressed with what he heard of Evagrius' astute sense of human nature and requested that he be presented for ordination to the episcopate. Taking the advice of the desert tradition, Evagrius ardently avoided women and bishops, seeking to maintain his life of strict asceticism. He remembered what a snare ambition had been for him before.

He was the first important writer of Desert Monasticism, the first to organize a coherent system for others to follow. But more important to the subject of mysticism, it was Evagrius, the master psychologist, who articulated for the Church the inner workings of the human mind as it undergoes the invisible combat of the spiritual life. It was he who gave us the list of the eight deadly passions that lead us away from God. They are gluttony, fornication, covetousness, anger, sadness, boredom, vainglory, and pride.

We find in Evagrius an early study of the human psyche, in a specifically Christian context. This may seem startling to those who have dabbled in modern psychology, but we must always remember that the Truth we seek about God and ourselves is not a "modern" phenomenon. Even without the aid of diagnostic analysis and group therapy, the Mystics down through the centuries have understood the necessity of integration between our "dark side" or "lower nature" and our divinely etched image. Evagrius, unlike some Mystics, gives credence to the benefits humanity derives from our natural passions, that contrary to seeking to eradicate them, we need to understand and control them for our good and for the glory of God.

True prayer, for Evagrius, is entering into a void or an emptying of all thoughts in order that the monk may receive, in his deepest consciousness, the glorious presence of interior light. This he calls "Pure Prayer" and sees as man's ultimate end: to experience God immediately as light without the medium of any sense, thought, concept or image.

Light is one of the images frequently used by the Mystics. Other common images a reader will encounter are fire, heat, lover, beloved, bride, and bridegroom. Evagrius prefers the image of light, which he sees as the transforming agent, shining into the depths of a person's spirit, bringing one into the divine life of shared experience with God.

Pseudo-Dionysius
the Areopagite
5th to 6th Century
APOPHATIC
SPECULATIVE

We move on to a writer who had far reaching influence on medieval mysticism and in whom the Eastern tradition comes to a climax (and in a certain sense, an end). He is known as Pseudo-Dionysius the Areopagite and it was supposedly he who heard St. Paul preach in Athens on Mars Hill.[15] However, since his writings date only as far back as the early 6th Century, his claim to being Paul's disciple is highly suspect. Whoever he

---

[15] We hear of him referred to as St. Denis by the Medieval French Church.

was, his influence had one of the greatest impacts on Mystical theology for several centuries.

Dionysius was probably a Syrian anchorite.[16] We can most definitely categorize him as an apophatic/speculative mystic.[17] The writings he left are not extensive in number nor expansive in discourse, but they are a distinctly vivid portrayal of the early Christian's use of Neo-Platonic philosophy in explaining how humanity finds fulfillment in God.[18]

Articulated in Dionysius is a particular philosophical theology. Following in the path cut by Gregory of Nyssa and Evagrius Ponticus, Dionysius defines the mystery of spiritual growth in terms of cloud and darkness, but central to his theme and peculiar to him is the imagery of hierarchical order. This structure is spelled out in the nine choirs of angels, who are the emanations from the throne of God. The point is not so much their ordered place as that they are in reciprocal relationship with God. It is a give and take, an ebb and flow. The closer one is to God, the more readily one expresses the Divine attributes. One might think of this in more modern terms. Instead of the angelic order the concept can be played out using the symbols of molecules, atoms, cells, etc. The purpose of this hierarchy is to provide a place for purification, and so there is a constant communication flowing between the various gradations of creation. This will find

---

[16] one who lives alone, usually isolated from others by a specific enclosure
[17] one who deals primarily with the intellect and without images
[18] Neo-Platonism is a philosophic discipline which promotes the duality of nature, the definite distinction between matter and spirit.

its ultimate expression in "deiformity," being conformed to the Divine nature.

This mysticism is primarily derived from Hellenistic sources, although Dionysius also makes use of Jewish concepts. The whole of it is adapted to form a highly developed system, much of which is fleshed out by later mystics. For Dionysius, whatever *is* is part of the Divine Love and Life. Each order in its turn necessarily helps the others and thus provides support for the process of purification, illumination, and union.

To Dionysius, the Divine Love is an eternal circle. It flows from its Source of goodness, through the virtue of goodness, and back again to Ultimate Goodness. This concept might be easily compared with Julian of Norwich:[19] "Who showed it you? Love! What did He show you? Love! How did he show you? By Love!" By these parallels we can begin to see the influence Dionysius had on the medieval mind. Whereas their concentration lay with thoughts of the Beatific Vision, Dionysius provided a structure for them to proceed from the purification of an image whose origin was divine, through illumination of the soul, and ultimately to reunion.

But I have jumped ahead a century by speaking of Dionysius. I did so in order to follow a fairly consistent line in the Early Church's development of her spiritual life. I said that with Dionysius Eastern mysticism comes to a climax and a sort of end. Why an end? It is because we find that dogmatic and spiritual theology slowed to a turtle's pace at this time in the Eastern Church. It never again regained the momen-

---

[19] English 14th-Century Mystic

tum it had in the age of the Great Councils. Orthodoxy of the East settled down to the beauty and wonder it possessed then and refrained from venturing past those triumphs.

It seems as though revelation stopped for the Orthodox by the 8th Century. Once the battle over iconoclasm[20] was won at the Seventh Ecumenical Council (780 A.D.), it is as if they picked up their toys and went home, declining to discuss any more theological issues. Of course, the final split between East and West did not occur until 1054 A.D., but that seems more a political formality.

This is, of course, a gross oversimplification and does not do justice to the wonderful heritage of Orthodox spirituality. Historically we must recall that in the 6th Century there was a rise of the Islamic religion, and much of the Eastern Church was preoccupied with simply surviving. The Moslem empire began to swallow up the entire Middle East—the heart of Patristic thought—and so it is inevitable that systematic and mystical theology shifts to the West.

Augustine of Hippo
345 – 430
KATAPHATIC
AFFECTIVE

Now I want to back up a few steps to the middle of the 4th Century. We leave the Middle East and travel along the northern coast of Africa, to the city of Hippo. If you guessed that our next stop is with Augustine, you are right.

Augustine is extremely important in the expansion of theology in the Western Church. He is known

---

[20] the use of icons in worship

primarily for his prowess in defending the Faith against heresy, especially that of Pelagianism.[21] But he is also a loved and respected teacher of the spiritual life. With Augustine the Church begins to define itself as distinct from the East. Augustine, along with Tertullian, makes up a bridge between Oriental and Occidental thought. One thing we need to keep in mind, however, is that the Western Church has read the works of the Eastern Fathers primarily through Augustine's eyes. Only in more recent studies do we find a purer presentation of Eastern spirituality.

It is in Augustine that a preoccupation with sins of the flesh, particularly sex,[22] become the primary battleground for the pursuit of holiness. Because of his own struggles in this area, he viewed humanity as ultimately unable to reach perfection. For him, man could do nothing without Divine Aid—Grace. We may be reminded of a Protestant leaning in this direction: a downplaying of human worth.

Possibly what we owe to Augustine, above all other mystics of this early period, is gratitude for his honesty and skill in revealing himself so humbly to his readers. To agree or disagree with his thesis of God and man is a matter for theological debate and quite beyond the scope of this presentation. For the purposes of this pilgrimage, it is vital to note Augustine's candor concerning his own spiritual development. It is this aspect of the Bishop of Hippo with which we can best identify, even if it does make us somewhat uncomfortable. He was a man of passion and that pas-

---

[21] Pelagius was the British monk who promoted the idea that man takes the prime initiative in his own salvation.
[22] for him sex was inherently sinful

sion, coupled with his keen mind, draws us irresistibly to listen to him.

We need also to remember the time in which he wrote. It was the end of the reign of Rome, when all its glory had turned to debauchery and filth. Invasion from the barbarous hordes proved its ultimate downfall. Augustine wrote his mammoth work, *The City of God*, in an attempt to refocus the eyes of the wounded Church upon a city that was Eternal in Heaven rather than on Rome, thought to be the eternal city here on earth. Augustine's spirituality was by no means an ethereal piosity, but a hardcore certainty of life, dealing with "this" man in "this" place at "this" time.

Augustine helps us journey into the inner sanctum of the soul. He charts the way, through his own spiritual biography and through a countless number of ponderings on theological themes. He fleshes out, in concrete terms, the failings of philosophy alone and sets a standard which theologians and mystics follow even to the present. There is no doubt that Augustine, for good or for bad, is a force to be dealt with at some point on the spiritual journey.

Maximus the Confessor
580 – 662
APOPHATIC
SPECULATIVE

Discussion of the Mystics of the Early Church cannot end until some mention is made of Maximus the Confessor. Maximus illustrates for us a 7th-Century defense of Orthodoxy. The heresy of his day, Monothelitism, claimed that there was only one "will" in the God-Man, Christ. Orthodox Christianity claims two wills, corresponding with the two natures of divinity and humanity. Accordingly, Maximus saw in the heresy a blatant attack against the mystery of the Incarnation, the Word made flesh. For him, the Word Incarnate was the center of his theology and his spirituality and he would not abide any distortion of that Divine reality. Maximus spent his life and his ministry in the discussion and the defense of how the Divine nature operates within humanity.

Maximus made his principal contribution to the mystic tradition by rescuing Dionysius' structure of Neo-Platonic Christianity from its detractors.[23] It was here that Maximus had his primary struggle with the heretics. Rousing Pope Martin I to join in the battle for orthodoxy, they both met a seeming defeat. The Emperor Constantius II, a supporter of the Monothelitic cause, exiled the Pope and sent Maximus with two of his companions to be exiled and tortured. After a scourging, these brave defenders of the Faith had their right hands cut off and their tongues pulled out. Consequently their time in exile was short because they died of their wounds.

Remembering that this early period of the Church's life was spent in continual struggles over doctrinal purity, it took men like Athanasius and Maximus to keep the balance between dogma and spirituality. The latter's interpretation of the works of Dionysius characterizes a grounding in the tradition of the Cappadocian Fathers and perpetuates, for all

---

[23] Dionysius, as was noted earlier, had created a synthesis between Neo-Platonism and Christianity, two disciplines that were otherwise hostile toward each other. In this synthesis there came to be seen an intimate union between God and the soul and the progressive deification of humanity.

time, the *via negativa* or apophatic spirituality proposed by Gregory of Nyssa and Dionysius. Maximus also carried on the system of purification, illumination, and unification which Dionysius inaugurated. According to Maximus, true knowledge of God could only be acquired through mystic contemplation. The ultimate deification of a soul was brought about by the cleansing of love and a merging of the will with that of the Divine.

Among Maximus' spiritual affirmations are those that influenced Bernard of Clairvaux concerning the significance of ecstasy, as the soul moves in Divine charity. Central to that point of view is *philautie*, the love of the self for the sake of God.[24] Maximus promoted a true humility of loving the self for God's sake rather than our own. It is a hard balance to maintain and one which continues to be misunderstood. Clearly Maximus brings an important doctrine to bear on the Church's life and teaching; namely, that the end of all creation is the deification of humanity.

---

[24] We have seen the pendulum swing from a complete distrust and loathing of self to the completely opposite attitude of total self-conceit.

Chapter 3
the Monastic Ideal

We travel from Hippo back to the desert of Egypt. Much of the spirituality within this survey overlaps from one era, school of thought, or ethnic background to another. Sometimes this movement is almost indistinguishable so that it is practically impossible to define the distinctions in solid terms. Mysticism, as you may be finding out, is not an exact science—and neither is the study of it. One cannot cut it up into tidy compartments, though there are many theologians, philosophers, and psychologists who have tried to claim that "THIS" is mysticism. Rather, one should remain open-minded and view the mystic tradition as overlapping spheres of experience and a comprehension and articulation of those experiences.

It is important to discuss the Monastic phenomenon in looking at any aspect of Mysticism because so much of what we classically understand of the spirituality of mysticism comes from the monastic tradition. I am convinced that anyone who does not understand the essential elements of the monastic tradition will not be able to comprehend the mystical tradition. There has always been, in the Christian heritage, a vital link between these two foundations. However, it must also be remembered that they are distinct and separate spiritualities.

The Monastic Movement began in earnest roughly about the time when the Emperor Constantine legally sanctioned Christianity as the official religion of the empire. Opening these doors, making Christianity not only welcome but also fashionable, brought a dissipation of its ideals and a relaxation of the struggle after perfection. The emphasis moved from sanctification of persons to the right ordering and administration of the growing institution of the Church.

Up to this time holiness was equated with martyrdom, the gaining of the crown of righteousness through death. Now, no more were men and women to win their glory in the arena or by the sword, so a new way of sacrifice was sought. The true and devout disciple escaped the lowering standards of the Church by a solitary pursuit in the desert.[25] These people would seek their crown through the subjection of their bodies and minds to the rigors of the desert and the sacrifice of all "worldly" pleasures.

Remember that the marriage of religious faith with philosophical thought had been consummated by Clement and Origen. So these "Desert Fathers" had a fertile spiritual and psychological field to cultivate in their own unique way. The desert experience began tangibly with people like Anthony and Pachomius, but it came to blossom under the guidance of Evagrius Ponticus, Macarius of Egypt, and John Cassian.

Macarius of Egypt
300 - 390
Kataphatic
Speculative

Macarius was one of the outstanding spokesmen for the "charismatic" Christians of the 4th Century. It is sup-

---

[25] thus the diminutive, "White Martyrdom", as opposed to the "Red Martyrdom" of spilled blood

posed that he lived as a hermit in the desert of Scetis in Egypt for sixty years and was renowned for his gifts of discernment, healing, spiritual direction, and prophecy. His name in Greek means "Blessed One", but whether it was actually his name or a term of respect is open for speculation. So, too, do scholars debate his actual place of residence, whether it was in Egypt or in northern Syria. In any case, his distinction as a wise man gives us an extraordinary example of the ideals of early desert spirituality. Of particular value to us are his *Fifty Spiritual Homilies*, which have attracted the attention of many devotees of mysticism through the centuries.

One aspect of interest is Macarius' perspective on the spiritual life as a continuous baptism in the Holy Spirit. He views this process as a soul's willingness to wage constant war against personal evils and a yearning for complete conversion of life. The outcome of this pursuit is a soul filled with Divine Light. Indeed, light is a key symbol for Macarius as he describes the indwelling of the Holy Spirit.[26]

Macarius' eloquence leads the reader to a perspective that the only circumstance worth striving after in this life is a complete merger of the soul with the Divine will of God. In this is Christian excellence, though Macarius is realistic enough to acknowledge that it is a state rarely reached by the average person. Living out one's Baptismal covenant and surrendering to the gifts of faith, hope and love, mark his discipline of normal Christian living. Within this framework he asserts the redemptive power of the Holy Spirit as a continuation of the Incarnation within our

---

[26] i.e., light is indicative of the presence of the Holy

lives. Since God loved us enough to move within the reach of man by the act of Incarnation, it would be impious to degrade the value of humanity. Though austerity and sacrifice mark Macarius' expectation of daily living, the devaluation of human nature holds no place in his spirituality.

In fact, both Macarius and John Cassian hold similar views in this regard. Cassian's major work, the *Conferences*, speaks of asceticism in moderation, trying to keep in balance the values of renunciation and self-abnegation with common sense and a right perspective of the whole person.

John Cassian
360 - 435
APOPHATIC
AFFECTIVE

John Cassian was a colleague of Evagrius and takes primary responsibility for transporting monastic spirituality and theology to the West. It was he who, along with Evagrius, set down in writing the precepts of desert monasticism which Benedict applied in liberal measure in the formation of his famous Rule a century later. His was a teaching characterized by a spiritual realism with a surprising optimism toward the nature of humanity. Of particular interest to us in the study of mysticism are two concepts held by Cassian. The first is his image of "the fire of love" and the second, his conviction of the balance between the practical life and the contemplative life.

Cassian's image of holy fire can be related to Macarius' image of light. For him, fire is indicative of the presence of God in the soul. Light, heat, and fire are common images for mystics when relating to an experience of the holy; later on in this study one will see that this fire described by Cassian plays an important precursor role to the writings of an English mystic of the 14th Century, Richard Rolle. In Cassian, light is flame, and so the two images are in reality a single image. In our 21st-Century mind we can make a distinction between these two images which appear much more extensive than they obviously would for someone in the 4th Century.

The second concept that holds interest for us is that of the balance between the actual or practical side of the spiritual life and that of the contemplative or theoretical. This can be found particularly in his treatment of the life of prayer. In the *Conferences* Cassian expresses concern over the proper balance between private and corporate worship as well as between the fundamental business of daily sanctification through the correction of faults or acquisition of virtues and the pursuit of continual prayer. The primary goal of a monk is unceasing prayer; prayer so intensely intimate between the soul and God as to be ecstasy. So practically and theoretically speaking, the life of the monk, in Cassian's view, is to be a zealous expectation of Heaven.

Benedict of Nursia
480 – 550
KATAPHATIC
SPECULATIVE

Closely allied to this understanding of balance stands the next major influence in the monastic way—Benedict of Nursia. He is probably the most well-known of Religious, and was the first monastic founder to have his name used as synonymous with his Religious foundation—Benedictines. And through this endowment he provided the pattern for the whole of Western monasticism from the 5th Century to the present day. Anglicanism particularly takes much of its spirituality from the Benedictine tradition, and there has come a revival of study of the Benedictine Rule even among the laity of our present time.

Benedict is best known for his "Rule," and though much of it is not original in thought, having borrowed heavily from Cassian and Basil, the compilation of it into such a form is. Perhaps this marks the greatest of Benedict's contributions to the Church. It stands as a Rule of moderation, but for him, perfection did not consist in tranquility and contemplation, but rather in Charity. The Prologue to the Rule exhorts the brethren to turn from evil and do good. By such perfection in charity could be cultivated a true sense of monastic humility and obedience. If contemplation followed, it would be recognized as a gift from God and not the attainment of individual struggle.

Benedict's system or "Rule" promoted the signal role of the Abbot within the monastic structure. Sanctification would come by obedience to a monastery's superior. The hermit need only obey what he perceives as the Will of God, but the monk, in community, must also obey the human agent of God, putting trust in the institution as representative of one's true obedience to Christ. What we find distinctive here is Benedict's assertion that the "coenobitic" life[27] is far superior to the "hermitical" life.[28] The monastery thus becomes a "school of the Lord's service". Obedience, humility, and commitment to a single monastic house mark

---

[27] life in community
[28] life as a hermit or solitary

the Benedictine pursuit of holiness and also provide us with yet another pathway to union with God.

John Climacus John Scotus Erigena & Simeon the new Theologian
570 – 1022
KATAPHATIC
SPECULATIVE

We next meet three mystics who provide us with other aspects of the spiritual pilgrimage. Each became Abbot of his respective monastery, but none of them made his mark as a founder or reformer of a monastic tradition. They are John Climacus, John Scotus Erigena and Simeon the New Theologian. It is imperative that I place them in this particular discussion of the monastic influence because each gave to it, or passed on to it, an important theory of mystic insight.

John Climacus (570–649) was originally known as John Scholasticus and lived sometime during the end of the 6th Century. His name change came as the result of his important work, *The Ladder of Divine Ascent*, or *klimax tou paradeisou*, as it was known in Greek. He was the Abbot of Sinai, but beyond that we know very little about him personally.

What little we do know of the man is found within the pages of his treatise on the pursuit toward God. For Climacus, pure contemplation, being drawn into a "holy quiet", culminates the human experience. He recognized readily the difficulty a person would naturally have in attaining the sort of solitude which contemplation demands, and therefore his suggestions and counsel were both practical and systematic. Both layperson and monastic have benefited from his effective counsel on prayer and the development of the virtues, for he recognized the varied needs and differences of persons. Not all, he admits, have the same capacity for contemplative union, but all do have their own need for purification. It is of interest for us to note Climacus' comprehension of the psychology of human behavior. His wisdom recognized the mental deceptions people use to get around the difficult task of surrender to God's Will, and his sensitivity to the tension between self-love and self-surrender makes him one of the more companionable of mystic guides.

Climacus wrote *The Ladder of Divine Ascent* for monks, but anyone with patience and knowledge can derive good benefit from its pages. Climacus would possibly be a popular psychologist and spiritual director today by virtue of the fact that one of his main insights in the spiritual journey is self-knowledge. According to him, this would bring about an internal harmony as one seeks to progress through the various stages of sanctification.

It cannot be stressed too much—and in fact will be reiterated throughout this study—that any reading of the works of a mystic or theologian must always be accompanied by a grasp of the historical and religious setting of the author. To do less would be to read these saints in a vacuum and hinder them in their true significance and classic quality.

With that in mind, we move to John Scotus Erigena (810–877), whose very name is a redundancy. Both Scotus and Erigena point to the Irish heritage from which he came. In the 9th Century, when this John was a notable figure, Ireland was known by both the names "Scotia" and "Erin".[29] Other theologians went by the name John the Scot, so we learn to identify this mystic by the name Erigena.

This John was also not a monastic founder; nevertheless, he was an important figure in the development of Medieval philosophy. Scholars say that he provided the Middle Ages with its first metaphysical synthesis,[30] but more importantly for us, he translated both the writings of Pseudo-Dionysius the Areopagite and Maximus the Confessor from Greek into Latin, bringing these essential works into mainstream European thinking. The translation of Dionysius proved to have far-reaching effect on the Mystics of the later Middle Ages, from Meister Eckhart in the 12th to Julian of Norwich in the 14th and to John of the Cross in the 16th Centuries.

Erigena could be said to possess the most brilliant mind of the 9th Century and was certainly the supreme of the Celtic theologians. He not only mastered Greek beyond the normally held scholarship of the age, but he also successfully built a philosophical system concerning the division of nature. In this system we find his explanation of the active communication of God as in and through the things of this world.

There has been concern over his orthodoxy, in this regard, but as you may be discovering, original thinkers concern themselves with the essence and articulation of their theories and only later worry about how they fit into the accepted doctrinal system. It seems of primary importance to people like Origen and Erigena to see if their thesis holds water as a

---

[29] not to be confused with Scotland
[30] a system of religious thought gleaned from both Christian and pagan philosophies

theory and only secondarily whether it gains credence alongside established Christian doctrine. To me, they are the "theological mind-stretchers" of the Church and are sadly under-acknowledged.

One of Erigena's propositions that proved troubling to the Church was his idea of "theophany".[31] Because of this communication from within, the higher up the scale of created order, the more profound the theophany. Ultimately, he would say that man himself is a theophany and manifests, on a temporal level, the Divine Nature. We can possibly see here a similarity with the idea of "Deiformity" as found in Dionysius. It took several centuries to condemn this theory on the basis of "pantheism".[32]

Two stories of Erigena's death keep a person speculating as to what sort of man John Scotus Erigena really was. One story states that the monks of his own monastery murdered him, while another tells that his students stabbed him to death with their writing tools at the end of an impassioned lecture. This sort of information gives rise, in the student of spirituality, to an unsettling realization that holiness and mystical excellence are not couched in a fairy tale world of sweetness and calm. However, it also frees a person from the unnecessary dejection that comes from thinking that no one can ever be "good enough" to approach God on more intimate terms. These people earned the distinction of sainthood or holiness by their continued strivings rather than by the perfect

---

[31] God's self-revelation, communicating from within creation rather than transcendent from it

[32] the equation of God and nature as eternally necessary and coexistent

attainment of their desired goals. This is a lesson we often forget.

Between the 8th Century, which hosted the last great Ecumenical Council, and the 11th Century the voice of doctrinal and spiritual formation remained relatively mute. This is certainly not to insinuate that the period was dead or devoid of those theologians and mystics who kept alive the vision of Christian hope. However, it must be acknowledged that very little literary evidence has been passed down to us from these centuries concerning the mystic tradition.

One exception to this is the Eastern mystic, Simeon the New Theologian (949–1022), who exemplified the Byzantine religious culture. He was a true follower of Evagrius and Maximus, perpetuating the thought of the deification of humanity. Simeon acted as a compiler of the previous theologians' endeavors to examine and explain their theories, pronouncing them with devotion and authority. The monastic tradition of the East held on to this tradition as perpetuated by Simeon and continues to maintain a loyalty to this spirituality even today.

To his own credit, Simeon spoke out against a lax and corrupt ecclesiastical hierarchy. His demand for life filled with the grace and light of the Holy Spirit was a prerequisite for anyone who wanted to enjoy a reputation as a cleric. Suspicion and fear arose of the new "charismatic enthusiasm".

Simeon's teaching brought turmoil to the 10th-Century Byzantine Church. His apparent denial of the Church's hierarchical authority to forgive sins because of moral and spiritual corruption and his deduction that a "spirit-filled" monk, though not in holy orders, could pronounce absolution raised the furor of his detractors. The proposition of the primacy of the Holy Spirit's indwelling and emphasis on a personal experience of God brought Simeon under attack by the Archbishop of Constantinople and was the eventual cause of his exile to a small town on the shore of the Bosporus. However, his teaching was consistent with Patristic tradition and never condemned as heresy.

Primary to Simeon's imagery of the deification of man is the Divine Light, which already had strong emphasis in Evagrius' spirituality. Simeon elaborated on the "light" imagery, however, equating the holy name of Jesus to a beacon, which draws us to its source. Contemplation, also, is likened to the light, so that as a person enters more deeply into that experience, the uncreated light of divinity is discovered within. Simeon's thesis prompted him to be recognized as the father of hesychasm, a form of the Eastern mystical spirituality whereby a person seeks to so quiet his mind and body that he would ultimately arrive at the vision of this Uncreated Light, which is God. The word *hesychasm* comes from the Greek word for "quiet". We may recognize in this discipline our modern version of "the prayer of quiet" or "centering prayer" which has become a popular style of meditation.

| Bernard of Clairvaux |
| 1090 – 1153 |
| Apophatic |
| Affective |

Moving from East to West again and making a fairly large jump in time from the impact made by Benedict's innovative Rule, we begin to make the transition into the great medieval period. Bernard of Clairvaux stands as one of the bridges between the monasticism of Benedict's ideal and the Canons of the 12th and Friars of the 13th Centuries. With his reforming spirit, returning his monks to the essence of the monastic ideal, Bernard helps to transport the authority of the monastic vision into the common purview of ecclesial concern.

The mystical expression found in Bernard comes from a thorough grounding in the lives of the "Desert Fathers" besides a return to the essential Benedictine example. For him, the ultimate perfection in love comes by way of "Remembrance" and "Imitation". Developing the imagery of Spiritual Marriage, Bernard gives character to the Western spirituality of the next four hundred years. Thematic in his writings stands the Christ as spouse and lover of the soul. Love so dominates Bernard's writings that it becomes equated with the Divine Teacher who aids the soul in overcoming evil. Love teaches the soul through purification and illumination how to move from the desire for God alone.

The whole of medieval piety receives its affective nature through Bernard's belief in this love and the way of ecstasy.[33] This is done by way of mystic contemplation, discerning the Bridegroom as Love itself. One might be reminded of the love of which the Gospel and Epistles of John the Beloved speak. Not only was this spiritual expression a prime influence in Bernard's day, but it has filtered down to us by way of the Cistercian piety from whence it came, notably in the life and writings of Thomas Merton.

---

[33] moving out of oneself

fRancis of Assisi	**N**ot many years after the
1181 – 1226	death of Bernard, there was
KATAPHATIC	born in the Italian town of
AFFECTIVE	Assisi a man who pioneered his
	own mystical interpretation of

the monastic life. Francis bestowed upon the Religious Life a new countenance, bringing the monastery into the highways and byways of society. Francis, in his own unique way, ushered in what I consider the Golden Age of Mysticism, though his was not so much a spoken (or written) mysticism as a lived one. The writings he did leave were a few letters to his brethren and some spiritual counsels, but they are relatively unknown to the contemporary reader. Most of what we read of Francis is *about* Francis rather than anything original.

In Francis can be found a mystic of a different sort. The stigmata[34], which he received a couple of years before his death, is among the most celebrated mystical experiences of the Middle Ages. It is this extraordinary phenomenon which marked the summit of the poor man's radical identification with Christ and was to serve as the dominant symbol for subsequent medieval and Franciscan spirituality. However, a study of Francis as a mystic based on his own writings and amplified by the accounts of his early biographers remains yet to be written. Predominant before him was a speculative type of mysticism, following the pattern of classical metaphysics. He began a course, associated with what became known as the nature cult, of an affective form of mysticism which saw the

---

[34] Bodily wounds or pains considered, in the Christian context, as a visible sign of participation in Christ's passion.

Divine Life pulsating through all of creation.[35] His was an imitation of Christ through a mystical marriage with Lady Poverty and culminated in his own mystical crucifixion. Francis uniquely synthesized two facets of mystical tradition: that which was "anti-world" and that which viewed the world as a receptor of the Divine presence.

Conditioned by a 12th-Century understanding of Holy Scripture, Francis became interiorly transformed when he heard passages that concerned the love of God for man. Much of his piety reflects the Gospel of John. He was a visionary and even somewhat of a prophet, combining strict asceticism with unlimited love. The utmost humility represented for Francis the true relationship between God and man, and in him is medieval piety summarized.

For Francis, the fundamental truth of the Gospel was that God was recognized as Father, which has become one of the primary focuses of Franciscan spirituality. The charisms of humility, charity, and joy all spring from this confidence in our relationship with our Father God. Francis zeroed in on the goodness of God in the humanity of Christ, giving basis to a trend which spread throughout Western Christianity and creating a place for non-intellectual spirituality to flourish. This spirituality spoke in terms that were concrete, particular, human, and moral. It is consistently salvation-centered, whereby Jesus bridges the gap between humanity's sinfulness and God's magnanimous love.

---

[35] One can find similarities here with the Native American spirituality, which also views nature as inherently good because of its ability to reflect the Divine within itself.

Poverty provided the vehicle by which Francis pursued his ideal, seeking connection with God through a complete annihilation of the "lower" nature so that God would be unhindered in the transformation of the soul. Francis embraced poverty as the very image of the Lord. His purpose for vowing Holy Poverty was not for some sort of perverse denial, but rather for a holy detachment that would leave him free to adore God alone and be available to God completely. A follower of Francis sees poverty as a means of liberation, a liberation for the sake of love.

Another strong influence made by Francis and Franciscan piety is in the realm of Christian meditative prayer that finds its roots in this environment. Through meditation upon the earthly events of Our Lord's life, one has fertile ground for "religious thinking" and for entering into an event by way of the imagination and affections. For Francis, the way of mental prayer and interior detachment would lead a soul to contemplation and ultimately to mystic union. His chief study was to be free from all worldly occupations and concerns, lest the serenity of his mind be troubled, even momentarily. This he pleaded that his brethren copy. Unlike Benedict, Francis perceived that even manual labor and works of charity could distract a monk from his obligation to pure union with God. There is in this thought a hint of passivity that distinguishes the Franciscan piety from the Benedictine.

dominic
1170 – 1221
KATAPHATIC
SPECULATIVE

Until Francis and the Spaniard, Dominic, monastic institutions had in primary view the personal sanctification of their monks. The coenobitic communities did not, as a rule, consist of apostolic workers whose end was to evangelize the greater populace. However, these two spiritual giants entered the monastic scene and brought a whole new aspect to the Religious Life.

Dominic and Francis met on several occasions and Dominic said that he wished their two foundations were one, so closely were they allied. Dominic formed a company of preachers basing his Rule on that of St. Augustine, so that they were not only mendicant friars but also Canons Regular. These friars were bound to recite the Divine Office and to community life when their preaching did not demand otherwise of them. Dominic also focused on the conversion of souls, especially those caught in the heresy of "Albigensianism".[36] His Religious became known as Friars Preachers,[37] and they were truly the first "mixed" order, combining both an active apostolic spirit with a contemplative one. Though this was true of the men, the Dominican nuns remained entirely contemplative. However, the legacy that Dominic left was not completely original with him. Dominic, like Benedict, drew heavily from the spiritual teachings of John Cassian.

For Dominic, prayer uttered in the stillness of the night was a mere preamble to the glorious radiance of Christ's light uttered in the day of preaching. To proclaim the Gospel for the salvation of souls was Dominic's ideal. One difference between Dominic and Francis can be found in that Dominic wanted his monks to be educated and that the education should be broad, encompassing the sciences and philosophy

---

[36] a heresy of dualism which sees the spiritual as good and the physical as evil

[37] whereas Francis' brethren were known as Friars Minor

as well as theology. His desire was to ground himself and his followers firmly in the tradition of the Fathers of the early church—and that he did with profound success—but then to take that tradition into the highways and byways of society.

thomas Aquinas
1226 – 1274
APOPHATIC
SPECULATIVE

Dominican spirituality is built almost entirely upon scholastic theology and is therefore predominantly of a "speculative" nature. We know it primarily through the life and teaching of Thomas Aquinas. Since Dominic and his early disciples left no major writings of their own, it is best to discuss Dominican influences by speaking of Thomas. For many, Thomas is the most important theologian and philosopher of the medieval period, and some would even go so far as to say that he is the most important theologian in Christian history. Certainly he ranks with the greats: Augustine, Anselm, and Abelard.

Aquinas' system is built almost entirely on scholastic theology, which lays extreme importance upon Aristotelian philosophy and the preeminence of reason. It was he who so wedded faith and reason that reflection upon the great truths of Christianity without employing both disciplines is unthinkable.

A Dominican monk sometimes might have been excused from the Divine Office for the sake of study. In the Dominican school of mysticism both asceticism and mysticism were firmly connected with the gifts of the Holy Spirit. Also, Holy Wisdom was the agent that would bring about the desired union of the finite soul with the infinite God.

As brilliant as Aquinas was and after all the massive scholarship he produced, it was his own mystical encounters which best define his sanctity. He reckoned all his work as straw compared with the experience of union with God. Not many will attempt to read his famous *Summa Theologica* but all may be edified by the hymns he wrote in honor of the feast of Corpus Christi. These hymns remain among the most beloved for Eucharistic celebrations and are as relevant as they are timeless in the truths they proclaim.

With mystical understanding borrowed from Dionysius, Dominican writers such as Thomas specially insist on renunciation both of material possessions and personal will as well as the mortification of selfish desires. The point here was to so unite one's will with that of the Divine Will that a complete identification results. You must recognize that though this sounds very harsh and degrading for our 21st-Century understanding of the psyche, for men and women of the Middle Ages, it spoke of the good news of salvation. As in the teaching of St. Augustine, so in the Dominican school there was a marked tendency to consider the initial position of Divine action in the acquisition of holiness. Rather than condemn the material, as the Albigensian heresy did, Dominic and his famous disciple from Aquino promoted the goodness of humanity as it cooperated with Divine Grace. They taught that this was accomplished by gazing with theological sensibilities upon all of God's creation, especially by the integration of human, social, and religious realities.

So with the reforms of monasticism brought about by Francis and Dominic at the end of the 12th Century and the beginning of the 13th, we find our feet firmly planted in the Christianity of the medieval mind.

Rather than finding a depressing and "dark" time of history marked by famine, pestilence, and economic depression, a student of spirituality will discern here a lush vineyard of remarkable proportions. The monasteries, in particular, were the seedbed of the marvelous heritage of mystical experience and theology. Monasticism found its mission to be prophetic utterance, and that mission has been expertly accomplished through the scores of men and women who followed in the footsteps of Benedict, Francis, and Dominic.

Chapter 4
the Rhineland School

ow we move into what I consider to be the Heart and Soul of the Mystical laboratory, the Middle Ages. Because of the multitude of mystics and their particular expressions that characterize this period, I will begin by dividing the "schools" into separate sections, endeavoring to encapsulate each one in sketch form.

This period, both ascetic and dogmatic, lies before us like a vast forest full of life and exceedingly dense. It is, therefore, of prime importance to cut a path that will enable one to pass through it with the least amount of struggle. At the outset, I feel it is important for the reader to go easy on the various details and try to grasp the overall impact of this period. There are many mystics who had much to say about their experiences, and for the "first-time" explorer of mystical theology, it is best to take it in as a panorama rather than in finely etched details. The details will come later on as one continues to study this tradition.

The spirituality of the Middle Ages is to be encountered first in the great monastic traditions which formed "schools" of thought. In these, asceticism and mysticism developed in accordance with the spirit proper to each foundation. Four monastic schools, above all, left their mark on the spirituality of the early part of the Middle Ages, and their influence is still felt in our present time: the Benedictine, the Franciscan and Dominican traditions, and the order of Canons

Regular of St. Augustine.[38] In the Later Middle Ages there will come a dominance of the Carmelite and Jesuit influences, but for now, these four orders are the major institutions of concern. Each had its place and each has left its mark upon our own understanding of the spiritual life.

The ultimate goals within each of these traditions, while being fundamentally and substantially similar, nevertheless differ in emphasis and vision. In other words, their approach, their spiritual understanding, provides distinctive flavors to the backdrop of mystic experience. The reader must also recognize that geographical and national distinctions also begin to dominate this period, taking note where and how those monastic influences operate within the societal structure.[39]

Each of these "schools" accommodated members who maintained one of the three concepts of mystical science:

1) *The practical and affective aspect,* which touches the heart rather than the mind.
2) *The speculative,* which builds up theories rather than concerning itself with outward piety.
3) *An integration of the affective and speculative,* which includes both sentiment and reason.

---

[38] also known as the Austin Canons
[39] the Benedictines and Dominicans in the Rhineland region, the Franciscans in England and Italy, the Canons Regular in the Rhineland and England, and later the Carmelites and Jesuits in Spain and France

Such a concept of mysticism as a science had its foundation in the Early Church but was expanded into an "institution" of its own during the High Middle Ages.

One must briefly look at the social, environmental, and political influences at work during this period to gain a true understanding of the spirituality that was fostered there. The great prophetic mysticism of the 13th and 14th Centuries came to fruition amid a declining and decaying Church structure and the devastating violence of war and disease. Within the Church the morality of the clergy and even the hierarchy was no less than appalling. Popes became political pawns of kings and emperors. Money and other tributes were squeezed out of the common man to assuage the greed of the princes of the land and of the Church.

The country we know as Germany was, at that time, a multitude of small principalities continually at odds with each other. France and England were engaged in the Hundred Years' War. The Eastern and Western Christian Empires (including the Church) split permanently with each other. And if this was not enough to edge people toward despair, the Black Death (Plague) leveled the population in Europe by a third in some places, by a half in others. Comparing this with the problems of today—leaving out the threat of nuclear holocaust—can we wonder why the thoughts of so many were on Heaven and a reality other than this world?

It was mentioned in Chapter 2 that with Tertullian and Augustine there came an institutionalizing of Christianity. What they began this period brought to full flower. The primary concern of man was his salvation, and much of his time was spent in the search for an assurance that he would make it to heaven. For this reason, "Indulgences" became readily accepted by the people, and we see the Church taking over more and more control of the mental, moral, and spiritual aspects of its people. These "Indulgences" were, in essence, a buying of "time off" in Purgatory, so as to reach Paradise or Heaven more quickly. The Church made her living by this crude sort of extortion for many years and found it a convenient way to keep a controlling influence on the culture.

It appears that God, in order to aid the drive for reform and religious fervor, raised up a kind of prophetic mysticism during this period, to check the tide of moral decay. Women such as Hildegard of Bingen in the 12th Century and Bridget of Sweden and Catherine of Siena in the 14th exerted this gift of mystical prophesy, not fearing to reprimand priests, bishops, popes, and even kings. So with this in mind, let us begin to look more closely at the life and times of these medieval prophets.

We journey first to the Rhineland, to a school that is distinctive more for its geographical base than its monastic base. Since much of the theory and practice intertwines and crisscrosses in the discipline of the mystical tradition, it would be useful to the reader to imagine the connection between the various mystics as the interlocking of circles rather than separate and distinct squares. Many of us tend to compartmentalize information, but when dealing with spirituality, and mysticism in particular, it is best to try to synthesize or integrate information.

The development of mysticism in Germany and Flanders is notable for the number of women who contributed to the movement. These women—Hildegard of Bingen, Mechthild of Magdeburg, Hadewijch of Antwerp, Beatrice of Nazareth, Mechthild of Hackenborn, Elizabeth of Schonau and Gertrude the Great—are among the most celebrated and added to the richness of ascetic reform in the 12th Century. In briefest outline of their theory, they described the union between God and the human soul as the birth of the "Word" in the "Ground" or "Spark" of the soul. In order that this might take place, the soul must renounce all created things in order to practice complete detachment or abandonment. They go beyond the assumption that union takes place simply in the intellectual mode of life and at times portray a very passionate mysticism. The majority of these women felt that the intellect knows or conceptualizes God through images, but in its "Ground," the soul is free from images; therefore, God can unite Himself to the soul freely, without form. This "grounding" is the union of the simple essence of the soul with the Being of God. Summing up this specific mystical expression one might view it from three perspectives: the total renunciation of the self, an intelligence stripped naked, and a unifying of essences.

hildegard of Bingen
1098 – 1179
APOPHATIC
SPECULATIVE

Taking a closer look at these prophetic mystics, let us begin with Hildegard. Around the turn of the 12th Century, little Hildegard would remember Holy Roman Emperor, Henry IV of Canossa fame, being brought to her father's castle as a prisoner one Christmas Eve. Not only Germany, but the whole Christian empire, had been torn by the long struggle between the Papacy and the Emperor. A moral decline of the Church due to lax piety and doctrinal heresy was broad. The times needed and were primed for a reformer. That fact undoubtedly lent to Hildegard's visionary life a prophetic flavor. She appeared in a time of political and religious conflict and was strong enough to raise her voice, demanding that conflict cease and the minds of men be directed to worthier things. This prophet, sometimes called the "Sibyl of the Rhine," treated civil power as a God-given and God-governed institution, and therefore she dealt with the civil authorities in as straightforward a manner as she would the ecclesiastical. This view gave Hildegard courage enough to rebuke a later Emperor, Frederick Barbarossa, through a letter when he questioned the Church's authority.

Legend has it that Hildegard miraculously possessed the ability to read and write by Divine source rather than acquiring the skills in the normal way. Though her Latin was not the most scholarly, she was in fact a woman of great skill and genius. Her power of prophesy and foresight was what filled her contemporaries with awe, a sense of the supernatural shining through everything she did and impressing all with whom she came into contact.

The particular mystical symbol that Hildegard was noted for was what she called "A Living Light". This light that came to her showed her revelations which she was interiorly compelled to make known. Any hesitancy on her part to express these revelations brought with it a physical illness that immobilized her until she agreed to disclose her vision.

We are very apt to psychologize a phenomenon like this as some sort of religious hysteria or delusion, but we must always keep in mind that the era from which a woman like Hildegard came knew nothing of the language of modern psychology. These people acted and reacted upon such circumstances and phenomena with a completely different mindset. God's will and His revelations came to many of the mystics in the common circumstances that they met on their spiritual journeys.

We recognize nothing of the idle contemplative about Hildegard. While deeply interested in the politics of her time and the reform of the Church, she was also kept busy in attending to those who sought medical advice from her. She was reputed to be skilled in medicine and the use of herbs, and her mystical writings are sprinkled liberally with thoughts on these subjects. Thus, even though her day might begin with a vision of the transcendent light, it might end with a cure for an earache. In essence, Hildegard was a practitioner of what we now call "holistic medicine".

It was in the year 1141 that Hildegard's greatest prophetic period really began, for it was then that she began to write down her symbolic visions in a book called *Scivias* or *Scito Domini*.[40] In this work she describes the nature of these visions and their spiritual content. The "voice" within her vision describes himself as "The Living Light" which illumines the darkness. This manifestation of the Living Light was the presence of God who was to reveal or illumine the mysteries of life to her. It took her nine years to fully accept the direction to write these things down, but reluctantly she did complete the task.

This is the first time in this pilgrimage of the mystical tradition that we have touched on the "Extraordinary" phenomena of mystical experience. I asked you, in fact, to dispel from your mind the sweet, young

---

[40] Know the ways of the Lord

girl levitating over her prayer desk. This was necessary so that we could begin to build an understanding of the "ordinary" aspects of mysticism rather than dwell on the infrequent and "extraordinary" aspects. Now, with the Tradition firmly rooted in the common life of the believing Church, I think it is safe to begin dealing with some of the ecstatic experiences. From the perspective of the whole mystic tradition these experiences are neither necessary nor, in many cases, welcome by the Saints. Some went so far as to call them a nuisance to their spiritual life. However, it seems that the mystics of this period were able to accept and articulate these supernatural experiences more freely than any other.

hadewijch of Antwerp
c. mid-13th Century
KATAPHATIC
AFFECTIVE

Moving on to the 13th Century, which was a time of emotional stirrings and impulses, we begin to encounter the literary genre of epic poetry and heroic sagas. It was the time of the Minnesingers and their joy in nature, in birds and flowers. But this was also a time of continued spiritual awakening. Somehow, the newborn joy in natural beauty was transfused with spiritual longing. While the nobles were off on Crusades, their sisters were being called to serve a celestial chivalry. Into this age Hadewijch of Antwerp was born.

The Rhineland school encompasses not only Germany but also the countries we know as Holland and Belgium, or the "Low Countries". Unlike Hildegard, Hadewijch was not a nun. She was a Beguine from Flanders. Beguines were laywoman who lived a devout life of voluntary poverty and contemplative prayer but without taking vows. Many lived alone in their own homes, but some, like Hadewijch, lived in communal groups. These women supported themselves by their common work of caring for the sick or other manual labor. Hadewijch became the "Mistress" or leader of one of these communal groups until, at some point, her leadership became unacceptable to the women under her and she was expelled, ending her days homeless.

Hadewijch comes to us as something of a mystery; very little is known of her personal biography. She lived in the first half of the 13th Century and has been identified as coming from either Brussels or Antwerp. However, she wrote in the Brabant dialect that is a form of medieval Dutch. Such personal enigma contrasts dramatically with the vivid and vibrant literary portraits she left behind. What can be even more confusing in her regard is that we have not only one mystic by the name of Hadewijch, but two. Scholars distinguish them as Hadewijch I and Hadewijch II. However, for this study, the most important and influential is Hadewijch I. She dates between Hildegard and Meister Eckhart and, in fact, greatly inspired Eckhart's own spiritual development. Both he and Jan van Ruysbroeck quoted liberally from her letters and poems, and Ruysbroeck in particular undertook to ground her lofty notions of love in a solid theological base.

From Hadewijch's writings we have some of the most glorious examples of "Love Mysticism" of the medieval period. Her theology is centered in Christ and the Trinitarian relationship of love as the binding force between the divine persons. Her visions reveal the prophetic nature of her mysticism, and the mystical passion exemplified in her poetry and prose give her a distinctive style. What distinguishes Hadewijch's concept of the love relationship between God and the soul from the concept of so many of the other mystics presents itself in the fact that Hadewijch perceived and taught that this love relationship could be lived in the present. Hers was not a mysticism of negation of all that we experience in this life, focusing solely on the rewards of eternity; rather, the daily experiences of love, of God's constant presence, caught Hadewijch's attention and imagination. Writing in the tradition of "courtly" or chivalrous love, as the love between a "lady" and her "knight errant", she created a heretofore unknown genre of mystical expression: God as Trinity and Trinity as unity, from the Love which makes them One.

Hadewijch took as her standard of All Love. By participation in Christ, humanity reaches the sublime levels of the beatific, even in the present moment. Her love for Christ is passionate, and sometimes even erotic. One of the main characteristics of such a love, for Hadewijch, shows itself in her refusal to separate the love of God from the love of neighbor. They became two sides of the same coin.

Mechthild of Magdeburg
1210 - 1280
KATAPHATIC
AFFECTIVE

Mechthild of Magdeburg was born into the same milieu as Hadewijch. It is said of her that from the age of twelve she was under the influence and guidance of the Holy Spirit to such a degree that she could no longer be tempted to serious daily sin. By her early twenties, like Hadewijch, she began to live the life of a Beguine. She lived for many years in Magdeburg in this state, later moving to Helfta where she lived out her days in the Cistercian convent there.

The mystic mantle of Hildegard seems to have fallen on Mechthild. The Church was in as depressed a shape as ever, suffering from neglectful clergy and a materialistic hierarchy. Mechthild spoke out in denunciation of these abuses, but this led to persecution at the hands of those she condemned. Her ideals were so high that even the Sisters with whom she lived despised her. Bitter complaints from all quarters led to the imposition of an "Interdict" against her by the Church. This meant that she was forbidden to receive Holy Communion or to recite the Daily Offices. Some of the charges against her were as banal as that she was "unlearned", a member of the laity, and worst of all: "a woman!"

It is quite possible that her writings were known in Italy by 1300 and were read by Dante. It is speculated that she even appears as one of the characters in his *Divine Comedy*. In her book of visions entitled, *Flowing Light from the Godhead Christ*, the beautiful youth is depicted as the personification of love. Like Hildegard, she was commanded by God to make her mystical experiences known and, like Hildegard, suffered physical ailment when she refused to obey the command.

There are two directions her writings take: the prophetic and the contemplative. Love, that common mystical theme, is the basis of Mechthild's book. She speaks of Love as the source of her very essence, and only Love can liberate her from this world. On the prophetic side Mechthild derives her influence from Hildegard as well as Elizabeth of Schonau, a Benedictine nun who was a friend of the mystic of Bingen, as well as a fellow visionary. On the contemplative side she owes much to Richard of St. Victor and Bernard of Clairvaux, following the path of "Love alone".

Gertrude the Great
1256 - 1302
KATAPHATIC
AFFECTIVE

Mechthild was never formally canonized by the Church, and neither was Gertrude the Great, the most famous pupil of another Rhineland mystic, Mechthild of Hackeborn. Theirs was a deep and abiding friendship that leads one to conclude that Gertrude's spirituality was influenced to some extent by the Mechthilds. However, her visionary experiences were more subjective in nature and she was the least politically or socially active of these holy ladies of the Rhineland.

Gertrude's book, *The Messenger of Divine Love*, was of a delicate and feminine nature. Her writings, as well as the writings of the other women of this early Rhineland school, did much to influence the devotion to the Sacred Heart of Jesus. Prior to this period, the "humanity" of Christ had not been the subject of popular veneration, but from these women from the Rhineland school there began a popular reverence among the faithful in Germany. The Divine nature of Christ had been emphasized for so long that until this period the Human nature of Christ had been obscured.

Gertrude was an ardent scholar, yet she relinquished her love of secular study to devote herself more fully to the Lord's call. Her keen intellect shows up in the deeply Trinitarian structure of her spirituality. No half-measures are allowed when contemplating the Divine attributes, even though there is also an almost childlike simplicity about her. *The Revelations of St. Gertrude* as well as *The Exercises of St. Gertrude* make for quite easy reading and provide for the reader a glimpse into the heart of a woman wholly betrothed and wholly absorbed in her Beloved Jesus.

It provides a curiosity for those of us today—who are surrounded by "the feminist cause"—to realize the power and impact of these women upon the religious and even secular culture of their day. We need to understand in this context that women far outnumbered the men in this period and were in a position to be more attentive to the moving of the Spirit in their midst. More and more Religious foundations for women were springing up, both within the guidelines of older establishments as well as new and innovative styles. It was to these new communities that our next three personalities found themselves acting as spiritual guides.

Meister Eckhart
1260 – 1327
Apophatic
Speculative

We move now to a very integral point in Rhenish mysticism. We begin with a sketch of Meister Eckhart. Born Johannes Eckhart in the village of Hockheim, his father was a steward of a knight's castle in the province of Thuringia. At the age of 15, Johannes entered the Dominican monastery at Erfurt and became its prior by the time he was 30. From this point on, Eckhart began a preaching career which increased his fame in both Germany and France. A degree of Licentiate and Master of Theology was conferred on him by the College of Paris in 1302 and from this point onward, he became known as Meister Eckhart, a title that has remained to the present.

Though we find in Eckhart the epitome of the speculative theologian, he also had a profound insight into the ways of the human heart. This Dominican preacher diligently searched for the source of the human desire for union with God. His conclusions were that questions concerning divinity inevitably encompassed questions of human existence. The reverse proved true as well, in that the ultimate questions about humanity involve answers intimately related to God. In this, Eckhart echoes the theology of St. Augustine, upon which Dominican spirituality is based.

Meister Eckhart made a theological distinction between the God whom the human soul comes to know in intimacy and the Godhead who is totally transcendent. This God we know in intimacy comes to birth within us as Jesus was brought forth from the Virgin Mary. The Godhead lies beyond any concept of God. In this Eckhart's mystical theology shows similarities with the Jewish mystical tradition of the Kabbalah, which was being formulated about the same time. Kabbalah mysticism describes God in terms of the Ten Sefirot, or ten attributes of God. Beyond these attributes and yet encompassing them exists the Ein Sof, the God of total ineffability.

Due partly to the scholastic rivalry between Franciscan and Dominican Orders and partly to the ambiguous language of mystical theology, Eckhart became a controversial figure in his own day and to some extent has remained so ever since. By the end of Eckhart's life, however, he had been condemned for teaching heresy by the court of the Archbishop of Cologne, who happened to be a Franciscan. He appealed to the Pope but died before the pontiff had given a verdict in his case.

The question of heresy was caused by the fact that Eckhart had an intense interest in the speculative question concerning the nature of the soul's union with God.[41] His speculation was that the "Ground" of God's nature and the "Ground" of the human soul's nature are essentially the same. Basically, in Eckhart's scheme of the soul's essence, unity between God and man is attained when man reaches the depths of his own center. But in Eckhart's effort to articulate this Truth, the language he used seemed to border on Pantheism, a heresy held by some of the pseudo-religious movements of his day. Pope John XXII condemned 28 separate points made in Eckhart's writings yet never condemned their author. These propositions, taken from his works and standing in isolation, are exaggerated and incorrect, but there is little doubt for scholars today that his intention was utterly orthodox. We may recall that Origen had a similar problem.

Eckhart was a popular preacher in his day and he was innovative in the fact that his sermons were not written out completely but were preached simply from notes or outlines. He delivered them in his own vernacular—German rather than the customary Latin—and it is said that Eckhart did for the German language what Dante did for Italian.

Johannes Tauler
1300 – 1361
APOPHATIC
SPECULATIVE

Seeing what treatment Eckhart received, his disciple, Johannes Tauler, became a bit

---

[41] and what mystic wasn't interested in this?

more cautious in his presentation while retaining the essence of Eckhart's teaching. Also a Dominican, Tauler lay stress on the transcendence of God, the Unity in which all multiplicity is transcended.[42]

What makes Tauler a unique individual in the mystical realm of his day lies in that he delivered most of his teaching in sermons for the liturgical year. These sermons were meant as much for the common laity as for the religious and orthodox Beghards and Beguines. It stands to reason that the mystical standpoint does not, by its own authority, free a person from the contemporary environment of opinion and prepossession. Therefore, his sermons contained a foundational language of his day to the effect that all spiritual life is to strive earnestly to rid itself of sin and detach itself from anything which would stand in the way of union with God. Though this may seem like a "tall order" for a humble soul, there existed in his German mind a mystical tendency which explains how to encapsulate these truths within his heart and to express them with his whole moral being. This approach became known as "high spirituality".

The secret of Johannes Tauler's influence comes through in the way in which he holds together the concept of a revival of heartfelt devotion within one's piety and the necessity for respect of the established methods of Mother Church. For him, piety was as vital to the laity as to the cleric. He begins to bridge the gap in a social structure which had separated these two "classes" for several generations.

---

[42] who is Being and Becoming, who is Rest and Motion

henry Suso
1295 – 1366
KATAPHATIC
SPECULATIVE

A mystic of a different sort, but of the same tutelage as Tauler, was one Henry Suso. Following the teachings of Eckhart and being a Dominican puts Suso very much in this particular Rhineland school. It is instructive to glance through his book entitled, *The Little Book of Truth*, which is highly mystical in flavor. This work treats the union with God as abandonment. With awareness of the condemnation of Eckhart's teaching, Suso is more cautious and separates the image of Christ as the sole proper image of the Father, and we are rather in the image of the conjoined Trinity.

In a style reminiscent of St. Francis, Suso wedded himself to Lady Wisdom, seeing her as the personification of the Divine, in which the soul loses all consciousness of present reality. In the literary style of the time, other similarities can also be noted, such as the dialogue between Lady Wisdom and the Servant, as the Spaniard Ramon Lull writes in dialogue between the Lover and the Beloved. These three spiritual masters make up a firm pedestal upon which a distinctive mystic style is given credence.

John van Ruysbroeck
1283 – 1381
APOPHATIC
SPECULATIVE

Following in their wake is another master, who is neither Dominican nor German, and yet belongs very surely to the Rhineland school: John van Ruysbroeck (often spelled Ruusbroec). Born in Flanders toward the end of the 13th Century, Ruysbroeck carried the heritage of apophatic, speculative mysticism to a hermitage called Groenendaal, or Green Valley. This move was probably the most advantageous event of this young priest's life since the infamous Black Death was soon to wipe out one-third to one-half of the population of Europe. The spread of the contagion was more drastic in cities and towns because people lived together in such close quarters. Plague was carried by flea-infested rodents and then passed from one diseased person to the next with rapidity. Those who fled to the country, for whatever reason, were much less likely to contract the disease.

It is necessary in this sketch of the mystics to pause briefly to discuss the impact this Plague had on the environment, even the spiritual environment of Ruysbroeck's day. The devastation by this epidemic nightmare reached into the very soul of the people, besides changing the face of the social, political, and economic landscape. A disproportionate number of clerics died of the Plague, perhaps because of the dedication with which they performed their ministries. The results of this sort of disaster could be seen in the increased number of "plural benefices" held by fewer and fewer men.[43] There was also widespread closing of monasteries and parish churches.

This sort of deprivation led to younger and ill-trained clergy taking over larger congregational responsibilities, causing a weakening in the spiritual and organizational structure. There came then an easy infiltration within the church by reformers and heretics,

---

[43] a *benefice* is an ecclesiastical office to which a monetary endowment is attached

which allowed for an increase in spiritual dissipation and confusion among the masses.

One group of reformers which had a fairly wide influence during this time were the "Flagellants".[44] These people processed, as on pilgrimage, from village to village where they would ceremonially whip themselves with heavy scourges. The purpose was to perform public penance for their sins and to beg God's mercy concerning the spread of the Plague. Their messianic pretensions soon ran them into conflict with the Church as they began to denounce the hierarchy as well as to ridicule the Church's sacramental nature.

There is endless evidence of the instability and excesses that characterizes all unsettled times. Besides the Flagellants, another phenomenon that arose was the mass persecution of the Jews all over Europe. Rumors spread of the Jews' responsibility for the Plague by their tainting of the drinking water. Large-scale persecutions arose around these rumors and fears, creating some outlet for the mass hysteria occurring at the time. To John van Ruysbroeck, these were dark and forbidding times. His answers to the questions of life lay in the realm of the blissful union of the soul with God. Instead of looking at the horror and devastation around him, he sought perfection, beauty, and rest in holy contemplation.

Piety was to become a matter of great urgency. Not only was the whole of Europe being ravaged by the Black Death, but also the Church was being ravaged from within by political intrigue, economic corruption, and organizational strife. In the Rhineland, as elsewhere, the matter of the dwindling clergy and the

---

[44] also known as the Brethren of the Cross

ecclesial inadequacies among those who tried to pick up the pieces left the Church with a combination of spiritual and organizational weakness amid a greater financial prosperity. This proved to be a disastrous combination because it fostered contempt and distrust by the people who most desperately needed the Church's ministry and instruction.

As one begins to read the mystics, it becomes apparent that they should never be considered by their spiritual merit alone. So much of their writings come out of a response to environmental as well as spiritual reflection. Such is the case with Ruysbroeck. We need to be aware that he was immersed in a stream of human history and directly influenced by the conscious and subconscious impact it had upon him.

By way of example, in his *Little Book of Enlightenment*, Ruysbroeck summarized his understanding of union with God in order to confute the false mystics of his time, called The Free Spirit Brethren. For him, union consisted of three levels: union with an intermediary, union without an intermediary, and union without difference or distinction. Union with a medium is achieved through God's grace given in the sacraments and through the virtues. One might say it is simply a union by grace and good works. The union without an intermediary or medium happens when a soul's will becomes one with God's or becomes exalted through love of God so much as to truly die to self. The union without difference is that spiritual marriage, the supreme degree of union and ecstatic love, such as is the love between the three Persons of the Holy Trinity. In order to clarify how Ruysbroeck wished these levels to be understood, one must remember that he was always speaking in terms of a concurrent spirituality instead of a successive one. All of these stages of unity always coexist in this life as well as the life to come.

It must also be said that though much of Ruysbroeck's thinking and writings were very "otherworldly" in character, his ecclesiology was highly germane to the times in which he lived. He was fully aware of the faults and schisms of Mother Church, but he also held firmly to the Petrine foundation and the apostolic tradition found there. He was adamant in his obedience to the hierarchy of Church and Sacrament and saw in them the channels of God's grace, especially the grace received from Christ the Bridegroom, in the means of the Blessed Sacrament.

Ruysbroeck's life was a blending of contemplation and action, which characterizes the religious life in the late Middle Ages. The institutional Church offered less and less stability and hope for a world in agony, so it was left to the mystics and reformers, the mendicant orders and those desiring a new devotional model, to rediscover meaning and truth. Pious devotion grew up around the mysteries of the Passion and the homely accounts of our Lord's life. The "Angelus" and the "Ave Maria" became established in definitive form, and the Rosary became more widely used. Personal needs of redemption and sanctification were stressed more and more urgently so as to deal with the waves of fear and doubt.

The scholastic realm of logic and reason gave way to a growing domination of religious emotion. The mystics of the 14th and 15th Centuries were capable of firing a believing soul's imagination, be it the soul of a scholar or of a ploughman, a craftsman or a monk. This period of the Church's spiritual history has remained unique in its moral decadence in contrast with its fecund mystical tradition. It makes a person of our century curious as to the parallels that might be made between the environmental traumas and moral decline of our own time with that of the later Middle Ages.

Shortly after the effulgence with which the 14th-Century mystic giants bathed a terrorized populace in spiritual light, a major shift began to occur within the realm of common devotion. The piety that had been relatively controlled by the hierarchical system of Mother Church gradually shifted to a more subjective approach. As the "individual" gained in importance under the rise of both secular and Christian humanism, so did religious sentiment and practice take on a keener expression of personal and individual piety.

Gerard Groote
1340 – 1384
Kataphatic
Affective

Toward the end of the 14th Century a new mystical movement came to birth, known as the *New Devotion*, or *Devotio Moderna*. Ruysbroeck is known to have influenced one of the leading pioneers of this movement, a holy cleric by the name of Gerard Groote. Groote founded a quasi-monastic community that later took the name Brethren of the Common Life and derived their spirit from the Canons Regular of St. Augustine. This group was highly influential as an active order, dedicated to the ministry of education. Their works are noted primarily through the establishment of schools and as copyists of religious books. As a body, they took no vows and received no alms but were entirely self-supporting through their work.

Groote was a Dutchman and of a respected family but lived a rather unspectacular life. He is not distinguished for ecstatic experiences nor profound mystical insights. However, his influence brought genuine reform in the spiritual life of Germany, Flanders, and France, probably helping to set the stage for a greater acceptance of the Protestant rebellion that occurred some 150 years later.

thomas à kempis
1380 – 1471
KATAPHATIC
AFFECTIVE

Another quiet yet major figure who assisted in this transition to "Modern" devotion was himself a copyist of Groote's Brethren: Thomas à Kempis. He is possibly the most well-known writer of this period due to his *Imitation of Christ*. There has been speculation of his actual authorship of this book; nevertheless, it does set forth his own spirituality that stresses a wholly inward conversion. This conversion leads the soul to complete renunciation of the self as the condition one must accept in order to win union with God.

It has been expressed by some scholars that à Kempis possessed a magnetism upon his own culture, and the interest he still holds upon our own religious sensibilities has been more harmful than good. The reason for this is because of the extreme denial within his spirituality of the goodness of the creature. According to his notion, all creatures or creatureliness is an obstacle to be overcome instead of a wonder to be embraced. So it is intriguing that his book, *The Imitation of Christ*, has been read with such trust and devotion, possibly second only to Holy Scripture in its popularity. Certainly it is an established "classic" of the spiritual life, ranking with the 17th-Century classic, *Pilgrim's Progress*. This being the case, it is not difficult to see

the way being paved for the doctrines of man's deprav-
ity that sprung up with the rise of Protestantism.

Chapter 5

The Victorine and English Schools

W hy do mystics write? To praise God? To make a record of their experiences? To instruct others? I believe that it is safe to say that mystical writers are unlikely to have been and to be interested in conveying that very thing which attracts us to them. These holy people know that the mystical life cannot be experienced vicariously by their readers; therefore, we must not be deluded into thinking that we can have the same experiences simply by reading about them.

While it is true that the saints fit into their own historical era, the fit is by no means a static one. Part of their spiritual genius escapes from the boundaries of history because they each carry in their soul that which is timeless. The essential message—that which springs from the depths of their souls—is for every age. That is why the literature of these bygone centuries is still so pertinent today. As we read the documents of mystical encounters, of poetry and of reflections on the holy life, we might even feel as though they were meant specifically for us. Such writings both confirm and correct our own spiritual journeys toward the deeper love of God.

Backtracking a few centuries, from 15th-Century Flanders to the early 12th Century in France, we seek out a small but dynamic school of mysticism—the School of St. Victor.

Taking the habit of the Canons of St. Augustine, William of Champeaux founded a monastery of clerks at the oratory of St. Victor just outside of Paris. To this house three influential figures eventually came, bringing depth and substance to a foundation based upon a synthesis of scholasticism and regular monastic observance. These men became known as the Victorines.

Adam of St. Victor
c.1177 – 1192
APOPHATIC
AFFECTIVE

Adam of St. Victor, a poet and the least known of this group, survives for the devotee of mystical theology through a few scant poems by which he added a richness to the otherwise academic tenor of the Victorine school. The other men, Hugh and Richard, each in his turn influenced the mystical expression of later Rhenish and English writers. In fact, by the time their influence reached the English shores, the spirituality they promoted was no longer referred to as Augustinian, but Victorine. 14th-Century England was to become saturated with this spirit and shows its typification in Julian of Norwich's *Revelations of Divine Love*. A few "verbatim" quotations of Hugh are even found in the writings of the English mystic, Aelred of Rievaulx.

Hugh of St. Victor
c. 1096 – 1141
APOPHATIC
AFFECTIVE

Following in the footsteps of the Victorine founder, Hugh of St. Victor succeeded William as Master of the school until his death. Hugh was a native of Saxony and belonged to a family of Counts. He took the habit of the Canons Regular of St. Augustine in 1115 and it was he who really established the identity of Victorine spirituality, gaining much from the tradition of Pseudo-Dionysius. Hugh saw the goal of spirituality as a synthesis of study and mystic contemplation. For him, no learning was a superfluous act; rather, any and all learning has benefit for spiritual growth. This dominated the Victorine pedagogy.

Being grounded in the study of Holy Scripture, Hugh's philosophical and theological positions have a very strong Christo-centric base. He used Dionysius' *Celestial Hierarchy* to describe his own understanding and experience of salvation history, but his chief concerns were with the monastic ideal and growth in the interior life. By following this ideal one would be led from natural thought into intuitive thought which, according to Hugh's process, would ultimately lead then to mystic contemplation. Of course, he also recognized that love is the prime mover and end result of the contemplative process.

An interesting notation to Hugh's concept of this temporal world lay in his belief that nothing is for itself alone but always for a greater end. Therefore, no understanding of science or the scientific process is an end in itself; rather, it is destined to culminate in a contemplative act. Every avenue of the arts and sciences known in Hugh's time expressed its ultimate fulfillment by a restoration of God's image in humanity. In this scheme, all knowledge works to the benefit of mystical union. This view is very reminiscent of Origen's philosophy as he strove to unite Hellenistic thought with Christian theology. It also foreshadows a later mystic/theologian, Teilhard de Chardin.

There are very few spiritual masters in this period whose powers of synthesis were equal to Hugh. He combined the use of the dialectic method, rational investigation, with faith augmented by love to reach his goal. That goal was toward the divine perfection. Hugh saw that the perfection which humanity seeks in this world is a reflection of that which is divine. Philosophy and theology are the disciplines which lead us toward that perfection.

Richard of St. Victor
Died c. 1173
APOPHATIC
AFFECTIVE

As with Hugh, Richard of St. Victor moved toward a synthesis between secular and mystical knowledge. By 1162 Richard was made prior of the abbey of St. Victor, a position he held until his death in 1173. Beyond this very little is known of his life. It is supposed that he was born in Scotland and that he entered the Abbey approximately ten years after Hugh's death.

Richard was able to assimilate the Victorine tradition through the writings left by Hugh, and though so little is known of the man himself, he became the most well-known of the Victorine school. He holds the distinction of being a master of mystical theology, and both Bonaventure and Dante will extol him in their own writings a century later.

From the solid foundation of a biblically based and liturgically sensitive theology, Richard became the first Christian author of the medieval period to compose a systematic teaching on contemplative asceticism. The two treatises which he composed, *The Book of the Twelve Patriarchs* and *The Mystical Ark*,[45] offer us the best view of his analysis of contemplative prayer and the process by which one attains to that state.

Taking his cue, as did Hugh, from the mystical theology of Dionysius, Richard discussed the process and levels of prayer and contemplation. He made a distinction between the ordinary activities of prayer and that which we would call infused or supernatural. He also introduced a trend of using Scripture as the foundation of mystical theology. Beginning with the theological premise, Richard would find his justification in the Scriptures and then synthesize that scriptural interpretation (exegesis) with the science of the observed phenomena of the natural world. This was a subtle change from the prevailing scholastic method that began with a scriptural text and then extrapolated from it a theological premise. From this process he developed a somewhat holistic approach to theology.

As with Evagrius Ponticus, the desert father of the 4th Century, Richard also seems to have excelled in the area of human psychology. He was fascinated by the mental process and showed extreme concern for the growth of the individual person rather than being interested only in abstract theological systems. Interpersonal relationships, particularly in the monastic community, concerned him. This concern reveals one of the subtle differences between the Benedictine approach to community and the Augustinian approach in which Charity is a hallmark.

---

[45] also known as *Benjamin Minor* and *Benjamin Major*, respectively

In his treatise "On the Trinity", we find Richard's standard of measure for Charity. There, in fact, he used the interpersonal relationship between the persons of the Trinity as the pattern for human relationships. He perceived our love as the reflection of the Divine and described the true nature of charity as that which draws us ever closer to our potential union with God.

It is the Victorine school which promoted the process of "meditation" in which orderliness coupled with personal temperament provided a portal for growth in union with God. Through a methodical and yet personal approach to the symbolism of material existence, a person can find the ultimate meaning or truth hidden there. Hugh and Richard each recognized that God teaches humanity about Himself through creation. To them, the whole of the universe had been restored by Christ, so all natural science and philosophy are an extension or continuation of the perfecting of truth in grace.

Because the Victorines played such an important role in the development of the English school, it makes sense to have spoken of them before delving into the unique flavor of early English spirituality. These English saints not only sprung from the Church in England, which had its own distinctive flavor, but their very essence is marked by their race and culture. The English are independent in spirit, lovers of freedom, brave in their championship of the poor and the oppressed. They are outspoken and sometimes indiscreet. In spiritual matters their Englishness shows itself in their urgent emphasis on the personal relationship each soul must cultivate with Jesus; not a religion only for the aristocracy but very much encouraged for the "even Christian"—the common folk.

The times in which these English mystics lived were packed with interest and incident. Life was neither stale nor stagnant. It might best be described as an age of awakening. The old order was disintegrating and a new one was pressing in. This was the age of the emancipation of the serf. The Hundred Years' War (1337–1453) introduced the efficiency of the archer with his long bow as equal worth to the knight in armor. The common laborer enhanced his value as the population declined seriously through the horror of the plague. Craftsmanship began to prove that "Jack" was as good as his master.

As these facts show us, it was inevitable that in the raising up of the common man, the vernacular language would become more and more important. Books written in English were more accessible to people who had little or no knowledge of Latin. Therefore, one didn't need to be a scholar to receive spiritual aid from the written word. The possibility of being tried in a court of law, hearing one's native language, increased justice. To be wooed or entertained by the poet expanded one's view of life. This was the age of *Piers Plowman*, *The Canterbury Tales*, and John Wyclif's translation of the Bible into English.

In many ways the English Mystics ushered in this trend toward more personal and vernacular religion. Much of the genre in which they wrote resounded with the romantic strains of their contemporary secular literature. These mystics penned their religious experiences in a context set amidst the atmosphere of the

"Miracle Plays" and Gothic sculpture.[46] Thus, spirituality came into reach of every person.

Yet another influence on the composition of a particularly English spirituality flourished as Benedictine monasticism, specifically in the Cistercian form. Before the Norman Conquest in 1066, England was known as the land of the Benedictines.[47] The most obvious legacy of this influence comes to us in the development of the *Book of Common Prayer* as a by-product of the monastic recitation of the Divine Office.

Aelred of Rievaulx
1110 - 1167
KATAPHATIC
AFFECTIVE

The first of these amazing English mystics I have chosen for this study is the Cistercian monk Aelred of Rievaulx. He was instrumental in planting the Benedictine model of monastic and mystical spirituality upon English soil. The ruins of Rievaulx Abbey lie in a subtly beautiful valley of the river Rye in Yorkshire. These ruins are the most important of any of the Cistercian monasteries in the British Isles because they stand as a veritable historical document in stone of the life which thrived there, particularly during Aelred's time.

Of this 12th-Century abbot we know two things. First, we know that Aelred was influenced largely by the Roman orator Cicero and his treatise on friendship.

---

[46] Miracle plays began as liturgical drama as an aid to the teaching of Bible stories to illiterate congregations. They grew into popular pageants organized by guilds and performed in guild halls and theaters.
[47] in this period of the 14th Century it could have conceivably been called the land of the Cistercians

Second, we also know that he was a popular and respected member of the court of King David of Scotland. Whatever the exact nature of his position there can be no doubt that Aelred's life at court and his life as head of a monastic foundation at Rievaulx were intimately linked. His success in the one seemed to spill over into the other, but each found its impetus from a commitment to the centrality of friendship.

While on a mission to York for his Archbishop, Aelred made a visit to the monastery of Rievaulx. The Cistercian foundation so impressed him that he immediately asked to be admitted. It didn't take many years before the monks realized Aelred's genius, and they expressed their confidence in him by electing him Abbot.

In his youth Aelred had the opportunity to travel to Rome and en route met the great Bernard of Clairvaux. Aelred so impressed Bernard with his abilities and sense of the Holy that Bernard commissioned him to write of Love as it had been revealed to Aelred. He accepted this task as an obedience and produced *Mirror of Charity*. Later, as Abbot of Rievaulx, Aelred produced his best-known work, *Spiritual Friendship*.

Aelred took an amazing departure from the traditional view and language of spiritual thought and portrayed an Incarnational spirituality in a completely unique way. Instead of the ethereal Bride-and-Bridegroom imagery common to the mystics of the time, Aelred exalted the chaste love of friendship as the symbol of spiritual union. He took a radical stance by raising the earthy and earthly state of filial affection to that of the sacramental. This view is diametrically opposed to a more prevalent spirituality throughout history which seems always to desire a negation of natural human emotion.

For Aelred, friendship was a way to Christ. Through the intimacy of holding another human being up to the healing power of Christ, a person receives a double portion of "affection passing into affection." Not only does love for Christ grow, but love for neighbor grows as well. Embracing a friend thus, according to Aelred, we rise to that state whereby we also embrace the living God.

Through this expression of mystical thought the Incarnation is brought to a level that each of us may touch, not with the logic of discursive reason, but rather with the depth of our affective spirit. Aelred's thesis exemplifies the notion that mysticism is not a separate religion for special people. Instead, it models an ordinary system in which prayer, sacrament, self-surrender, and fellowship intensify as a person draws closer to the throne of a relational God.

Richard Rolle
1295 - 1349
KATAPHATIC
AFFECTIVE

Another mystic who exemplified this attitude of a common or ordinary mystical life was Richard Rolle. Educated at Oxford at the time when the Franciscans dominated southern England, some scholars claim that he was the most widely read of the mystics from his time to one hundred fifty years after his death. Because of his orthodox teachings, Rolle's works were greatly favored during the Counter-Reformation.

What we know of Richard's life comes from a Latin office written in anticipation of his beatification in the 1380s. Though never officially canonized, his cause did inspire a flourishing cult in the north of England and on the Continent for nearly two hundred years. This office depicts for us a young man of fiery temperament who, after a few years at Oxford, at age eighteen resolutely abandoned society and what he called his sinful youth. Borrowing a garment from his sister, Rolle fashioned for himself a hermit's robe and spent the next thirty-one years living the hermit's life. He spent his time writing and giving spiritual guidance to those who sought him out.

During the first six years of his new life, Rolle experienced special spiritual graces but did not try to describe them until much later. He related his spiritual progress in four provocative images: the open door, heat, song, and sweetness. Each of those images records a stage in attaining union with God. In Rolle's writings, the state of union is ultimately expressed in the image of a medieval feast, with all exuberance of fine music, the savor of fine foods, and with the Lord of Love presiding over the banquet.

Imagery of heat, fire, music, sweetness, touch, or sexual union is very common in the writings of all the mystics in the Judeo-Christian tradition. Those aspects of life which characterize humanity and life at its most intense and meaningful are those which tend to be used, even when what they ultimately symbolize is totally ineffable. One only tends to use analogies that are intimately known, even though language and images are incomplete and imperfect representations of the mystery being expressed.

Rolle was a prolific writer, but his works fail to fall into a uniform pattern or theological structure. We can categorize them into three groups, each of which corresponds to a particular stage in his own religious development: 1) didactic writings, such as commentaries on scripture texts; 2) devotional writings, showing Rolle's personality and theological understanding; and 3) letters of spiritual direction, which show his practical nature.

Rolle taught a spirituality of a very affective timbre. He stressed Jesus at the center of devotion and strongly encouraged the laity to aspire to personal union with God. In recognizing the hierarchy of loves, as did the contemporary Italian mystic Dante, Rolle emphasized to the ordinary churchgoer the vitality of the exchange of love between the human soul and God. No matter the inequality of the exchange, love must be told. Rolle pointed to a God who is lovely as well as loving. His writings remind the Church that the Body has a heart as well as a mind, and though he may seem to us extravagant and effusive in his language, we must ask ourselves the question: "When is love not extravagant?"

Richard Rolle played an important part in the mystic tradition because of the encouragement he brought to the ordinary Christian. He was often compared to Francis of Assisi, since he never took Holy Orders and was one of the most unclerical and independent of mystics. Rolle leaves us with the impression of a "freelance" missionary and troubadour. Writing from the point of view of his wandering yet eremitic lifestyle, he spoke poetically of a passionate response to a God of love.

Julian of Norwich
1342 - 1413
APOPHATIC
AFFECTIVE

One of the best known of the 14th-Century English mystics is Julian of Norwich, an anchoress born a few years before Rolle died. The reconstruction of her anchorhold, attached to a small church in an industrial section of the city of Norwich, is hard to find but worth the effort. The life of a recluse might be hard for our modern minds to grasp. We may think it unnatural and uncommon to remain "walled up" within a small room of one's own free will. However, between the 11th and 16th Centuries, it was an established institution. So widespread did it become that there was not a single county or shire in England which did not at some time or other have a recluse's cell. There is evidence for the existence of at least seven hundred fifty cells, with the known names of over six hundred fifty hermits and anchorites.

Like Richard Rolle, Julian also painted a passionate image of intimacy and union with the Holy Other. This comes to us through her *Revelations of Divine Love*, which is currently printed in several different editions and is among the most popular spiritual reading today.

The formal difference in her literary style comes through as a report of visions or "showings" she experienced. The first version, written shortly after the series of sixteen visions occurred, is rather short, telling only what she witnessed in her visions. This version was followed by a longer one which came as a result of Julian's reflections upon those visions some ten to twenty years later. Her ecstatic experiences are unique in that Julian sought not only to relate the events as they pertained to her own soul but also to lay out the theme of a divine plan of salvation for all souls. The revelations offered answers to fundamental questions of human existence, and this the anchoress desired to offer for public edification of her "showings". Though it is possible to list them as sixteen separate episodes which lasted for a mere five hours, none of them really stand on their own without reference to each other. All the revelations relate back to the first, namely, the precious crowning of Christ with thorns. The first showing included and demonstrated to Julian the mystery of the Holy Trinity as well as the Incarnation and the unity between the human soul and God. We should recognize here, in the first revelation, that Julian was laying out her Christology.[48] The focus of her theology is in the Passion of Christ. The complexity of this theology is astounding in its depth and profundity, especially as Julian refers to herself as a "fool" and as a "simple creature".

"Divine Love" is the primary theme of Julian's revelations and whatever else may be spoken of in the content of these revelations, Love remains the central focus. For Julian all wisdom and knowledge must be rooted in love, and from this it becomes transformed into a loving knowledge of God. This approach to the mystic experience has many parallels in continental visionary literature; however, Julian's sobriety painted a less flowery picture than the rest. Continental predecessors such as Ramon Lull or Jacopone da Todi tended toward the more effusive language of passion and presented a more poetic genre of mystic literature. Julian, consciously inspired by Holy Scripture, showed more of an interest in the practical problems of teaching the laity something about mystical prayer and was less interested in the literary expression which that took. Basic to Julian's theology is a perspective of the soul as

---

[48] her understanding of Jesus as the second person of the Holy Trinity

having a like substance with its Creator. She uses the term "Substance" while other Mystics refer to the "Ground" or "Spark" of the soul. However, the intention is the same: the substance of our soul is that point at which we are immediately present to God and He to us. We are made conscious of that connection through our Sensuality, according to the anchoress. Sensuality, in this context, does not signify base nor merely animal instincts; rather, it functions as the seat of human sensibilities. This brings God into the very dailiness or otherwise mundane facets of our lives. This aids in the divinization of our souls by bringing us back to our intended nature.

Julian viewed sin as that which keeps us from connecting our Sensuality with our Substance. In her opinion, sin keeps us broken and unavailable to experience our true potential as extensions of the Divine nature. This is not at all foreign to our current understanding of the damage caused by compulsive behavior as regards human wholeness.

MARGERY KEMPE
1373 - 1433
KATAPHATIC
AFFECTIVE

Another woman, contemporary with Julian, offered yet one more style or journal of mystic experience. Margery Kempe, married with fourteen children, proved to be one of England's most controversial mystics of this Medieval period. By her own account Margery recognized herself as a pioneering feminist within the Church. Many who read her *Book* find her an infuriating or exasperating person, yet scholars such as Martin Thornton defend her as expressing the core of English spirituality and providing a bridge from the Middle Ages to the Modern Era.

Margery's eccentric nature comes through in the descriptions of her own rushes of ecstasy and fantasies in which she saw herself participating in the birth of the Virgin Mary and Jesus. Although this may appear rather bizarre to us, the early 14th Century saw an increase in a recognizable type of feminine piety, exemplified by its ecstatic phenomena and centered in particularly human accounts of the Gospel narratives. Literally thousands of women tried to live quasi-religious lives while they remained in the world. Margery Kempe was such a one.

By carrying a stream of pastoral and ascetical tradition through a turbulent period of reform, Margery's gift to the student of mysticism is found in her singular devotion. For whatever else might be said of her, Margery possessed a stick-to-it courage which never failed as she made her life's pilgrimage for the love of Christ.

the "Cloud" author
c. 1349 - 1396
APOPHATIC
AFFECTIVE

The mystery of God's call to the soul receives examination and explanation by another 14th-Century Englishman who has remained completely anonymous to all but God and to those who knew him personally. He is known to us only as The Author of the *Cloud of Unknowing*. Educated guesses have been made that he was a cleric and possibly a monk.[49]

---

[49] some speculate that he was a Carthusian

In the *Cloud* and in the short *Book of Privy Counsel* this author dealt with the varied problems of the spiritual life, and we can detect by them that his mystical doctrine is at once traditional and church-centered, humane and humorous. It is not generally known that there are six other treatises from his pen, shorter in length but of similar value and interest. They can be found in the Classics of western Spirituality series from Paulist Press, under the title, *The Pursuit of Wisdom*.

The best known work, *The Cloud of Unknowing*, expresses the apophatic tradition and from the 14th Century onwards dominates spiritual writing in the western Church until the Reformation. Discernible in the Cloud are the influences of the Dionysian school of spirituality, which were filtered down to him through the Victorines. The Dionysian world view, or "cosmic theology", was taken for granted by the *Cloud* author. By the 14th Century it had become his own milieu. He, in turn, influenced the 16th Century Spanish mystic, John of the Cross, along the way of the *via negativa*.

Germane to its proposition, the Cloud described the spiritual stages of illumination by using thematic imagery of ascent through mist, rain, and cloud. The land of sunshine represented, for this author, the end of the pilgrimage, where the soul would feel the heat of God's affection "aflamed with the fire of His love". The four stages which the Cloud author defined as that ascent or evolution of the person on the way were:

1) *The Common*—those folks who are simply in the habit of attending church and saying the prayers they learned as children;

2) *The Special*—those who have felt the desire to go further into the spiritual life;

3) *The Singular*—those who have heard a specific call from the Lord to live more completely for him and dedicate their entire lives for his sake; and

4) *The Perfect*—the ones we recognize as saints. The first three stages are obtainable to us in this life, but the fourth stage we can only begin here, awaiting our completion in the Heavenly Kingdom.

There are subtle but non-essential differences among these writers. They are subtle between the *Cloud* and Richard Rolle's fire of love. They are non-essential between the passion for Christ as expressed in Julian's *Revelations* and the *Book of Margery Kempe*. What gives the English school its distinctive flavor are the curious idioms of expressed love such as "Christ's own dearworthy darling", "homely dalliance", and "listy" behavior which become impossible to translate fully into modern vernacular.

WaLteR hilton
c. 1340–1396
KATAPHATIC
SPECULATIVE

If our sensibilities are, at first, put off by the intensity with which the English Medieval art and literature dwell on the realistic conceptualization of the Passion and Crucifixion of Christ, we must keep in mind their intent. Realism and homeliness constantly reappear in English devotions to incite feelings of love and contrition for sin. The intent was to manipulate the emotions in order to cultivate a greater ardor of these icons of the English spiritual tradition. The one recognized as master of "Ghostly Counsel" is Walter Hilton. A priest, a solitary, and eventually a monk in the Diocese of Lincoln, Hilton lived in the early period of the 15th Century. Little is known about his life, but Hilton is survived by his massive work, *Scale of Perfection*. This spiritual treatise comprises so wide and diverse an approach that almost any reader can find a place which speaks to his or her own spiritual condition. It remained for centuries the most popular of English spiritual works.

The *Scale* was evidently comprised of two works: the first written for a female recluse and the second for a larger audience. The devout middle and upper classes of Hilton's day sought experiential union with God, which Hilton tried to nurture by providing guidance in the ways of contemplative prayer. Throughout the *Scale* Hilton tried to direct his readers within the complexities of affectivity, the leading of the senses and emotions toward the conversion of the whole person. Since the totality of a human being is engaged in the process of union with God, our intellect and our emotions must each undergo a conversion and a progressive purification if they are to reach the ultimate goal of transformation in Christ. He based this progression upon the twin virtues of meekness and love.

Hilton, like the rest of the English school, sought to wed the affective with the speculative mystical tradition. His hopeful expectation of spiritual progress for those who cooperate with divine grace characterizes the catholic tradition in that he saw humanity not as depraved or beyond hope but as actually participating in redemption and sanctification. Putting it simply, Hilton proposed that we help God to help us. He also condemned any spirituality which neglected the practicalities of life such as child-rearing or manual labor.

Hilton, however, was also a man who was loyal to the authority of the Church. For him, the grace of God was not some magic formula which, when sprinkled liberally upon a soul, would bring a sort of immediate holiness. Struggle and pain are necessary aspects upon the pilgrimage, and Hilton viewed the Church and sacraments as a vital remedy for the moral dilemmas which accost the soul on its journey. Within the framework of the Church's institution, Hilton endorsed a pursuit of virtue. Duty might have inaugurated this pursuit but pure love for God would be the final motivator.

Solidly grounded in Holy Scripture, English piety expressed itself through encouragement to all "goodly souls" to read and meditate on those verses which speak of God's love for the soul. The mystics of 14th-Century England pioneered the translation of Scripture passages into the vernacular even before the famous John Wyclif. The age was surely alive and introduced the fashion of "common" prayer that was to develop into a distinctive Anglican form two centuries later.

Chapter 6
The Italian School

The spiritual setting of 13th-Century Italy concerned a return to the Gospel and the desire for a spirituality focused on the humanity of Christ, especially his suffering and crucifixion. This intent has already been stated in the discussion of St. Francis of Assisi, from whom a deep Christo-centric rationale was preached. Francis set the stage and Franciscan spirituality certainly dominated the Italian drama.

Bonaventure
1217 – 1274
APOPHATIC
SPECULATIVE

Pre-eminent among the followers of St. Francis was Bonaventure, a central figure of the Church's spiritual, scholastic, and political life in the 13th Century. Affective in nature and akin to the spirituality of Bernard of Clairvaux and the Victorines as much as that of St. Francis, he taught as a professor at the University of Paris during the time when his Dominican counterpart, Thomas Aquinas, was there. For a time Bonaventure also acted as the Minister General of the Franciscan Order.

What Francis began with his followers Bonaventure solidified by grounding that particular mendicant lifestyle and charism firmly with a theological underpinning. He was able to accomplish this because he lived in a period of history which had not yet separated theology from spirituality. These two disciplines had not yet become distinct; therefore, Bonaventure was able to draw on a wide variety of sources in order to build a systematic defense of Francis' ideal.

As with any bright idea—even those of divine origin—which becomes an institution, dissension and controversy often follow. For Francis and his band, this came relatively quickly. Among his own brethren there were those who wanted a mitigated interpretation of poverty, a less harsh living out of the Franciscan charism. By the time Bonaventure was well-established as a member of the Order, the controversy between the "Spirituals" and the "Conventuals" was full-blown. The Spirituals wanted to keep Francis' absolute ideal of poverty. They also preferred an eremitical style of living and were opposed to ecclesiastical advancements and the pursuit of scholarship. Their whole outlook was apocalyptic in nature and they saw their role as instruments of reform in a decadent church. They believed they ushered in an era of mystical enlightenment. On the other side were the Brothers of the Community, as the Conventuals were sometimes known. They pursued the mitigated rule, living out the Franciscan spirit as scholars in universities and at the heart of urban affairs.

Pope Alexander IV intervened in this controversy by asking for the resignation of the Minister General of the Franciscans, one John of Parma, who leaned heavily in favor of the Spirituals. The Pope then appointed Bonaventure as John's successor. Bonaventure was known to be a moderate and a stabilizing influence, and he served in the capacity of Minister General for seventeen years. He guided the Order in such a way as to cultivate in its ethos a spirit of humility with sound learning, and his genius balanced the cultivation of knowledge without undermining the spirit of prayer.

In effect, Bonaventure wedded the speculative and affective natures of true devotion and because of this success has been credited as the Franciscan's second founder.

A spirituality focused on the passion and poverty of Christ not only had its practical application but, as we see in Bonaventure, was also part and parcel of the intellectual milieu of the 13th Century. Bonaventure expressed a deep devotion to the Passion of Christ and his writings mark a milestone in the development of this love for Christ's suffering. To this end, be composed the *Tree of Life*, hoping to assist the faithful in their meditation on this aspect of our Lord's life. In this work, Bonaventure depicts Jesus as a mystical tree who bears the fruits of our redemption in the various actions of his earthly ministry. He tells us that as we apprehend these fruits in our own lives, delighting in their sweetness, we allow divine nourishment to accomplish its work in us. Of all the fruits born of Christ, those which spring from His Passion provide the richest sustenance. Also important in the spirituality of Bonaventure are his theory on the purgative, illuminative, and unitive way and his views on contemplation. For the first time, a complete exposition on the distinction between the three ways of the spiritual life is established. Progress in this threefold way comes about by employing another triad: meditation, prayer, and contemplation.

As Francis and Dominic were so alike and yet so different, so theological reflection of the highest caliber associated the Franciscan Bonaventure with the Dominican Thomas Aquinas, bringing the spirits of their founders from the pragmatic struggles of living out their visions to the systematic theology of the Church.

On the opposite side of the Franciscan controversy stood Jacopone da Todi, one of the Spirituals who lived contemporaneously with Mechthild of Magdeburg, Gertrude the Great and Meister Eckhart and offered a poet's heart to the Italian school. Though a member of the upper class of Italian society, Jacopone threw himself into the life of a "bizzocone"[50] upon the unexpected death of his young wife. After ten years of this rigorous life, he sought entrance into the Order of Francis, the Friars Minor.

Although Jacopone did not possess the mystical sagacity of Francis nor the literary brilliance of Dante,[51] he still played a visible and vital role in the mystic tradition of 13th-Century Europe. The torment which consumed him, with regard to his personal life, with questions of God, and with the institutional Church leaves little doubt as to his earnest devotion.

Because Jacopone allied himself with the Franciscan Spiritualist party, he came into direct conflict with Pope Boniface VIII who supported the Conventuals of the Franciscan Order. In the end serious hostilities erupted, ending in bloodshed or imprisonment. Jacopone threw in his lot with the fate of the spirituals and spent several years in prison. Benedict XI, Boniface's successor, pardoned him, but prison life had been so harsh that he died within three years of his release.

Powerful poetry, both spiritually and politically, marks Jacopone's *Lauds* as the premier verse in Italy

---

[50] a public penitent and beggar
[51] though he does hold the distinction of being the author of the beautiful hymn, the "Stabat Mater"

prior to Dante. Responding to the intense corruption of the Church and beginning with the papal office, Jacopone's sensitivities compelled him to stand apart from the political machine and even somewhat from his own brethren. The Spirituals found some small deliverance from persecution in the support given to them in 1294 by the newly elected Pope Celestine V, who drew them under his protection by incorporating them as the "Poor Hermits of Celestine". That protection was short-lived, since the Pope abdicated his office only five months after his enthronement. At that time, the Church—particularly the papacy—bent under the heavy thumb of the King of Naples and succumbed to moral decay. Flowing from the pen of an impassioned poet came both Jacopone's fury and his love.

Intense emotions flamed within Jacopone's poetry. It speaks of the austere and the gracious. It depicts Franciscan piety of this age well. Characteristic of his style, Jacopone displayed metaphysical doctrines with such color and enthusiasm that a person can be dazed by the thought that, like John of the Cross, his most impressive works were written in prison. His *Lauds* delight and inform the reader by their distinctive flavor and diverse subject matter. One poem laments the neglect of humility and love in the keeping of a Religious Rule, while another gently caresses images of the Nativity. Jacopone resembled a troubadour, free and given to altered moods to suit the circumstances around and within him. He gave integrity to Franciscan spirituality through his own convictions and his own devotion, lending a more serious note to the joy of the Poverello's[52] ideals.

---

[52] "The poor one", a popular nickname for Francis of Assisi

Angela of Foligno 1248 – 1309 KATAPHATIC AFFECTIVE	

Yet another of the Franciscan band who favored the Spirituals, though of the Third Order, was Angela of Foligno, an Umbrian mystic. She vigorously encouraged faithfulness to the primitive Rule of St. Francis, and she herself lived a strict vow of poverty.

Angela was a married woman whose husband, sons, and mother all died within a short span of time, just after her conversion. What we know of her comes to us through a writing which she dictated to her confessor, the Franciscan Brother Arnaldo. As is common in the realm of medieval history, little else is known about the details concerning Angela's life.

Angela tells us that she was a woman of means and that prior to her conversion she enjoyed all manner of impetuous living and luxury, even to the extent of immorality. Being as rich and beautiful as she is said to have been it is not difficult to imagine some of what Angela may have thought necessary to repent of in her full confession. That confession proved integral to her conversion process. Though she was not formally educated, her mind was open, active, and exceptionally cultivated.

For the first five years after her conversion, spiritual progress was rather slight, as she struggled with the difficulties of letting go of a pleasure-seeking past. However, in 1291, Angela and some companions decided to make a pilgrimage to Assisi and there to beg the intercession of the Saint. She desired that he might obtain for her the grace to experience the presence of Christ in her soul and to help her attain to a true spirit of poverty. During this pilgrimage, Angela had several visions and behaved with such strange ecstasies that she was asked to leave Assisi and never return.[53] Regardless of the rebuke, Angela received abundant graces and was in fact transformed by this event. She was filled with a tremendous sense of peace and intimacy with the Lord, which never left her.

The Brother who had reprimanded Angela during her pilgrimage, asking her to leave, was none other than Brother Arnaldo, her own cousin. It was he who later became her confessor. On being transferred to Foligno, Arnaldo began to foster Angela's spiritual life with growing interest. His prompting and questionings resulted in the dictated account of Angela's spiritual experiences. This has since become known as *The Book of Blessed Angela of Foligno*. Through the relating of what she experienced, Angela passed on to Brother Arnaldo her spiritual journey up to that point. The first part of the *Book of Visions and Instructions*, called "The Memorial", describes what Angela calls the "thirty steps of mystical ascent". There she tells of frequent visions concerning the Passion of our Lord, and because of this she reflects early Franciscan spirituality in its highest form. The second part of her book, called "The Instructions", is made up of letters of spiritual advice and of further accounts of visionary events in her life. Angela often used the metaphor of an embrace to describe the experience of Christ's authentic presence in one's life. She also described the uniqueness of each divine ecstasy. No two visions, no two meetings with the Lord are ever the same. Encountering the Divine is ever new and original.

---

[53] One is reminded of the embarrassing behavior of Margery Kempe.

dante Alighieri
1265 – 1321
KATAPHATIC
AFFECTIVE

Of Italian literary giants, one of the most well known and most loved is another one whom not many people would have considered in the category of "mystic". He is the poet Dante, who wrote the famous *Divine Comedy*. Neither a priest nor a monk, Dante Alighieri was born in Florence in 1265, where his father worked as a notary. His family was an old and noble one. His mother died shortly after his birth, and although his father married again and had two more children, he too died while Dante was still just a boy.

Impossible to fit into a defined category of mysticism, Dante's life and work yet remain extremely important to those who pursue a deeper comprehension of the spiritual life. While no evidence has survived of Dante's personal mystical encounters, his *Divine Comedy* continues as the world's best poetic specimen of the reality of sin, reparation, redemption, and beatitude. An earlier work, the *Vita Nuova*, stands as a precursor to the masterpiece in that it introduces us to the revelation of Love (Beatrice) for whom Dante began his pilgrimage. It would be of benefit to the reader to begin the study of the *Commedia* with the reading of this small book.

Not only was *The Divine Comedy* a religious allegory, but also it is a political one. Here we find Dante reflecting the state of affairs at the time. The poem describes the political and religious milieu of a divided Italy, where dominion seesawed between the Guelfs[54]

---

[54] supporters of the papacy

and the Ghibellines.[55] It was in the second volume, Canto Six of *Purgatorio*, where Dante characterized his homeland as a brothel and a pilotless ship.

In its volumes *Inferno* (Hell) and *Paradiso* (Heaven), Dante treats of the Church's traditional teaching on these two aspects of eternal life. Through them he voyaged as a mere spectator, guided by the spirits of Virgil, the great poet of antiquity, and Bernard, the mystic of Clairvaux. All that is portrayed there conforms to the orthodox teaching of the Holy Scriptures and of the Roman Catholic Church. *Purgatorio*, the middle volume, is unique to the trilogy and is portrayed through Dante's own imagination. Traditional teaching has purgatory as being a subterranean region, whereas Dante depicts it as a lofty mountain of pilgrimage. Dante's Purgatory is less shrouded by dogma and depicts a type of passionate game in which those who have lived wasteful and neglectful lives must spend the same amount of time in that place striving to rid themselves of their sinful natures. Here Dante actively participates in the action of the story.

Dante did not entitle his work *The Divine Comedy*, but simply, *The Comedy*. The word "Divine" was added by later publishers. While it is a story which certainly has a divine nature, it is also a very human story. We need to understand what is meant by the word "comedy". In this context it does not mean something amusing or funny; rather, in the literary sense, a comedy is the opposite of tragedy. In other words, it has a happy ending, though as one reads through the first volume, *Inferno*, the difficulty of keeping this in mind becomes quite apparent. For Dante, no question

---

[55] allies of the emperor

of a happy ending arose. His religious convictions stood firm in the assurance of Eternal Life for those who love God, no matter how difficult the journey from this life to the next. Thus, *The Divine Comedy* is a drama of the soul's ultimate choices and is one of Christianity's finest allegories. It derives its power from the Christian revelation of eternal reward and punishment as seen traditionally through its apocalyptic literature. The *"Commedia"* suggests, without using much theological detail, the three stages of return to God: purgation, illumination, and perfection. In this, his theology is completely in line with Catholic teaching which maintains that every soul in the world must make the choice between accepting or rejecting God and that life is a process of sanctification.

Politically, Dante was far ahead of his time. As doctrinally orthodox as he was, Dante belonged to the Ghibelline party[56] which supported the Emperor over the Pope. In a treatise concerning this state of affairs, Dante supported the notion of a separation of Church and State. He acknowledged the Pope's authority over the Church but felt that the Emperor should be the supreme authority when it came to civil affairs. Ideally, he felt that they should govern their jurisdictions side by side and compatibly. As an exile from Florence for his political views, Dante spent the rest of his life in Ravenna.

A bizarre anecdote ends the story of Dante. After the years of political rivalry were ended and Dante had won the acclaim of the world for his literary genius, Florence desired to have her "favorite" son's remains returned to the city for interment. Ravenna refused to

---

[56] though his family had been firmly Guelfs

give up the body. After many years of this discussion and firm refusal, Dante's grave was finally opened and there was nothing found therein. Legend grew up around this incident that Dante had returned to the nether-regions which he had so eloquently described. However, in the 19th Century, when construction workers were making a hole in a monastery wall in order to install some pipes, a coffin was found bearing the name "Dante Alighieri". It is supposed that during the hot debates about the claims on Dante's remains, some pious folk hid him from possible Florentine grave robbers. But they hid him so well that the people of Ravenna did not even know where he was. So in Ravenna his mortal remains remain.

Catherine of Siena
1347 – 1380
KATAPHATIC
AFFECTIVE

There can be no doubt about the mystical genius of our next Italian mystic, Catherine of Siena. This "Doctor of the Church" pursued a social as well as a religious mission which she expressed in a consistent manner. This won for her the admiration and attention of both the political and ecclesial aristocracy of the 14th Century. A contemporary of Julian of Norwich, this Catherine epitomized affective spirituality through the path of "Mystical Marriage". In her espousal to Christ, she saw as her primary responsibility the winning of souls and restoration of the unity within the Body of Christ.

The mysticism of Catherine inclined toward learning, and as a Dominican she remained faithful to the teaching of Thomas Aquinas. Creation, for her, was a pronouncement of God's own Goodness, and thus all that He created remained dependent upon Him. As with Thomas, Catherine allowed that sin put a wrinkle in God's creation. By repentance and suffering, truth could be restored to creation and a pristine freshness which is Christ's own gift.

While extremely active as an ambassador of God's Love to a crippled Church, Catherine remained a devout contemplative within the enclosure of her heart. Her early discipline of a solitary life in a small room of her Father's house grounded her in a singularity of will, mind, and heart as the Bride of Christ. As one of the greatest "spiritual mothers" of the Middle Ages, she kept up a massive correspondence with her many disciples. Approximately four hundred letters have survived and provide portholes through which a fresh spiritual breeze still blows.

The *Dialogues*, Catherine's best known work, has similar qualities as *The Revelations of Divine Love* of Julian. In it Catherine explained the Love of God as it had been revealed to her and expounded upon the theological attributes which go into the relationship between Creator and Creation. As with Julian, Catherine is very Christo-centric, a central theme of the *Dialogues* showing Christ as "the Bridge". All of her discussions end with a reaffirming of personal fulfillment as found only in the Godhead, revealed by Christ. Love, grounded in true humility, is the divine motive and love the proper response of the soul.

Girded about by love's colloquy in the south and in the northwest of Europe, between Catherine of Siena and Julian of Norwich, a strong strain of self-awareness began to dominate the pursuit of union with God. Major shifts in approach to human value came to birth under the gentle guidance of these two women, yet always proclaimed within the life of traditional monastic austerity. Humanity was seen as less and less of a blight upon creation. The soul began to be recognized as God's dwelling place here on earth and, therefore, commanded more respect.

Catherine of Genoa
1447 – 1510
KATAPHATIC
SPECULATIVE

A hundred years later another Catherine dominated the Italian scene. Unlike the virgin of Siena, Catherine of Genoa was tied to a political marriage in her early years. Her father, who died prior to her birth, had been the viceroy of Naples, and the family saw fit to use this daughter as a pawn for the benefit of themselves rather than in her best interest. Though Catherine ardently desired to enter the convent of the Augustinian canonesses in Genoa, she was too young to make that decision and her family intervened. Her marriage was one which left her unhappy and neglected.

After ten years in this unholy alliance, Catherine had an intense conversion experience and asked to be released from her marital obligations. She then began an active ministry to the sick and needy. Later on, her husband also had a change of heart and placed himself under rule as a Franciscan Tertiary. They continued to live together in a celibate relationship until his death in 1497.

Less visionary and more philosophic than the previous Catherine, this mystic of Genoa found her balance between the active and contemplative states. She became noted as a philanthropist and administrator of the women's ward of the hospital in Genoa. In this she proved to be a competent and courageous caregiver, laboring tirelessly during the fever epidemic of 1493.

Catherine's major contribution to mystical theology and her primary regard lie in the perfected harmony between the human soul and Divine Love as won in Purgatory. The soul in Purgatory had its imperfections burned away through suffering, much as rust is burned away from a pure metal. Catherine viewed sin as a parasite which hid the soul from the rays of Divine Love and caused the soul to wither. Suffering provided the refiner's fire by which the parasite was removed and enabled the soul's capacity for God to grow to final union.

That Catherine met and knew suffering cannot be doubted. Many of the works of mercy she performed suspended her precariously over the seething cauldron of the Black Death. In such a woman, no separation exists between belief and action. They are of a piece, melded together by the identification of pure love in union with God.

An extraordinary aspect of Catherine's spiritual life showed itself in her inability to eat during the Church's penitential season. These fasts, particularly the long fast of Lent, did not leave her weak or emaciated. Modern psychologists might diagnose this inability to eat as a severe case of anorexia, but the fact that her life was enhanced rather than depleted by the experience keeps us from labeling her with a psychological illness, especially in the fact that at the end of these extreme fasts, Catherine was able to partake of a complete meal with no negative effects.

Chapter 7
The Spanish School

ithout a doubt, no thoughtful traveler or pilgrim can spend much time in Spain without perceiving the deeply ingrained sense of the spiritual which is inborn in its people. The close association with the mystical realm comes through in her history, her art, and her literature. Therefore it cannot be an exaggeration to say that the mystical writings of Spain's golden age, the 16th Century, have had a universal influence of dynamic proportions. The religious literature of this period numbered into the thousands, yet relatively few have made their way into the English-speaking world. The treasures which have come to us have been initially due to the translations and scholarship of a professor of the University of Leeds, E. Allison Peers, who published many translations early in the 20th Century.

The 16th Century was the age of the Spanish conquests, of prosperity and genius. Significant also, this period realized the unification of the Spanish nation. Reclaiming Spain from the Moslems bred a fiercely militant and crusading brand of Christianity, for once the Moors were expelled or forcibly converted, the Spaniards went to work on the Jews and those suspected of Protestantism. The Spanish Inquisition earned its reputation as one of the most infamous movements of the Counter-Reformation but also fostered an expression of spiritual fervor and renewal. The Spanish mystics reflect this side of the movement.

In what ways do the Spanish mystics differ from their English or German counterparts? Some scholars feel that the difference is found in the intensity of their devotion and the strong injection of vibrant personal experience. Theirs is a vibrant passion which could almost be described as an abandonment bordering on intoxication. It was the Spanish who gave to the Church the vivid symbol of the crucifix and who took the Church into the New World.

Ramon Lull
1235 – 1315
KATAPHATIC
AFFECTIVE

Intoxication easily describes the evangelistic passion of Ramon Lull, a contemporary of Angela of Foligno and Dante. For this Spaniard, mysticism had no vestige of cool, speculative reason. Rather it was something mobile, fluid, and as impassioned as the chivalry of the age. Lull's imagery leaned toward the exotic, with an affectivity similar to Jacopone da Todi. Yet there was a sense of wild abandon in Lull that leaves the reader emotionally stirred.

In his youth Lull prided himself on being quite a "ladies' man". His conversion came in the midst of some rather ridiculous extramarital affairs. The story runs that, in spite of his wife's affection and the children which she bore him, he was passionately enamored of a Genoese lady who kept spurning his advances. On one occasion he is said to have ridden his horse right into a church where she was engaged in prayer. The lady endeavored on many occasions to rid herself of Lull and when this proved unsuccessful, she summoned him to her. She then revealed to him her breasts which he had so often extolled in his love poems. To his horror Ramon saw that her breast was being slowly eaten away by a malignant cancer.

By his own account, Lull shows us the amazing generosity of God toward a thick-headed sinner, for while in the midst of yet another love poem to yet another object of his infatuation, Lull became aware of the crucified Lord standing at his side. On this initial vision he quickly left the room. On the second appearance of Our Lord to Ramon, he went into hiding under the blankets on his bed. It took the Lord a total of five appearances before Ramon allowed the metanoia to be completed within him. His conversion complete, Ramon turned his pen from the amorous poems for his mistresses to an effusion of passionate affection toward God. In his mystical works *The Tree of Love* and *The Book of the Lover and the Beloved* one can witness how Lull combined a philosophical vocabulary with a language best suited for the boudoir.

Clearly taken by the mysticism of Islam, a prevalent influence in the Spain of his day, Ramon mirrored the Islamic literary style in his own work. In fact, Lull's first Christian script, *The Book of Contemplation*, was written in Arabic. This influence comes through also in Lull's obsession with number concepts and applications of logic to any and all situations. His adept mental capacity for Arabic mathematics helped earmark his favorite work, *Ars Magna*, as a mental alchemy or a cybernetic machine in that it was an extremely well organized system which tried to capture all manner of knowledge and place it within the framework of the basic building blocks of the created order. In other words, each piece of knowledge fits under a category of one of the elemental principles of the universe. This type of writing distinguished it from the poetry and other works of the age, and yet it still exuded passion and convincing motivation for conversion.

Lull seemed determined to change the world—or more precisely, he desired to bring it back into the original alignment which God had given it at the beginning of creation. Ramon proposed that humanity fits into a natural hierarchy corresponding to the divine vocation of each person. He perceived it to be the duty of the individual to perfectly reflect the purpose for which each was created. Once this was accomplished, complete communication could exist in the world via a common language, a common law and a common religion. We could consider this Ramon's image of utopia.

His affinity for the Islamic and Judaic religious traditions in no way hindered Ramon from an all-out evangelistic campaign for their conversion. He saw his own purpose in life as the winning of converts from these two cultures, and his primary tool for spreading the Gospel came from the system he had devised in the *Ars Magna*. The undergirding of this system he viewed as the transformation of chaos into order. Tirelessly Ramon pursued his fantasy as a soldier of the Cross, and legend has it that he won the martyr's crown in one of his many excursions to evangelize the Moslems of North Africa.

For the student of mysticism, the centerpiece of Ramon's work is his *Book of the Lover and the Beloved*. Here Lull offered his reader the essentially mystical figure of the Beloved (God) and the Lover (the contemplative soul). He not only uses romantic and picturesque language to describe the Incarnation, Passion, and Crucifixion of Jesus, but also he points to those who have fallen in love with God, who embrace the glories of the mystical life, which lead the soul to that sublime goal of perpetual union with God. The book itself is contained within a larger book, *Blanquerna*, a narrative story of a young man's pursuit of God. Also contained within that narrative work is another book which compliments *Lover and Beloved*. It is *The Art of Contemplation*, and it illustrates Ramon's love of method. We might call it his practical manual of devotion, which acts as a guide book for those on the lower slopes of the ascent to God. While *Lover and Beloved* shows us Ramon as mystic, *Contemplation* reveals Ramon as teacher.

Ignatius of Loyola
1495 – 1556
KATAPHATIC
SPECULATIVE

Perhaps a better known soldier for Christ, and one whose battlefield lay completely within the bounds of the Christian church rather than in evangelizing the heathen, was Ignatius of Loyola. Some scholars claim that Ignatius originated one of the greatest eruptions of spiritual energy in the history of the Church, immersed as he was in the controversy of the Reformation and Counter-Reformation.

A poor writer, literarily speaking, Ignatius nevertheless gave the Church one of the best-known and best-loved systems for synthesizing the contemplative process for the common man. Instead of visual or auditory ecstasies, he received experiences of infused comprehension, understanding profound spiritual truths without the aid of academic discipline. By this means the spiritual life opened to him its many faces, and Ignatius desired most deeply to pass his understanding on to his followers.

With Ignatius, another style of religious literature makes an appearance, though it is not usually considered as a mystical writing. While other mystics produced dialogues and treatises or sermons, Ignatius constructed a "how to" manual. He was a mystic who had a great distrust of mysticism, and he was a man of action who sought to balance active participation with a passive reception of Divine Grace.

The Spiritual Exercises of Ignatius were meant to be *used*, not just read. His primary audience was his band of followers, a barefooted lot, wearing long gray smocks and calling themselves "Inigo's preachers". This manual helped them as they endeavored to direct others in the now-famous Thirty Day Retreat. The ragtag band of followers was the first of an order Ignatius called The Society of Jesus, known more commonly as The Jesuits. Their influence, as engendered by their founder, has made an impressive mark on the world. Along with the powerful Carmelite tradition, the Jesuits dominated the later period of the Middle Ages and indeed the subsequent eras as well.

Ignatius' own mystical experience and conversion came during his recuperation from a battle wound. While convalescing, he began reading *The Life of Christ*, written by the German Carthusian, Ludolph of Saxony. Another book which had great influence in his early devotion was The Golden Legend by the Italian author, Jacopo de Voragine. These books filled Ignatius with the desire to do great things for God. In fact, he described himself at this period as possessing a heart inflamed with the love of God. As soon as his recovery was complete, he sought out the solitude of prayer and reflection in a retreat at the monastery of Montserrat, where he made the ultimate warrior's sacrifice of hanging up his sword and dagger before the altar of Our Lady.[57]

Traditionally the *Exercises* are meant to be the spiritual director's guide for those making a thirty-day retreat, but this retreat has also been successfully compressed into a retreat of eight days. No matter the length, the retreat is not meant as an isolated experience but rather the foundation upon which a person's whole life will be transformed.

The key to Ignatian mysticism is its dynamism, which renders the Christian life transparent. As with Dante, Ignatius' mystical style is totally image-oriented, or kataphatic. *The Spiritual Exercises* are certainly a paradigm of the *via positiva*. Ignatius desired his followers to focus on the Divine Mysteries, the earthiness and the heavenliness of Jesus' life. He wanted them to experience the Christ life in such a way as to make that life experience a salvific event in itself, and in this he succeeded.

teResa of avila
1515 – 1582
Kataphatic
Speculative

Another phenomenal specimen of the Spanish school, and one of the best-known and most loved of the mystics, is Teresa Sánchez de Cepeda y Ahumada, known to the Church as Teresa of Avila. Gifted as an administrator and writer, Teresa lived submerged in the milieu of the infamous Spanish Inquisition, when all vernacular writing and especially the writings of women were

---

[57] Legend has it that St. Mary herself dictated *The Spiritual Exercises* to Ignatius. Be that true or not, it is undisputed that the *Exercises* are truly inspired.

forcefully denounced. Though she taught her people to speak the language of the angels, Teresa herself experienced the trauma of having to burn her entire library. Her brilliant faculties and intuitions were tried in the fire of holy obedience as she authored many works under one confessor and was then commanded to destroy them at the behest of another. It is truly remarkable that so much of Teresa's brilliance remains for us to savor.

Teresa's life is set in the turbulent era of the Counter-Reformation and the lofty romance of the Spanish conquest of the New World. As it is virtually impossible to ignore cultural temperament, we can well imagine that Teresa displayed all the idealistic tendencies of the age. Her writings portray a woman who is at once pragmatic and passionate. Her interest lay not in the perpetuation of a mystical theory; rather, she relates what transpired in her own soul. All the stages and psychological interpretations Teresa describes amount to an intimate disclosure of autobiographical design.

Teresa commanded a powerful influence through her life and in her writings. Through both we can see that she was a real person with a real life and real feelings which she is not ashamed to show. In her we find a saint who sang, danced, cooked, and cleaned. Her sincerity, integrity, and personality have the ring of authenticity, which helps us not to hesitate to read her works, though we acknowledge her as a Doctor of the Church.

Besides her *Autobiography*, Teresa's best-known mystical works are *The Interior Castle* and *The Way of Perfection*. While *The Way* was written as a guide for her nuns, *The Interior Castle* is the journal of her experiences in mystical prayer. The enormous invest-ment of her energy in the experience and meaning of prayer pervades this work. The stages and struggles of praying occupied her continually, and here she reports them in nuanced detail.

Theologically significant and contrary to the popular aspirations of a growing Protestant spirituality, Teresa countered the view of that disembodied piety (spiritualism) with her own very anthropological Chris-tology. Realism expressed the centrality of Teresa's spirituality. With her spirit so enfolded in the love of the Incarnate Lord, it appears obvious that a natural object of interest would be the Mystical Body of Christ, and this is personified in her love for the Church. By uniting herself to her Spouse through untiring interest in ecclesial challenges, Teresa urged the lover of God to embrace that humanity which Christ assumed and to minister to the great need found there.

There can be no doubt that Teresa's greatest brilliance for the contemporary reader resides in her teaching on prayer, of which *The Interior Castle* gives such excellent description. Always compelling a person to stretch supposed capabilities, to stimulate recollec-tion one step at a time, Teresa assures us that it is the Lord's good pleasure to meet us on our own terms if we but make the effort. Hers was no theory of spiritual doctrine but what she experienced within herself as a true and valid approach to God.

Although a cloistered Religious, Teresa did as much in missionary fervor as any under a mendicant rule. The number of souls she influenced in her lifetime established Carmelite spirituality as a cardinal institu-tion for the propagation of contemplative prayer and mystic union even in our own age. When one thinks of mysticism, Teresa of Avila naturally comes to mind, and along with the image of a great lady also comes images of the classic exemplifier of the ecstatic experience. Much of what we have come to accept as vision, revelation, or mystical ecstasy is because, as has been said, she was not loath to give descriptive accounts from her own experience. We have learned to judge spirituality using as criteria her life and example.

John of the Cross
1542 – 1591
APOPHATIC
AFFECTIVE

One such soul who came directly under Teresa's sphere of influence was her young confessor, Fray Juan de la Cruz, better known to us as John of the Cross. The Yepes family, into which John was born, had its secrets. As were Teresa's family, the Yepes' were of Jewish extraction and lived in a period when that was not an acceptable heritage. The year 1492 is best remembered by us as the year when Columbus, through financing by the Spanish monarchy, "discovered" America. Few recall that it was also the year that the Jews, who had held consequential influence in Spain, were forcibly expelled.

John's parents married in love and defiance of family wishes and so were cut off from any financial assistance as they began their struggle to raise a family. His father died when John was about seven years old, which meant that at a very young age John learned responsibility by helping to support his mother and brothers. For several years he lived and worked at a hospital for derelicts, developing a compassion for humanity with an intensity at which many marveled. Through this experience John began a persistent pilgrimage toward God and discovered along the way that sanctity consisted of searching for and finding God in the very substance of humanity.

John's connection with the famous—or to some infamous—Teresa led him into troubles with the Carmelite order. Teresa had been appointed prioress of the Convent of the Incarnation in order to curb her adamant reforms toward a stricter rule. But, as circumstances would have it, John, as her confessor, was sympathetic to the reform and encouraged Teresa to pursue her vision. The brethren who opposed the more primitive observance had him kidnapped from his home in Avila, flogged publicly, and thrown into prison.

As dreadful as that experience must have been, living only in the dank recess of an unventilated cell which was no more than six feet by ten and with scarcely enough food for survival, Fray Juan used the time to compose his first mystical work, *The Spiritual Canticle*. No stranger to suffering nor "the dark night", his genius picked up on the apophatic style of mysticism and expounded upon complicated and abstruse doctrine.

The chief characteristic of John's mystical scheme is his analysis of purification. He describes these purifications as stages that one passes through in order to cleanse the soul completely before being drawn into God. Using the imagery of mystical nights, John devotes his two other well-known works, *Ascent of Mount Carmel* and *The Dark Night of the Soul*, to the explanation of this spiritual cleansing. The first book deals with the activity of the individual preparing for more intimate union with God and was written for those who have already begun the mystical journey. The second deals with the passive side of purification, which is God's initiative working upon the soul, drawing out of the person those blemishes hidden deeply within. At this point in the mystical journey John asserts that God changes "light" into "darkness", whereby transformation of the soul's inner resources takes place.

Both works are classics and of the highest caliber of mystical writing and should be accepted as volumes one and two because of the dominant theme which they share. But each needs also to be read in the context of the history and environment out of which they came, understanding that John wrote for people with a special vocation to the solitary life. However, those of different lifestyle and spirituality can benefit greatly from reading him.

In tracing out the traits which are particular to Fray Juan, gentleness is one which comes most readily into focus. Serenity, calm, and peace in his own personal life, despite the harsh and cruel persecutions he endured, stand out in bold relief. He counsels his brethren to cultivate humility, meekness, and patience of soul, cautioning them that souls focused on self rather than God grow very hard. If one were to summarize John's life, particularly as seen in his writings, it would be safe to say that he taught that the way to God was through total self-surrender.

Discussion of the Spanish school of mysticism has overlapped a period of ecclesial history which needs to be dealt with separately. The Protestant Rebellion and subsequent Counter-Reformation provide a very fascinating turn of events in the golden age of the mystical tradition. While Ignatius, Teresa, and John of the Cross culminated the Great Medieval Period of Catholic spirituality, they did so while Western society was well into the period known as the Renaissance. There is an overlap which may cause consternation to the history "buff", but it is not always easy to delineate between periods of spirituality. Truly Teresa, John, and Ignatius could be considered mystics of the Renaissance just as could the Rhinelanders Eckhart and Tauler, but one needs to remember that they were also linked most profoundly with classical age of Medieval spirituality. I would propose that the best way to view these holy ones is as the transitional ties which link the Medieval with the Modern eras. Had it not been for their dynamic influence, possibly mysticism would have faded into obscurity. As it stands, the essence of mysticism remains as fresh for us today as when these Spanish masters began their pilgrimage.

Chapter 8
Spirituality takes a turn

he period of history between the mid-15th Century and the end of the 16th Century becomes critically important as one moves into the study of modern and contemporary spirituality. A dramatic turn in the life of the Church and in all of Western society promulgated new doctrines as well as new interpretations of old and established ones. Of course, this did not happen suddenly nor at the motivation of one momentous event such as Luther's challenge at Wittenburg; rather, change was brought about by the several effects of significant intellectual, political, economic, and social factors which evolved over the course of this epoch. As these cultural shifts affected religious practice and thought, they also pushed the whole spectrum of spirituality into an intricate and complex framework.

No longer did there remain one continuous thread of thought or piety as had been fairly traceable from the Apostolic Church through the Scholastic period, or "High Middle Ages". The most striking departure, to my mind, was the shift from a collective (we) mentality to that of the individual (me) mentality—the secularization of society having done much to foster this change.

From this point on one must be more or less specific, making decisions about the variety of mystical piety one desires to pursue. Rather than the choice of an "historical" period, as has been mapped out in previous chapters, deliberate selection must be made along denominational lines. At this point, the structure of the

Church shatters into definitive species and subspecies, if you will. Accompanying this splintering along denominational boundaries, spirituality took on a multifaceted appearance. Even within groups one can discern differing spiritual formulae. For this reason, this chapter will endeavor to lay the sketch of a foundation of the period known as the Reformation. It necessarily must leave off discussing the spiritual biographies of individuals in order to set the stage for the displacement of classical theology.

As noted earlier in this study, the Church's structure and authority came under scrutiny in the Middle Ages. Mystics such as Catherine of Siena or Hildegard of Bingen felt compelled to remonstrative relationships with their religious and civic superiors when they perceived a laxity in Christian observance or morals. Conditions, however, worsened in subsequent centuries, so much so that by the 15th Century the moral decay and political rivalry that infected the Church left it with few unbiased advocates and even less power to control its own jurisdiction.

While the Church struggled internally, a major shift was taking place in the cultural milieu of Western Europe itself. From the conversion of the first Holy Roman Emperor, Charlemagne, in the 9th Century until this era of the late Middle Ages, there was an accepted world view that historians have called "Christendom". Within this view, all those who shared a common religious influence[58] desired to organize ALL of human society under its common precepts and authority. It could be considered, in effect, a medieval utopia in which the hierarchical structures of society were

---

[58] i.e., the Church of Rome

arranged in accordance with God's Will and intention. This was the age of feudalism, whereby everyone was born into a social rank and out of which no one could, by will, change or advance. The late Middle Ages, however, witnessed a gradual alteration of this structure. Where once the purview was a world governed by divine providence, it began to give way to one in which human power and plans authored the chosen destiny. The shift of control from feudal manors to cities and from sovereigns to magnates of commerce and banking precipitated the secularization of Western Europe. The decentralization of authority also gave rise to diversity of intellectual thought and ultimately to religious principles.

The advance of the secular state helped to bring about the decline of ecclesiastical influence in political and social matters and can be traced to such phenomena as the expansion of urban economies and the increased use of secular or native languages. As peasants moved off the land and into the cities, a spirit of liberation cultivated a linguistic independence as well. This became especially important as translations of Holy Scripture were made accessible to people in their common tongue. Also, the preaching of sermons in the vernacular languages became the rule rather than the exception. Innovated by such spiritual masters as Meister Eckhart in Germany and John Wyclif in England, these changes helped engender within the "common folk" an arena for developing a spiritual acumen apart from the monastic or scholastic systems that had hitherto dominated religious thinking.

Apart from spiritual masters such as the ones just mentioned, the educational level of the ordinary clergy had declined dramatically. Such being the case, the standard of instruction that they passed on inadequately met the needs of the people. As populations rose, so did the demand for education. Since the religious establishments could no longer be counted on, the people were forced to establish schools apart from the traditional ecclesial foundations. Princes began receiving tutelage from lay masters instead of monks. As the ignorance of the clergy became more readily recognized and civil administrations fell into the laity's hands, the Church lost its hold on the intellectual circles of Europe.

As urbanization and linguistic diversity served to modify the thinking of a pre-Reformation society, so too did a desire for autonomy and defense of individual interests. In other words, nationalism promoted a rationalism whose main interest was productivity and capital gain. Factors that stimulated these developments included the increased contact with cultures outside of Europe and the conquest of lands in which the exploitation and subjugation of native peoples became a prime motivator. Conversion also played a role in foreign conquests, but it took a back seat to the political and economic elements.

By the 15th Century, European society had become a mosaic of cultures and cultural interests rather than a single, unified Christendom. The norms established by political domains were, in essence, those of medieval Europe, but they no longer held cohesively within any theological or spiritual context. The intellectual movement called Humanism offered a significant creative alternative to theology, reacquainting society with the pagan philosophies and literature of ancient Greece and Rome. Thus this aspect of the period known as the Renaissance served to erode the Church's influence while it received patronage from its prelates. Danger of subversive thought threatened to topple the Christian perspective of God's dominance, allowing the humanistic perspective to dominate.

A strategic tumult at the middle of the 15th Century left the Western Church vulnerable on its eastern borders. In 1453, Moslem Turks swept over Eastern Europe, posing a serious threat to the Catholic West. The capture of Constantinople marks, for some historians, the end of the Middle Ages. Yet for others 1517, the year of Luther's challenge, delineates the beginning of the Modern era. Either view spelled serious trouble for a Church that no longer dominated society.

The Protestant Reformation amounted to a social as well as a religious revolution. Marriages and divorce, large sections of land and its rights of patronage had all been under the authority and jurisdiction of the Papacy.[59] Lay folk fell under subjugation to both ecclesial and civil jurisprudence, while the clergy were exempt from trial or prosecution in civil courts, a double standard which had become intolerable. We can see how closely allied were the religious and social struggles in the example of the swearing of oaths. Whereas before, civil oaths had been taken by swearing upon the Missal,[60] from this time on, oaths must be made upon the Bible only.

Prior to complete partition of religious factions, subtle rebellion began to take place. In France, for example, preachers stopped genuflecting to candles and statues. They also began reciting the Lord's Prayer before sermons instead of the Ave Maria. These gestures

---

[59] i.e., the Church
[60] the priest's altar book

were acts of defiance that spoke more directly to the common people and had a longer-lasting influence than the intellectual debates of scholars and theologians.

The spiritual battle waged between Protestant and Catholic forces centered upon the doctrines of salvation—of grace and faith and humanity's ability or inability to help itself toward holiness. Protestant spirituality did away with all forms or methods of mediation between the soul and God and even refused the notion that people could do anything at all to merit eternal life. For those of the reform traditions, this pushed the necessity for any institution or system of religious authority into serious controversy. Protestant piety, likewise, took an extremely passive stance. Since no virtue could be found within humanity, in essence humanity cannot help itself draw to the heart of God. Sacraments and other external acts were seen as vain and idolatrous and therefore needed to be abolished. This holds true more in the Calvinist reforms than in the Lutheran. Luther continued to hold a strong sense of the sacramental, primarily in Baptism and Eucharist, but he refined these doctrines in order to rid them of any superstitious elements. Calvin, on the other hand, promoted the idea that externals in piety are useless—even corrupt—and therefore should be viewed with suspicion.

By this assumption of human inability for good, all human activity or pious devotion was rendered as pointless. One could not win or merit salvation, since it is solely a gift, and an undeserved one at that. With this notion enters the doctrine of predestination. Reformers depended upon the writings of St. Paul and Augustine in their advocacy of a justification only by faith and a predestined election to the heavenly realm, whereas Catholicism held an explicit as well as implicit trust in God's mercy through the effectiveness of the grace in sacraments and sacramentals. Reformers elevated the certainty of salvation to the solitary predispositioned clemency of God. They could not be bothered with any other doctrinal debate, for no other was of any consequence to the human soul.

As Luther and John Calvin engineered the major reforms of Western Europe, other forces were at work within a decaying Catholic Church, striving to bring about a transformation. This movement became known as the Counter-Reformation and ran concurrently with the protesting faction. In countries where the dissolution of the wealthy monasteries was effected by secular powers, the reassessment of the Church's position became imperative. To meet the changing conditions, the Church in France, Spain, and Italy encouraged the revival of its religious orders and sought compensation for their repression at the hands of civil authorities. New orders and groups of religious organizations also formed. Both the established and the new foundations gained strength in a new paradigm of poverty and the mystic tradition, but these were of primarily localized instigation and did not carry the clout which former institutions had. Unlike the medieval orders, the new foundations were predominantly lay rather than clerical.

A major exception to this, the Society of Jesus founded by Ignatius, became an international force with far-reaching influence. That influence extended into the New World. Ignatius' followers typified the leadership of the Counter-Reformation. This leadership was primarily spiritual, however, and never enabled the Church to regain its former stature in the political arena.

The Catholic revival and its new religious orders chose to fight the growing secularism and Protestant infiltration by means of active spirituality and charitable works. St. Vincent de Paul, for one, succeeded in recruiting many women for the purpose of this apostolic ministry. Though religious in effect if not in name, these women and others like them opened schools, hospitals, orphanages, and other varieties of social support. Despite papal disapproval, they made a significant mark with such uncloistered activism.[61] Unlike the monastic foundations of the early Middle Ages, these orders sought to immerse themselves within the society to which they ministered rather than to withdraw from it.

Their style of worship drew one into a personal relationship with God as a reaction against the formal pomp and ceremony of the medieval Church. Ignatius' system exemplified that personal commitment through the routine of regular prayer and meditation. Significant also was the break with the more traditional forms of prayer and the encouragement to find God in all things, the natural as well as the supernatural. The spirit of individualism grew and affected the piety as well as the social order in this regard. With an emphasis on personal illumination and openness to divine intervention, the laity continued to seek independence implicit to the spirit of the age. It is curious to note that the mystic tradition had always been comfortable with the personal dimension but always with a strong determination that the person recognize that each is only a part of the whole.

In both Protestant and Catholic reforms there developed a popular Christianized form of humanism.

---

[61] Rome doesn't always like what it can't control

This stressed a personal piety of the heart with a downplay of the intellect. The shift of resources from dogma to devotion altered the spiritual and social battlefield between these factions. Each side synthesized in its own way the new scientific spirit of experimentation and practical application. The more complete the division between religious groups, the stronger became the hold of secularism, so much so that by the 17th Century, Western civilization had become religiously undermined.

The years of persecution and debate ended in a stalemate with the Peace of Westphalia in 1648, which provided that each political jurisdiction should worship according to the inclinations of its Prince. Such was the triumph of nationalism. No longer would the Church decide the criteria for political alignments, nor would it be a factor in the balance of power in the World. Society became increasingly emancipated from the dictates of ecclesiastical judgments, and though much psychological control continued to be maintained by the various religious structures, they no longer supplied the base for national decisionmaking. The Reformation took spirituality out of the cloister and promoted it in the home.

The advance of industrial technology and scientific investigation dramatically reshaped the association of faith and reason. Deity took on a different role as civilization learned to manipulate its environment. The question of purpose grew and along with it a utilitarian attitude toward life. Education veered from the pursuit of eternal truths to an occupation and pursuit of temporal responsibilities. Can it be a wonder why spirituality moved from being a vocation to an avocation? From a primary profession to a respectable pastime?

Somewhere a balance must be struck between Catholic piety and Protestant individuality.

From this period onward, the student of spirituality must make decisions as to which "brand" of the faith tradition he/she wishes to pursue. The choices are many and each has its own fascination. Lutheran, Anglican, Reform, or Roman Catholic are the major divisions one finds and within each of these are groups and subgroups of spiritual consequence. The expansion of Europe through colonization brings us eventually to the realization that we will end up this discussion on a global[62] perspective, and as an Anglican, I have chosen to include some of the figures who are important to that branch of the Christian Church.

---

[62] i.e., international and interdenominational

Chapter 9
The Modern Era: France

he transition from the Medieval world to the Modern, from the rigid structures of the pre-Reformation church to the factious denominational mindset, simply staggers the imagination. As Nationalism and the Enlightenment took over the mentality of the populace, a gulf widened between the sacred and the secular. The international prestige of the institutional church began an eclipse from which it has never fully emerged.

The most serious challenge to religion's authority stemmed from the emancipation of the intellect in the period from the mid-16th Century. Such liberty made it more possible to imagine that one's duty to God and His Church was not the primary reason for living. At this point, a person felt freer to question the "ultimate truths", which before was the sacrosanct privilege of the scholars. The monolithic dominance of the institutional church gave way to personal interpretations, and the uniform religious culture gave way to broader subjective piety. A revival of skepticism, stoicism, and other pre-Christian philosophies infiltrated the thinking of religious people and produced a new bend in spirituality. The primary gift of this period was the fostering of the depth and intricacies of the mystic life to the common person. No longer was contemplation and godly union the sole domain of the cloistered monastic or the university scholar. The language and pursuit of holiness of life were now a matter of conversation in parlors and drawing rooms.

One must assume that because of these changes, spirituality gained its importance in the daily life of the multitude. In France alone, between the middle of the 16th and 17th Centuries, almost every spiritual classic was in publication and available to everyone. Indeed, the 17th Century proved to be a time of religious revival for France, out of which came two prominent devotions: the adherence to the Word Incarnate through devotion to the Child Jesus and to the Sacred Heart of Jesus. Mysticism became the vogue and along with it a keen fascination with the miraculous and visionary.

fRancis de Sales
1567 – 1622
KATAPHATIC
AFFECTIVE

Into such an era were born Francis de Sales and Jane Frances de Chantal (1552–1641). It is difficult to speak of one without referring to the other at some point because their lives were so vitally interwoven and their spiritualities so indelibly linked. Even so, each of these fascinating mystics can stand independent scrutiny if one chooses to do so.

Francis de Sales, Bishop of Geneva, earned his ecclesial stripes in the missionary field of the Protestant stronghold of Switzerland. Spiritually he came under the influence of Madame Acarie, a Parisian laywoman, to whom most of the key figures of French Catholicism paid their respects at one time or another and who later went on to establish a Carmelite convent in Paris. From her he learned that simplicity leads a soul readily to the heights of mysticism, and this was the essential model he was to use for the rest of his life in the direction of souls. Warm affection characterized de Sales' style of direction. Rather than try to coerce others into a proper theology or into the rigors of ascetic practices, he displayed a deep charity that won souls to his practice of the devout life. No other spiritual master of the time carried more weight than did Francis, and few men have left such an impression of holiness upon the minds and hearts of those who knew him.

Alongside the immediate direction of souls, Francis affected the spiritual lives of countless numbers through his preaching, which he began in the Queen's own chapel. His sermons marked the beginning of a new form of preaching directly to the contemporary issues of daily life. They are at once simple yet profound, fluid yet systematic, and sought for the conversion of souls caught in Calvinistic doctrines or lackadaisical piety, as well as those whose overzealous practices could burn out quickly. What strikes us most about de Sales' sermons is the effect they had on the upper aristocracy, including the royal family.

For Francis, spiritual development was the result of a lifetime of hard work and the gift of God's abundant grace. His work with souls typifies the spirit of the age in which he helped to make accessible to the peasant as well as the courtier a delicate appreciation of the inner life. Francis' classic work, *An Introduction to the Devout Life*, stands as a model treatise of his intimate knowledge of the process of sanctification. It is both pragmatic and visionary and brings together the call of the cloister with the equally real call to live in the world, under ordinary circumstances. While it stripped away all elements of the superstitious and ostentatious from religious observance, it commanded a rudimentary response to God's love which was both passionate and effervescent. One intriguing aspect of Francis' spiritual direction was his encouragement of the use of books of devotion other than Holy Scripture. He affirmed the profitability of allowing the saints of the past to model Christian ideals, either through admiration or imitation, and so promoted the reading of histories and hagiographies. This countered the Protestant thrust of *Sola scriptura* and has been a consistent tool of spiritual guidance to the present day.

Salesian piety, as it has come to be known, is characterized by the "dailiness" of life. Those of the religious circles of Francis' day often derided him for teaching people that anyone could win a place in Heaven just by striving after virtue little-by-little instead of through monumental acts of piety. He wanted his spiritual children not so much to seek after heroic deeds but to accomplish common deeds with an heroic spirit. Francis' piety does not speak its devotion or its theology in terms of crisis but rather by the constancy and sincerity of the pilgrimage from one day to the next, one moment to the next, in humble attentiveness to the graces and sufferings present in those moments. As gentle a man and as gentle a spiritual guide as Francis was, the result of his instruction was to cut to the core of sin and error like a skilled surgeon. Nothing less than the intrinsic process of transformation into the image God intended for the soul was Francis' goal. His theological perspective concerning this process came through in his unshakable confidence in humanity's capacity to avail itself of God's grace and its inherent desire to move in that direction.

Jane Frances de Chantal
1552 – 1641
APOPHATIC
AFFECTIVE

This perspective was not wasted upon Francis' star pupil, Jane Frances de

Chantal. Soon after they had established a relationship of master and disciple, Francis began to turn Madame de Chantal's attention from the externals of her devotion to an interior attentiveness. The process took most of her life, but the process was the beneficence of one saint's spirit to another.[63]

Together Francis de Sales and Jane Frances de Chantal founded and fostered the charism of the religious community of the Visitation. This endeavor was an act, mentioned in the previous chapter, of the turn away from the strictly cloistered monasticism toward the more apostolic approach. It was a popular movement which advanced in number and influence immediately throughout France, carrying with it the vision of its founders to be a haven for those of weak constitution who desired above all to give themselves to the love of God and the service of their neighbors. Their interior devotion was to the Incarnate God brought to birth in the human being, and so their focus was toward His advent in the ordinary occurrences of life. The profound and the simple came together in the expression of the dedication of the Visitation, and Jane Frances thus stands as the prototype of the modern, apostolic religious.

Most of what we know of this remarkable woman is through her correspondence. Attentive to her fellow religious, especially those in charge of various houses of the Visitation community, Jane Frances supervised the well-being of each member of her congregation with a mother's love. It is regrettable that she herself burned the majority of her correspondence with

---

[63] One is reminded of the "spirit of Elijah resting on Elisha", related in Holy Scripture.

her spiritual mentor, Francis, but enough remains to give insight into the depth and quality of their holiness and their undeniable commitment to each other.

The Baroness de Chantal's early years of spiritual acumen were fostered by the Carmelite community in her native city of Dijon. Conversant with Blessed Anne of Jesus, who had been a companion of the great reformer, Teresa of Avila, Madame de Chantal picked up a comfort and fluency with the contemplative disposition. From this perspective she was able to lead to the sublimity of the Carmelite spirituality her daughters who otherwise would have caved in under the rigors of its noted austerities. Laughable to some, the establishment of the Visitation opened a channel of the corporate expression of Christian mysticism and contemplative life for those with less physical stamina to endure the harsher lifestyle of that institution.

Both de Chantal and de Sales write with a flair for the impassioned and embellished, underscoring their thoughts with colorful and romantic phrases. To our 21st-Century literary palate it may seem quite overdone and garish, but it must be remembered that theirs was the age of the Baroque and characterized by glitter and pomp set against a backdrop of severe simplicity. This Baroque flavor shows up in Francis' mystical work, *Treatise on the Love of God*, which he composed while very much under the influence of the newly founded order of the Visitation. Neither a political nor social work, the *Treatise* is filled with parables which demonstrate the many and various ways total love may be effective in practical application. Jane Frances, too, portrays Baroque characteristics in her many missives to her Sisters and to Francis. Where for us the salutation of "My Dear Daughter" would suffice, for Madame de

Chantal a greeting more to spirit and to the spirit of the times would read, "My Dearest Daughter, My Darling".

As flamboyant as it may seem, underneath these expressions lies a very practical approach to Christian perfection. Jane Frances struggled through her very earthly sorrow of widowhood and through the deaths of some of her children and other intimate relations as she strove to give herself entirely to God. Under Francis de Sales' tutelage, Jane Frances offered herself to her Lord not as a pseudo-festal virgin but as a matron, wise in the ways of the world and unafraid of facing passion as a loving wife and devoted mother. What she had given wholeheartedly and without reservation to her natural family she turned to give to her Community and, more especially, to Christ. Such a homely endeavor is augmented by yet another aspect of her spiritual life which brings consolation to those of lesser stature; namely, the struggle and temptation against the faith that followed her throughout her life.

PIERRE de BERULLE
1575– 1629
KATAPHATIC
AFFECTIVE

Contemporaneous with this dynamic spiritual couple is another devout prelate, Cardinal Pierre de Berulle. He too had a significant relationship with Madame Acarie which helped shape his mystic doctrine. And because Berulle helped her bring the Carmelite influence to Paris, its spirit can be noted in his own writings. These Carmelites quickly became the center for highborn, devout ladies of the Capitol, which included Marie d'Medici, the Queen.

Distinctive of Cardinal Berulle and the men who followed him (Jean-Jacques Olier and John Eudes) was the focus on the humanity of Christ, particularly in the devotion to the Sacred Heart of Jesus. For Berulle, a singular mystery of the Incarnation could be found in the self-humiliation of Divinity loving humanity so much that He would desire total identification, even in our dismal lowliness. Such an emphasis on the humanity of Jesus had been so lacking in religious teaching for so long that Berulle's message seemed rather radical, even suspect. Yet it was also met with enthusiasm.

Much of the teaching of this era of the early 17th Century came as a reaction against a growing Humanism, both secular and Christian. Under Berulle the mystic expression tried to strike a balance between a true self-abasement on the one hand and an enlivened dogmatic theology through experiential faith on the other. More often than not it tottered precariously in an uncomfortable tension, under attack by both Dominican and Jesuit scholars.

Politics and religion were so intertwined in the France of the 17th and 18th Centuries that reading the spirituality of this period is best accomplished after a preliminary study of the political history. Louis XIII, with his chief minister Cardinal Richelieu, battled the Protestant Huguenots through much of his monarchy, and the later struggles between Louis XIV and the Papacy over ecclesial appointments is reminiscent of those between the England of Henry VIII and Elizabeth I, though with markedly different results. Gallicanism is the term which describes this movement of the French monarchy's endeavor to loose itself from Rome's authority. It is naive, however, to think that this was the only line of religious strife operating at the time. Actually there were many fronts of opposition, many battle lines to note.

Cardinal Berulle was among those who knew controversy and this political tension. From the political angle he was at variance with Cardinal Richelieu's efforts to solidify the power of monarchy by opposing an alliance with Protestant Germany. On the spiritual front, Berulle came under fire for imposing vows of servitude of Jesus and Mary in the Carmelite convent he served as Visitor.

Servitude to Christ, in imitation of Christ's servitude to humanity, was a primary characteristic in Berullian spirituality. A second factor was found in the virtue of religion itself. The good Cardinal brought a renewed emphasis to the understanding of adoration of God for God's sake alone. This piety had fallen by the wayside in the institutional religious framework. Reverence for God, especially in the mysteries of the incarnation, is the hallmark of Berulle's devotion, and fundamental to his system was a revival of the Augustinian concept of grace, whereby humanity must depend on God alone rather than itself.

The chief end of the French school of spirituality under Berulle and his disciples was the reformation and sanctification of the clergy. As has already been mentioned, the clerical training of these past few centuries lay in a horrible state. This situation Berulle, Olier, and Eudes sought to correct by the founding of extremely fine seminaries. The results were the famed Oratory and the Society of St. Sulpice, which have passed down to us a legacy of two very useful methods of mental prayer known as the Oratorian and the Sulpician methods, respectively.

Explicit to the revived priestly spirituality of this period was the view of the priesthood from the standpoint of Christ rather than the merely human. The priest stood as the physical representation of Jesus in His sacrifice, and the primary function of the priest was that of giving God the adoration due Him. The priest was often likened to the Virgin Mary; for as she brought Jesus to birth in her physical body, the priest brought Him to birth in the Blessed Sacrament. Berulle's disciple, Olier, often described the priest as a "monster of sanctity".[64] This is a far cry from our contemporary view which denotes the priest's primary role as pastoral caregiver.

Mystic and anti-mystic factions rose up around this turbulent political era. The followers of Berulle spent much time and effort cautioning others about "abstract spirituality" which had become popular in many circles. Those who followed the abstract thinking easily fell into a negation of the necessity of Christ's mediation. This thinking was a stretching of the Dionysian apophatic tradition to its extreme and Berulle, as supportive as he was of the Dionysian structures, meant to keep a strong Christological base. This was where he relied heavily on Carmelite spirituality, with its strong Incarnational precepts.

BROTHER LAWRENCE
OF THE RESURRECTION
1605– 1691
KATAPHATIC
AFFECTIVE

Another mystic who portrays the powerful Carmelite Christology, though whose writings have none of the savor of the Baroque nor the intellect of the scholar, is the Carmelite lay-brother, Lawrence. Sim-

---

[64] coming from the French word *montrer*, meaning to show or manifest

plicity and directness characterize his scant work, but of all the spiritual writers of any century, except St. Paul, he is probably the most widely read and recognized of authors. *The Practice of the Presence of God*, compact in size but profound in its truth, travels easily in jacket pocket or purse and though it cannot possibly compete with the titans of spirituality like Augustine's *Confessions* or de Sales' *Treatise on the Love of God*, it has had wider influence on the prayer life of the average Christian than many of the others combined.

What makes Brother Lawrence's writing so intriguing is the timeless quality of his experiences as well as the ease with which he makes the unitive way available to the common soul. Heights of ecstasy and sublime visions have no place in Lawrence's theology. Quiet attentiveness to the present moment contains all the mystery and majesty necessary for the soul's intimate communion with the Divine Essence.

Brother Lawrence, like Ignatius of Loyola, had been a soldier in his younger years. Unlike Ignatius, however, he did not pursue intellectual or scholastic development but preferred the simplicity of a lay brother's duties in the monastery kitchen or shoe shop. He refused to separate piety from action but saw each as simply part of a single-minded effort to be in God's presence. Prayer, the primary focus of Lawrence's spiritual teaching, was not an isolated event of conversation with God but rather a way of life that combined all the elements of living into one's self-oblation. Simply put, true prayer meant living in such a way that all was done for the glory of God.

Some of us can take heart in the fact that this man was commonest of the common folk. He described himself as clumsy while others described him as "gross by nature". All the delicacy and propriety usually associated with sanctity was totally lost on Lawrence. His life illustrates for us the authenticity of our nature which God desires us to recognize and accept as graced, regardless of external appearances. Holiness becomes recognized in Lawrence as doing that for Jesus' sake which otherwise he commonly did for his own. Possibly his book could be retitled *Holiness for the Average Man*. So for those unable or afraid to follow John of the Cross in the ascent of Mount Carmel, Brother Lawrence, as a spiritual master, can lead a soul into the simplicity of holy attentiveness to the presence of God by a less exacting route.

If nothing other than a sense of balance is disclosed as one walks through this brief historical panorama of spirituality, then at least one major task has been accomplished. We cannot be bounced back and forth from the speculative or intellectual to the passive and affective approach to God without coming to some sort of awareness that there are no final spiritual revelations except the unique moment when the single soul is drawn into His essence by whatever means that happens. Through the ages, the language and the emphasis have oscillated from imagery to nothingness, from the mind to the heart. Sometimes each of these extremes has met congenially on some common ground to form a middle way. It then becomes important for us to remember that all of these expressions of the spiritual life are necessary and are woven together into a glorious tapestry of Christianity. The modern era of France holds for us a marvelous illustration of this balance, as the pendulum swings from the active to the passive, from the rational to the impassioned.

Blaise Pascal
1623– 1662
APOPHATIC
SPECULATIVE

Thus the humble, convivial approach to God, expressed by Francis de Sales, Jane Frances de Chantal, and Brother Lawrence, stands in striking contrast to their contemporary, Blaise Pascal, whose spiritual approach came by way of the Jansenist movement. Pascal, especially in his *Provincial Letters*, lashed out against what he describes as "easy virtue". Strict and severe, he sounds more like the prophet of doom, set against those who would not adhere to the Jansenist code of penitential morals. A key element in this theology was uncertainty, which purported that however sure one felt of being God's chosen, still the grace of that calling could be withdrawn at any moment.

Born of an intellectually astute family, Pascal's father undertook Blaise's primary education because of the boy's delicate health as well as his own expertise in academics. The social circle this family moved in brought Blaise into contact with René Descartes (1596– 1650), whose intellectual revolution utterly demolished traditional philosophy in France. Thus one can see that the upheavals of the secularization of Europe and the religious controversies of the Reformation era were at their height during Pascal's formative years. He would later go on to dispute the teachings of Descartes but only after he had become very well acquainted with them.

Part of the importance of Pascal's *Provincial Letters* is that they reflect the controversy between the "ultra-conservative" strain of Roman Catholicism and the more moderate strain, exemplified in the Jesuit and Carmelite influences. Indeed, the Letters were leveled specifically against the Jesuits, but alongside these salvos of contention rests Pascal's other and better known work, *The Pensees*, in which he expands upon the themes of salvation, conversion, and amendment of life. *The Pensees* was thus an apology on the Christian life as perceived through the eyes of a scientist and mathematician.

Pascal's intended audience was the cultured agnostics, the "free thinkers" of his country, who were more attracted to Cartesian rationalism than Catholic doctrine. His arguments appealed to the scientific mind of the 17th Century rather than those whose devotional preference remained in the seat of the emotions. Were Pascal living in the present society, he doubtless would write from the perspective of an astrophysicist or computer systems analyst. Pascal's view, which was innovative for his day, was that belief in God was a matter of personal choice. Prior to him, conventional belief amounted to a blind acquiescence to the cultural trappings of false security and false values. Pascal put to rest the error of honoring the facade while ignoring the shallow emptiness of one's cultural milieu. He was not interested so much in the "system" of doctrinal belief as with the "order" which led one ultimately to wholeness. For Pascal, any search for Truth implied an implicit search for the Author of that Truth and by its very nature demanded a coherent, volitional decision. The Calvinistic call to accept and believe what one is told to believe was in radical opposition to Pascal's understanding of the nature of religion.

The mystic element of Pascal's faith did not become known to the world until after his death when a servant, going through Pascal's effects, found a note sewn into the lining of his coat. On it was written, in his own hand, the account of an ecstatic occurrence that had transformed Pascal's faith in Eternal Reality. The account described, in true mystical language, an event that lasted for two hours, whereby he was enveloped in the "fire and love" of God's holiness. That event changed the direction of Pascal's pursuit for knowledge and led him away from the mere rational, cognitive quest to understand truth toward a personal desire to be joined to the truth, as found ultimately in Jesus Christ. From that point on, Pascal accepted that he was intimately related to everything that existed, as everything that existed was held in the Divine Being, and that relationship was what constituted true wholeness. Never to be separated from God would then become Pascal's fervent prayer.

Madame Guyon
1648 – 1717

François Fénelon
1651 – 1715
APOPHATIC
AFFECTIVE

While the Jansenist dispute was raging, another questionable spirituality was brewing in the salons of the aristocracy. The couple who caused this stir was Madame Jeanne Marie Guyon and the Archbishop of Cambrai, François Fénelon. Their relationship, as innocent and spiritually centered as that of de Sales and de Chantal, did not, however, produce the same cup of blessing; in fact, disgrace was their recompense.

Fénelon distinguished himself as an able prelate and an astute confessor/spiritual director early in his career. He was appointed by the Crown as tutor to Louis XIV's grandson, the Duke of Burgundy; it was just prior to his appointment as Archbishop of Cambrai when he met Madame Guyon. She was strongly attracted to Fénelon from their first meeting, but it took a short while before he succumbed to a reciprocal attraction. Guyon, having spent a good deal of time under "detention" in a Visitation convent, may have fashioned for herself a reprise of the relationship between the Visitation founders, de Sales and de Chantal. After one reads her autobiography, there can be little doubt that Madame Guyon was given to a very active imagination. Indeed, in some places, it reads very much like the fantastic accounts found in Margery Kempe's book.

Once won over to her argument, Fénelon fell into agreement that God's providence was at work in their relationship and that Madame Guyon would be a chief instrument in God's will for his life. As the controversy over her teachings grew, detractors of her doctrine tried to discredit them both by rumoring the illicit nature of their relationship. A close reading of their correspondence, however, quickly dispels such rumors.

The dispute escalated when Jacques Bossuet, Bishop of Meaux, denounced Madame Guyon's teachings—accusing her of the heresy of Quietism—and Archbishop Fénelon came to her defense. Quietism had been condemned by Pope Innocent XI, and Bossuet viewed Guyon as a dangerous promoter of it. The Quietist theology centered around an indifference or complete passivity in relation to God. This teaching urged the uselessness of desire or any activity in prayer, purporting that neither could bring a soul closer to spiritual perfection. Fénelon wrote the *Maxims of the Saints*, an apology[65] to this thesis, championing Madame Guyon's teaching. His argument settled upon three

---

[65] a formal justification or explanation

points. First was the concept of "disinterested love", an idea that a soul would love God for Himself alone, with never a thought of heavenly reward. The second argument promoted passive prayer, which required a person to remain in a totally inactive state, not even becoming resistant should the soul find itself destined to perdition. The third point of debate supported the thought that those few perfect souls, namely the great Saints, had weathered the trial of abandonment so completely that they possessed an irresistible conviction of their eternal loss and were content to remain damned for the sake of their pure love for God. It was these three concepts that Bossuet felt compelled to contest.

Bossuet adamantly argued from a Berullian perspective: man must abandon himself to God totally and accept that he must never surrender his hope of salvation or refrain from actively fleeing from sin. The soul must "fight like hell" to stay out of Hell! Where the Quietists promoted a passivity which led to a spiritual idleness, Bossuet encouraged an abandonment that directed one toward activity for and in the power of God. The controversy between Bossuet and Fénelon may seem to us hairsplitting and irrelevant; however, as technical as their arguments grew, it carried a serious theological consequence.[66] The argument between Bossuet and Fénelon revolved around a correct view of human nature. The thesis put forth by Fénelon pro-

---

[66] We must remember that a similar quarrel over technicalities rocked the early Church also. The struggle then seemed to be over a mere "iota": the difference between "homoousia" and "homoiousia". This, of course, was the Arian heresy; and we know that the real issue was not a jot, but the very nature of Christ.

posed a type of perfection that the Church labeled contrary to human nature and therefore contrary to the order of God's intended design for man.

Eventually Bossuet won the argument, and the Pope condemned Fénelon's views in 1699. Fénelon himself, however, was not denounced as a heretic nor removed from his pastoral office. In censuring Fénelon the Pope is said to have remarked that the Archbishop's fault was due to too ardent a love for God, while his opponents were at fault because of their lack of charity toward their brother. Such a censure then warns us against viewing Fénelon as anything but a devout and holy cleric. His Counsels and his Letters are well worth our reading, providing an edifying source of direction and spiritual comfort.

Just as Francis de Sales found his primary audience in the court of Henry IV and his queen, Marie d'Medici, so too did the Archbishop of Cambrai affect the hearts of a royal household. Fénelon's early champion was Madame de Maintenon, the second wife of Louis XIV. He brought a spiritual discipline to the court and encouraged those who wrote to him to pray even in the palace drawing rooms. The Archbishop's idea of a "holy worldliness" was built upon the legacy of those saints in the first half of the 17th Century: Francis de Sales, Vincent de Paul, and Cardinal Berulle.

Jean Pierre de Caussade
1675– 1751
KATAPHATIC
AFFECTIVE

While the struggle over the true nature of abandonment held the attention of the spiritual leaders, another holy cleric determined to enter the fray. Jean

Pierre de Caussade maintained a rather obscure profile during his life, but his spiritual instruction was powerful enough to survive all controversy and was posthumously published 110 years after his death.

Caussade sang a melody very similar to that of the Quietists, but his insistence upon the "sacrament of the present moment" made all the difference in his doctrine. That addition to the context of abandonment brought all the tediousness of daily life into the significance of God's will. Quietism floated beyond any sensitivity to the hard reality of daily living, and Caussade was determined rather to find God in it.

Relatively little is known about the life of Pere Caussade except what can be gleaned from his many letters to the various Visitation nuns with whom he corresponded. Although a Jesuit, his spirituality resembled the Salesian or French Carmelite schools more than that of the Spanish Ignatius. Fénelon's adversary, Bossuet, also had great influence on Caussade, which he makes mention of in one of his letters. So with such a spiritual foundation we can observe how he synthesizes the French mysticism of the 17th Century.

Pere Caussade's primary work, *Abandonment to Divine Providence*, is a compilation of his letters and conferences to the Visitation nuns of Nancy, France. They were edited first by another Jesuit, Fr. Henri Ramière, in 1861. Central to his view of abandonment was an acceptance of God's will as each Christian's duty. However, this abandonment should not suppress our active cooperation with the grace that would bring us true sanctification. Unlike Fénelon, who hypothetically would see the perfect soul abandon even his own salvation, Caussade links solidly God's glorification with man's sanctification; therefore man's pursuit of holiness also fulfills his duty to abandon himself to God's will. It is in this sense that Pere Caussade would urge a soul to unite his efforts with God in allowing God's grace to become active in him.

Reading *L'Abandon*, we must remember that its counsel was originally for Religious, who had already attained some degree of spiritual advancement. Caussade's cardinal principle that everything, every event or circumstance, helps draw us closer to God, needs to be wrapped then in a context of our own understanding of doctrinal truth. Without a solid foundation of theology under us, it would be easy to fall into distortions similar to those of Archbishop Fénelon and Madame Guyon.

Chapter 10
The Modern Era: England (Caroline Divines)

Parallel to the intellectual and spiritual controversies which demanded attention in 17th Century France are the ones which assaulted England of the same period. A sober Anglicanism vied with Puritan and Roman Catholic forces, but the political and social environment were markedly different from those which formed the French school. Whereas France's main struggle was between the supremacy of its own monarchy and what had been the Holy Roman Empire, England's contentions centered around more domestic issues of church and state. For a time, Anglicanism's fate tottered precariously while the major ecclesial sees were influenced by bishops sympathetic with the Puritan cause. The Crown and Parliament also became targets for a recalcitrant Roman Catholic minority, as evidenced in the fiasco known as the Gunpowder Plot.

When we think of the blood of martyrdom which seeds the faith of the Church, our minds naturally envisage those thrown to lions in the 2nd or 3rd Centuries or the brave missionaries whose courage and devotion inspire us as they faced savage and pagan cultures. It is a sobering fact, however, that the blood of the martyrs also spilled out over the consecrated stones of our own heritage, in an era of supposed civility and enlightenment. The Anglican Tradition came to birth amid the violence within the monarchies of Elizabeth I, James I, and Charles I. As a result of these contentions, two documents—the "Thirty-Nine Articles" and *The Book of Common Prayer*—became the means by which the Church of England made its definition and declaration of Faith.

The Anglican rule of faith based its doctrine upon the revelation of the Holy Scriptures of the Old and New Testaments, the three creeds of the Church, the first four ecumenical councils, and the teachings of the Fathers of the first five centuries. The "Thirty-Nine Articles" and *The Book of Common Prayer* set these tenets within the context of Anglican belief and practice and as such set the Church of England apart from both the continental reform tradition and that of the papacy. Calvinist doctrine held to Scripture alone as the rule of faith while Rome looked to Scripture, tradition, and the living "magisterium".[67]

Within Anglicanism the "Thirty-Nine Articles" spoke against the errors committed by Rome as well as the heretical tendencies of the radical Protestant factions. In them can be seen a surprising spirit of moderation and sound doctrine which characterizes the Anglican Divines and their espousal of the *via media*. *The Book of Common Prayer* gave shape to this moderate doctrine by means of worship and created a guiding rule of conduct unique to Anglicanism, namely *lex orandi, lex credendi*.[68] When asked to explain their belief, devout Anglicans might reply, "Come and participate in our worship, and you will then know what we profess as Truth."

The primary symbol of the conflict between Anglicanism and Puritanism could be found in the struggle between "altar" and pulpit". The Anglican

---

[67] the teaching body of the Roman Church under papal authority
[68] the law of worship is the law of belief

Church, while remaining loyal to the catholicity of its heritage, retained the altar as central to its focus and thereby typified the presence of God in the sacrament. Puritanism viewed this Anglican attitude as idolatry and looked instead to the pulpit, which typified enlightened humanity. The one concentrated on worship, while the other looked for instruction and intellect. Puritans even went so far as to remove the altar from its prescribed place at the east end of the Church and move it to a common place where it became the receptacle for hats and other paraphernalia.

Much of the writings and sermons of this period reflect these conflicting values and doctrines and are therefore less ephemeral in style than earlier mystical literature. Spiritual instruction became more practical and less aesthetic, more didactic and less visionary, than what would commonly be held as mystical writing.

I propose that one of the primary reasons these Divines are not widely read today is because our American literary culture has become lazy, spoiled by the media who transport people through the process of information and story in a short period of time. Who among us spends time on long, intricate treatises or reads over sermons unless it is for some academic necessity? Most of the authors of this period have not been re-edited in the modern terms and therefore are almost as difficult to read and understand as a work in a foreign tongue. Their use of language, idiom, and structure has become unintelligible to us without a deliberate effort to comprehend it.

As we must be aware, the Reformation was not a single event, but a long process which was not always uniform in orientation. In the spiritual sense, reform for Anglicanism involved a recovery of the lost or distorted integrity of the ancient Church. This process is readily discernible in the history of the Church of England, from Henry VIII's reign through that of Charles I.[69] By the time Charles I ascended the throne, the turning point in this religious controversy had occurred.

Lancelot Andrewes
1555– 1626
KATAPHATIC
SPECULATIVE

Two men critical to the solidifying of the Anglican stance were Lancelot Andrewes and William Laud (1573–1645). The eldest of thirteen children, Andrewes held a stunning academic career at Cambridge in the last quarter of the 16th Century. In his later ministry he was appointed privy councilor in both England and Scotland and was made Bishop of Ely and later transferred to Winchester. The majority of Andrewes' later sermons were preached in the Royal Chapel, where he had also been appointed Dean by James I. A far cry from the "country parson", he came down hard on the Calvinist doctrine which had invaded the Church's teaching. It was through his essential preaching that Andrewes has become recognized as a true father of the Anglican tradition.

Caught up in the establishment of James I as supreme head of both Church and State, Andrewes often preached in favor of the Divine Right of Kings. He was fond of using illustrations from Holy Scripture, primarily the Old Testament, to bring home his conviction that kingship promotes harmony and unity for

---

[69] The great Carolinian Age takes its name from Charles' reign, but its foundation was set in place through the turmoil and strife with which Elizabeth I and James I contended.

religion as well as for government. Bishop Andrewes called for respect toward the sacredness of kings because a king is made so by the will of God and therefore answerable to Him alone.

Lancelot Andrewes exhibited a principle which claimed prayer as the prerequisite to theology and indeed to all of Christian life. To his understanding, the holy life and therefore its theology were the natural outflow of a continuous communication with God; and not just a private devotion but an ongoing dialogue in the power of the Holy Spirit with the Fathers of the Church.

In Andrewes there emerges Anglicanism's continuing legacy of structure. His sermons were liberally laced with exegetical discussion which sought to give practical examples for daily living. Since the break with the Roman Church a spiritual and liturgical confusion had ensued, making the English people easy prey for the various strains of the Protestant reform. Andrewes urged a return to the stable ascetic practices of the Patristic Church, backing up his insights with a personal dedication to experience the Divine/Human interchange. It was Andrewes who led the movement which determined that the English Church should be Anglican rather than Calvinist.

Such personal inspiration manifested itself in Andrewes' intense prayer life. His *Preces Privatae*, a book of personal devotions which Andrewes compiled, reflects the conviction that the intellect must come under the scrutiny and illumination of the Holy Spirit if true religion is to be possible. With creativity Bishop Andrewes contributed most generously to the Anglican phenomenon and gave a particularity to its spirituality, raising the sense of morality to an integral position within the faith structure. By a synthesis of Scriptural and Patristic integrity, he laid the groundwork for the formation of a specific Anglo-Catholic piety upon which the later Oxford scholars would capitalize. Andrewes' piety was at once a sincere and sane balance which negated superficial emotionalism. He also followed up his piety with substantial acts of charity to the poor and displaced, often remaining anonymous in his giving.

William Laud
1573– 1645
APOPHATIC
SPECULATIVE

Archbishop Laud, one such successor to the loyalty and genius of Lancelot Andrewes, was one of the first "Anglican" martyrs, beheaded after the controlling faction of Puritan extremists tried him for treason because of his "Papist practices".[70] Throughout his life Laud firmly stood his ground and followed his conscience concerning religious practices. By maintaining the rites of the consecration of holy things, he refused to allow reverence to be thrown to the wind. This was an attitude passed on by his early mentor, Lancelot Andrewes, and it was no small matter to Laud that all things used by the Church and the faithful should be sanctified with prayer, a legacy which the Anglican tradition holds still.

The fight between the Church of England and the Puritans raged around such matters as the Real Presence in the Holy Eucharist, the necessity of Baptism, adherence to Episcopal Ordination, and the authority of the tradition handed down by the Fathers of the early

---

[70] Not long after, his champion and King, Charles I, also lost his head.

Church and her Ecumenical Councils. The Puritans scoffed at any relations with antiquity, reduced Baptism to a sign devoid of meaning, reviled the Blessed Sacrament, and held that anyone who fancied himself a minister of the Gospel could legally serve in such a capacity.[71] But those who held to the heart of the Anglican way viewed the denuding of religious practice by the Puritans as robbing pious practice of its nobility, its tenderness and gracefulness, and most of all its reverential qualities.

William Laud strove to retain these aspects of his religion. He had an innate sense of knowing that the best way to prevent the faithful from "fleeing to Rome" was to present the Church of England in all her rich fullness. By this he held up as worthy the worship from the *Book of Common Prayer* and all the rites and practices therein. He was determined that the Reformation in England would be more of a return to the ancient Church than the establishment of a new and ill-bred mongrel.

In the face of death, the sermon he preached after ascending the scaffold to be beheaded shows vividly the witness Laud bore Christ and His Church. There he professed the conviction and courage to follow Christ's example, even to death, for in such love he claimed the assurance of salvation. The sermon is ripe with biblical images, such as the Passover and the three children in the fiery furnace, and this helped to set the tone of vision and mission which Laud held. Such was the sense of vision and missionary zeal which Laud held throughout his life and to which he was

---

[71] Vestiges of these attitudes can be seen in the extreme fundamentalist churches of our present time, although moderation and ecumenical relations are on the rise.

faithful even in his martyrdom. It is no small thanks the Anglican Church owes to Archbishop Laud, and it should always look to his example for courage of conviction and the test of faith.

Two characteristics stand out as primary to Anglican spirituality. One is a keen interest in the tradition of the Greek fathers. Because liturgy plays an important part in Anglican worship, many of the Eastern devotions have found their way into the *Book of Common Prayer*. A modern example of this is found in the inclusion of the "Phos Hilaron" in the service of Evening Prayer. Most Roman Catholics are still unfamiliar with this prayer of light because it has not been used in their evening office.

The other characteristic of Anglican spirituality is a high regard for personal spiritual direction. There had been a convincing synthesis of doctrine and devotion in the 14th Century mystics which strongly encouraged personal guidance. In that golden age of English spirituality, the anchorites and hermits depended heavily upon their mentors and spiritual counselors. The Carolinian Age drew liberally from their ancestors' example and promoted that tradition but gave it a new face. Much spiritual counsel came to the people by way of the sermon. Anglican divines used the sermon as the platform from which to provide catechetical instruction and spiritual guidance as well as to expound upon the Word of God. We need to recall that the sermon was for the 17th-Century person what the Sunday afternoon football game is to the 21st-Century man. It was at once instruction and entertainment, the popular topic in the pubs or around the dinner table.

The common bond which united those of the Anglican persuasion was *The Book of Common Prayer*.

It engendered a consciousness of the family of God and was the vehicle by which the layman found his spiritual identity. Through the first few revisions of the Prayer Book, it is possible to trace the solidifying of Anglican tradition. This tradition leaned more toward a Catholicity rather than a Protestantism in terms of doctrine, but it would not be until the next century that the Church of England would regain, externally, the fullness of its liturgical and sacramental heritage. Always, however, was maintained a continuous synthesis between theology and piety.

Following Richard Hooker's recommendation, the Caroline Divines did not fear to follow the Roman Church when they perceived that Rome's teaching held to reason and truth. Never was Rome denigrated to be any less than a true limb of the Body of Christ, but where she was given to doctrinal error, the Church of England refused to acknowledge her position as legitimate. Two influences upon Anglican theologians helped maintain the catholic flavor of its spirituality: Thomistic thought and Benedictine piety. Each can be found as anchor points in the Prayer Book system of worship. Drawing on the speculative system of St. Thomas Aquinas and the affective quality of St. Bernard's teaching, the Caroline synthesis showed up predominantly in sermons, catechetical instruction, and in the mystical poetry of its Divines.

Just as the term "mystic" was not a popular expression for the Caroline theologians, neither was it used for another group of English spiritual masters. This other group has come to be known as the "Metaphysical Poets", a curious combination of layman or cleric, Anglican, Roman or Puritan. Their influence, however, was even more far-reaching and sublime than those in the forefront of the religious battle.

John Donne
1571–1631

George Herbert
1593–1633
KATAPHATIC
AFFECTIVE

The 17th Century produced a wide variety of cultural and literary art. Elizabethan English, coupled with the age of the romantic adventurer and the scientific philosopher, gave to poetry and drama a richness which has remained the undisputed pinnacle of the English heritage. Contemporaneous with William Shakespeare, Sir Francis Drake, Sir Walter Raleigh, and Sir Francis Bacon are two of Anglicanism's premier poets, John Donne and George Herbert.

A renegade from Roman Catholicism, John Donne was Dean of St. Paul's in London and a heralded preacher of the Jacobean and Carolinian periods. His passionate love for one woman brought him political and social ruin but also awakened within him a deep piety which he expressed especially in his poetry. Baroque in style and Medieval in sentiment, John Donne's poems are poignant and of the deepest sincerity; however, they are also somewhat haunting, even macabre.

George Herbert was born of an aristocratic family, being the younger brother of Lord Herbert of Cherbury. He had all the potential of a successful politician and yet chose instead the life of a simple country priest. From his rectory at Bemerton, Herbert modeled the virtuous life he felt that a man of the cloth should intend to live. There he also wrote the poetry and prose for which he has become so well known.

Compared to the pedestal upon which the priest was set in the French school, such idealism tumbled to the ground in the same period of English spirituality. It is not so much that the priest was degraded but that expectations for the laity were raised to that which had been reserved for religious and clerics. The priest in England became more of a first-among-equals.

This can be seen most clearly in the Prayer Book's order of worship and English devotions patterned after the Benedictine ideal. English spirituality became a "domestic" phenomenon where both the Benedictine system and the Prayer Book system were designed for an integrated and united society, predominantly "lay" in character. Distinctions between priest and layman were few except with regard to the service at the altar. This points to a definition by function rather than by character, as in the French scheme. The Benedictine and Prayer Book systems were for everyone within the community of faith, for which the priest was exhorted to set the example of obedience and dedication.

The priest's role took on a less sacerdotal function in the period characterized by the ministries of George Herbert and John Donne. These men spent a greater time in the pulpit than in the confessional or at the altar. Nevertheless, Herbert's concept of the priesthood continued along the perspective of mediator between God and man. To him, the priest was the model, the example to the faithful. He adopted the view that it was God's initiative which gave the priest the ability to mediate and to produce Christ, always leaving the impetus of that power in divine rather than human hands.

Rather than focus on the sacrifice at the altar, Herbert, and indeed Anglicanism in general, sought to bring the Incarnate Word to bear on the whole of life. The common man was enjoined to offer praise and worship in his own home by recitation of the Divine Office, making the Prayer Book a well-worn companion rather than a "coffee table" decoration. According to Herbert's ideal, the priest was called to place himself at the center of his congregation's life and to show them true devotion, calling for the ordering of one's entire life for the glory of God.

Whereas French spirituality emphasized the role of the priest as the mediator between God and man through the sacrificial offering at the altar, the English emphasized a pastoral mediation. The English priest took on the role of shepherd who was to guide his flock by example and encouragement. Pastor Herbert painted the picture of this shepherd through his poetry as well as his own priesthood. He saw both activities as acting in harmony to bring about the realization of God's loving presence to every soul.

Jeremy Taylor
1613– 1667
KATAPHATIC
SPECULATIVE

A protégé of Archbishop Laud, educated first at Cambridge and important to the Anglican movement, Jeremy Taylor gave English spirituality a pragmatic feature. He was ordained at a young age, 20, but nevertheless made a sensational impact as a preacher. Laud became aware of Taylor's exceptional gift and took him under his patronage, first sending him to Oxford, where Taylor took a Fellowship at All Souls. Laud extolled his talents but chided him on his youth. Taylor responded that with time he could rectify that problem.

A contemporary of George Herbert and a near-neighbor to the community at Little Gidding, Jeremy flourished in the environment of the Caroline Age. His heart leaned totally toward the royalist cause, resulting in three episodes in prison for his religious and political views. Taylor's heart was saddened by the Church, torn apart by political rivalries. He remained loyal to Prayer Book spirituality and the ecclesiastical structure of Anglicanism; one of Taylor's political exiles found him dependent upon the hospitality of Lord and Lady Carbery in Wales. While there he used his creative energy, composing some of his most spiritually moving and practically invigorating works. Sermons from this time demonstrate his keen abilities for beauty of concept and profound faith. It was on the Carbery estate, "Golden Grove", where Taylor wrote his two most famous and enduring works: *The Rule and Exercises of Holy Living* and *The Rule and Exercises of Holy Dying*.

Sympathetic yet extremely practical, we might consider these works by our own modern standards as "How To" books. In them Taylor outlines common sense answers to life's questions concerning Christian behavior, what to watch out for and what to attend to. Some have claimed that these books offer us a synopsis of Anglican piety.

In *Holy Living*, Taylor lays out the guidelines for fasting, almsgiving, prayer, and the keeping of festivals. His leanings toward Christian humanism come through in the manner in which he addresses issues such as temperance, humility, and chastity. We will find useful and beautiful prayers in the last portion of this book, composed for the common conditions of humanity and for the Church. Taylor wrote this book at the request of Lady Carbery, for her personal use. Like Ignatius' *Exercises*, it falls into the category of manual—something to be used, not just read and admired.

The same can be said of *Holy Dying*. This book Taylor wrote to help prepare those who were seriously ill for death. It helps a person contemplate the shortness of life, how to pray, and how to turn from sin. Ultimately it focuses on preparations for dying. Useful in our current era which fears the reality of death, tries to ignore it, or to escape it through fantasy, *Holy Dying* helps all those who read it to view illness and death from a truly Christian perspective, while also instructing those who minister to them. As with *Holy Living*, *Holy Dying* responds in a practical manner as well as a devotional one. For one who himself encountered much pain, hardship, and the loneliness of exile, Taylor's writing never betrays a dolorous attitude to the Christian life. His sense of the right order of things kept him from despair and his pastoral responses in *Holy Living* and *Holy Dying* acted as lighthouse beacons for those who would fear losing their way in the dark times of life.

thomas traherne
1636 – 1674
KATAPHATIC
AFFECTIVE

Another of the metaphysical poets, though not as well-known as Herbert, is Thomas Traherne. Born the son of a shoemaker and orphaned young, Traherne became an Oxford scholar, taking his first degree in 1656. Ordained a priest and sometime after his first cure, he served as private chaplain to the Lord Keeper of the Seals, Sir Orlando Bridgman. His place among the Caroline Divines has suffered from lack of recognition; nevertheless, Traherne deserves serious attention by those who claim fellowship in the Anglican tradition.

His best known work, and one which didn't see publication until two hundred years after his death, *Centuries of Meditations* reflects upon ethics and religion. Traherne wrote it for a friend, Mrs. Susan Hopton, who ran her household on the order of Ferrar's community at Little Gidding. It has been compared to à Kempis' *Imitation of Christ*, but with a less monastic spirit. Traherne writes of the natural world with the heart of a troubadour. Like Francis of Assisi, nature captivates his spirit, and he writes of it with such depth of conviction that the leaning toward pantheism is clearly recognizable.

Traherne renews our vision of God's creation, giving us a taste of that blessedness which still pervades the world even in the midst of its fallen state. He would tolerate no thought of conflict between the material and spiritual world. Felicity, (joy), under Traherne's assertion, draws out of the soul its real reason for existence. Happiness constituted his life's goal. Traherne delighted in life, in all that bears the mark of God. In contrast to the more somber Donne, Traherne's poetry exclaimed the mystery that God is both the object of our joy and the very means of that enjoyment. Here he follows closely the Victorine school of a creation-centered spirit.

Incarnational faith and awareness of human interdependence denote Traherne's theology. He loved the world because God loves it. He rejoiced in creation because God declared it to be Good. The *Centuries* offers instruction by a man in love for a woman in love— but not with each other. The unique friendship between Traherne and Mrs. Hopton was grounded in their mutual love of God. He dedicated *Centuries* to her, "to the friend of my best friend". The joy to which he gave witness, joy in creation coupled with the practicalities of living life in the spirit of God, hallmarks all of Traherne's work and makes him a joy to read even more than three centuries later.

William Law
1686 – 1761
APOPHATIC
SPECULATIVE

Moving into the 18th Century, England was in the midst of social and intellectual transition, and William Law stands as a pivotal figure of that troubled time. Born two years before the Glorious Revolution, Law maintained a loyalty to the Stuart monarchy even though it cost him his academic career at Cambridge. In the midst of continuing disturbance between the three parties of Anglicanism[72] and the two political parties,[73] the faith and practice reached its all-time low in England. There grew a pervasive attitude in society of materialism, comfort, and easy living—not unlike current American society. Few people took the Church seriously—except for matters of state importance—and most were put off by any spirit of "enthusiasm".[74] Religion was to be, above all else, reasonable and of proper form and rite.

An early mentor of John Wesley, William Law was thought of by his contemporaries as a mystic and a sound Anglican theologian. While his early writings dealt with the controversies pertaining to the issues of State versus Church, they have been compared to

---

[72] Liberals, Evangelicals, and Catholics
[73] Tories and Whigs
[74] a word coined to denote revival or spirit-filled worship

Pascal's *Provincial Letters.* His mystical works, *A Serious Call to the Devout and Holy Life, The Spirit of Prayer,* and *The Spirit of Love,* came later in his life and focused on the inner call of Christian perfection. Law was well-read in the Rhineland Mystics and influenced also by the writings of Francis de Sales and Francois Fénelon. At the apex of his mystical writings Law became much enamored with the German Protestant mystic, Jacob Boehme, whose works did much to influence Law's own spiritual formation.

Law brought to a close the Caroline Age but passed on to future Anglicans a solid tradition as based in the *Book of Common Prayer* and its piety, as well as the Anglican morality. His book *A Serious Call* was for the faithful in England what Francis de Sales' *Introduction to the Devout Life* was for France. Each enjoyed immediate success and popularity. Each laid down practical dictates of devotion, yet called readers to a transcendent love for God. And as with de Sales, William Law practiced what he affirmed for others.

The theme of *A Serious Call* centers around a Christian's daily life in terms of moral conduct, devotional practice, and the obligations of a person's state of life. Law himself lived out that theme in a semi-monastic setting shared with two like-minded women. Their daily round of prayer and a generosity in giving to the poor earned the little household, in Law's native town of King's Cliff, a reputation praised by admirers and scorned by detractors. Those of us who read Law now may find his standards for Christian living rigorous and uncomfortable, but that may well be because he had a much keener sense of sin than we do. Self-denial and humility are qualities no longer espoused or encouraged in our spiritual development, but they were integral to Law's understanding of Christian perfection. It must also be remembered that Law was evangelizing a dead church and a decadent society which needed to be reminded of responsibility connected to religious commitment. We would do well to take Law's precepts to heart, even if we find his understanding of sociology to be outdated. To devote oneself to the pursuit of heavenly wisdom and heavenly love, Law pleaded for every Christian's loyalty and determination, for he saw that whatever was not of heaven most certainly must be of hell—and thus to be avoided vehemently.

William Law was pivotal in English Church history because his devotional writings so influenced the next generation, ushering in the religious revival of John and Charles Wesley. His works also commanded the attention of John Keble and the stirring spirit of the Oxford Movement nearly one hundred years later. Whereas Law's earliest polemic works quickly became dated by the rush of history, the mystical works remain classics of relevance and pious wisdom, as characterizes the great masters of the mystic tradition.

Chapter 11

The Oxford Movement

he Anglican Tradition came to birth in England amid the struggles between Papal claims of supreme authority and that of the English Crown. This contentiousness dominated the political and religious panorama from King Henry VIII's (1491–1547) notorious rule until the Catholic Emancipation Acts by King George III in 1778. The spirituality of this period has little resemblance to that of the *Devotio Moderna*, with its highly "affective" expression. One might characterize it as devout but dry.

The doctrinal formulae known as the "Thirty-Nine Articles" (1563) and the publication of *The Book of Common Prayer* (1552) became the means by which the Church in England made its definitive statement of faith and through which it expressed its piety. The Articles were aimed against the errors committed by Rome as well as the heretical tendencies of the radical Protestant factions. In them will be seen a surprising spirit of moderation and sound doctrine which characterizes Anglican spirituality. *The Book of Common Prayer* gave shape to this moderate doctrine by means of its worship and claimed as a guiding rule of conduct central to Anglicanism, *lex orandi, lex credendi*.[75]

During the 19th Century, in England, there arose a religious movement which built upon this solid Anglican foundation and revitalized its significance and influence in the Body of Christ. Anglicans have striven

---

[75] the law of worship is the law of belief

throughout their history to synthesize their theological position to remain both truly catholic and truly Protestant. Then, in the mid-19th Century, England's famous Oxford University became the stage for Anglicanism's most dramatic offensive in the battle for political and theological stability. This has since become known as the "Oxford Movement" or the Anglo-Catholic Revival.

Those of us who worship in the Episcopal Church in the United States take for granted the various rites and ceremonies in which we participate. Weekly or even daily Eucharistic celebrations, the recitation of Morning and Evening Prayer, and the emphasis upon Scriptural truth and sound theology have become so much the standard of our piety that we never stop to think about the men who shaped our tradition. Because of this, we often flag in zeal and lack the depth to express fully our spiritual heritage. Those of us who begin to study our spiritual heritage are quickly mired in a network of political and religious history which is voluminous and confusing.

The political struggle between the Whigs and the Tories became also a struggle between the High Churchmen and the Low Churchmen, between the liberal parties and the conservatives. Catholic Emancipation, which allowed Roman Catholics to own property without taking an oath of denial and that priests would no longer be subject to persecution and imprisonment, left wounds still felt in religious attitudes today. The push for separation of Church and State is practically inconceivable to those of us who have grown up in such a different religious culture, but these things must not be disregarded if we are to comprehend the multifaceted crisis of this period.

One peculiarity of the Anglican tradition—and particularly the Oxford Movement—which has kept the Church vital and brought the always-neglected objective side of Truth into prominence is that it has never been under the guidance of any one man. This has saved it from disaster in times when a few prominent persons fell away and has also protected it from the narrowness of echoing any one man's opinions.

Oppositional forces were not only external to the Anglican Church but just as strongly established within it. Three major factions vied for dominance in the Church of England and remain distinct even today: the Evangelicals, the Liberals,[76] and the Anglo-Catholics.[77] Politically speaking the Evangelicals of Cambridge dominated in the 18th Century and continued to win a large following in the 19th. Their spirituality bordered on a more Calvinist approach, which maintained that only through faith could a soul be saved and that Scripture, rather than the Church, was the revealer of religious truth. They rejected the doctrine of Baptismal regeneration and the sacrifice of the Eucharist, which made them suspicious of and hostile to the Tractarians.

The Liberals were a group very much influenced by Erastian philosophy, an anthropocentric humanism which maintained the supremacy of reason but is inconsistent with Biblical and doctrinal orthodoxy. Their strengths, however, lay in their power to adapt to changing social and political conditions. They gave to Anglicanism a healthy respect for the skeptical approach until Christian revelation could be demonstrated

---

[76] also known as Latitudinarians
[77] or Tractarians

as truth. According to this group, religion must be straightforward and aboveboard, carrying with it a sound morality and common sense.

Anglo-Catholics, or Tractarians, sought a balance between faith and reason and proposed a middle way, the *via media*. In this was sought a medium between extremes, which ideally combined the advantages and shut out the evils of both. Characteristic of the *via media* was a striving after the maximum, the best possible guarantee for holiness, while maintaining a perfect balance between doctrinal and mystical response to the revelation of God's life.

The Oxford Movement was built upon a solid foundation of scholarship and devotion to the principles and doctrines established by the Patristic Church. Primary to its spirituality is the doctrine of the Incarnation and the Church as the extension of it. This became the foundation of the Oxford revival and in contrast with Protestantism, which claimed that religion's faith rests on a book, *Sola scripture*, the Anglican Church put faith in the Person of Christ. Central then to Anglicanism is the doctrine of *theosis*. It is the key to understanding their vision of Christian faith and life. Theosis is the deification of humanity or the participation of humanity in the Divine Life. For the Anglican, especially those of the Oxford period, theosis defines the consequence and completion of the Incarnation.

There were three distinct phases of the Anglo-Catholic revival: the Tractarian phase, the social phase of parochial missions, and the ritualistic phase, which is probably the best known period of the Anglo-Catholic revival. The Oxford Movement as a whole spanned three generations of expressing the Incarnational aspect of Christian life.

The first phase of the movement established the doctrinal basis or system of thought, which brought the Church of England to acknowledge its ancient catholic heritage. They made a firm stand that the "Church" is the continuation of the mystery of incarnational reality. The second phase moved the Oxford intellectuals out of the "common rooms" of the university and into the ghetto parishes and slums of the cities, to bring aid and comfort to the destitute. This was a further act of acknowledging the Incarnate Lord within the very heart of humanity. The third phase expressed its understanding of the Incarnation through form and ritual, attempting to bring the reality of God into every sense and fiber of a person's being.

Anglicanism's incarnationally centered spirituality strives to lead humanity toward its fullest potential. Traditional Anglicanism, built upon Patristic foundations and nurtured by the Caroline Divines of the 16th Century, was further solidified by the men of Oxford. Central to that Movement were John Keble (1792–1866), John Henry Newman (1801–1890), and Edward Bouverie Pusey (1800–1882).

John Keble
1792 – 1866
KATAPHATIC
SPECULATIVE

Keble inaugurated the movement with his "Assize" sermon, preached on July 14, 1833. This sermon, entitled "National Apostasy", is rather a bland statement in opposition to Parliament's interference in Church affairs. The English government had, at this point, dissolved ten Irish dioceses in order to re-route finances. Keble was the stable patriarch of the Oxford conspirators, to whom most of the others turned in time of crisis and confusion.

He provided solid guidance for the more brilliant and creative thinking of Pusey and Newman.

Professor of Poetry at Oxford, Keble's feel for the poetic coupled in an extraordinary way with his sense of traditional Anglicanism. In both he made an appeal for true reverence, laying the foundation for later ceremonial which would become a hallmark of the Catholic revival. His best known work, *The Christian Year*, poetically describes the festivals and seasons of the year in imagery reminiscent of the mystic's visions.

One is struck by the love of beauty which Keble gave to the great Truths of the Faith. He saw the mysteries of God wrapped in the tangible symbolism of the Church and in earth's natural phenomena. Yet the practical side of this professor of poetry demanded that a soul act upon the beauty of the world and the mysteries of the Faith by taking them into inner self and so to be transformed by them. Keble's theology, like that of Eastern Orthodoxy, could not separate the mystical from the dogmatic, the prayerful from the practical. Everything in Keble's teaching pointed toward holiness, the sanctification of the soul, and the Eucharist which he saw to be a prime vehicle for that work. It was such loves which John Keble, the genuinely gentle man from Oxford, passed on to Newman and Pusey.

John Henry Newman
1801 – 1890

Edward Bouverie Pusey
1800 – 1882
KATAPHATIC
SPECULATIVE

John Henry Newman, born in 1801, was the prime "mover and shaker" of the Catholic revival until he converted to the Roman Church in 1845. The process of his own search for Truth and the development of his moral conscience led Newman to build a method and means for theological argument. His was a genius—and a disturbed one at that—who paved the way for others to take confidence in the use of their personal reason to discover religious verity.

Between Edward Bouverie Pusey and Newman a solid and profound synthesis of Scriptural truth, the Apostolic Tradition, and sound thinking became the hallmark of the way Anglicans "do theology". For them, there was no distinction between spirituality and theology. Each man pursued a desire for holiness and that holiness was found in the informed reason of the conscience.

Pusey, a year older than Newman, entered Oxford a bit later, but so impressed him that Pusey won Newman's heart and imagination almost immediately, causing him to describe Pusey as a "saint" in one of his poems. Pusey's feelings for Newman were strong but lacked the element of the romantic which was more characteristic of Newman. In a letter to his fiancé, Pusey expressed his view of Newman as a valued and dear friend. They remained friends, though distant, throughout their lives, although after Newman's defection to the Roman cause, their meetings were very few.

A common denominator among all of the major figures of the Oxford Movement, and indeed distinguishing mark of Anglicanism, was their emphasis on conscience or moral character. I believe this to be the key to both Newman's conversion to Rome and Pusey's conviction to remain Anglican. They had followed the tradition of the Caroline Divines, to whom "casuistical" theology bore its greatest precepts. Casuistry is the science of bringing general moral principles to bear upon particular cases.

For each of them, "Holy Living" equaled a moral conscience and obedience to that conscience. But this "conscience" is something our present culture does not understand well because it has learned to function primarily on desire. Conscience, however, is key to comprehending the dynamics of Anglicanism and particularly the purpose of the Oxford Movement. Here again, we find a synthesis of the medieval casuistical thought with the modern enlightened thought.

The most important thing in Newman's mind was the ascertainment of religious truth and this he passed on to his followers in the Movement. He helped develop within them that passionate desire to bring the Church back into societal prominence, which it had lost in the rise of national and industrial development. The whole of the Movement asserted that the Church must govern society or society would eventually cease to be Christian. There are many within the Anglican Church today who would say that this has come to pass.

Newman and Pusey started out on surprisingly similar spiritual journeys, but concluded their search in radically different places. Both were Fellows at Oxford and both undertook rigorous scholastic campaigns which led them into the intricacies of Patristic theology. "Reading the Fathers" became each one's passion, but there the similarity ends. While Newman began to concentrate on the dynamics of the major heresies of the Early Church and how the Counsels maintained the Truth in the midst of such deviation, Pusey spent his time studying Semitic languages and the Greek Fathers. Pusey saw these as the archetypical pattern of God's self-communication, leading him to conclude that the

Anglican tradition was a continuing voice of God's revealing truth.

Newman was led to the other conclusion. The more he studied, the more he was convinced that the Anglican Church was an aberration of the true Church. He likened the Church of England to the Monophysites of the 5th Century. Monophysitism was a doctrine which professed a single nature in Christ and that nature held as Divine. Orthodoxy maintains that Christ has two natures, both human and divine. However, it was not the theology of monophysitism which led Newman to view the Anglican tradition as an aberration of the truth. Rather it appears to be in the subtly of definition that Newman saw the similarity. The many attempts made in the 5th and 6th Centuries to reconcile the Monophysites to the Catholics failed. Such could also be said of Anglicanism, in Newman's interpretation.

At the height of Newman's struggle with his conscience, the subtle differences between the Church of Rome and the Church of England grew to monumental importance, and the words of St. Augustine, *Securus judicat orbis terrarum*[78] which Newman read in an article which had been sent to him by a friend became the decisive turning point in Newman's thinking. Newman's view of the Church was that her mysteries were but the expression in human language of Truth, to which the human mind is unequal. It was Newman who raised the Oxford Movement to a higher plane than it would otherwise have been; therefore, he is considered its true leader.

The further Newman pursued the Anglican way, the further convinced he became of the necessity to

---

[78] literally, the world judges free from care

abide in the substantive tradition, which Roman Catholicism provided. The quote of St. Augustine. *Securus judicat orbis terrarum*, turned Newman's heart toward Rome and destroyed his faith in the *via media* completely. The desire of both Pusey and Newman, prior to Newman's conversion, had been to show that the doctrines of the Church of England were the continuous teachings of the Church through the ages, particularly of the teaching of the first five centuries. Anglicans have always made a special appeal to Antiquity and based their doctrinal claims upon fidelity to the Early Church.

But the obedience to conscience which led Newman from Anglicanism to Roman Catholicism was the same obedience to conscience which kept Pusey true to his Anglican roots. The question for Pusey as to which structure was right and which one was wrong became somehow irrelevant. He viewed the "Mission" of the Church as top priority, rather than "which" Church is in control. In his book *Eirenicon*, Pusey responded to an accusation by a Roman Catholic scholar, Dr. Manning, that the Church of England has claimed false superiority over the Roman Church. Pusey's reply was typically practical. He professed that in as much as the Church of England was the predominant denomination in the nation, then it naturally followed that it would be the best bulwark of infidelity for the English people.

Pusey, more than Newman, stood between the Papacy and Protestantism with a greater sense of theological balance and emotional equilibrium simply due to his personality. It is to be said that one distinguishing characteristic of Pusey's was that he shrank in every possible way from putting himself forth or allowing himself to be regarded as a leader. The Church is full of the history of those who, having gathered followers about themselves, have led them eventually out of the Church into a schismatic and sect condition. A true and loyal son of the church, ever submissive to her authority, Pusey, in the spirit of deep self-abnegation and humility, shunned what would be called leadership. Unlike his dear friend Newman, who was of a speculative mind and passed through many forms of belief, Pusey was always unexcitable concerning authority. The voice of God came to him through "The Church", which he defined as whole and continuous, and this gave grandeur and solidity to his convictions. He felt most deeply that Christianity's greatest weakness lay in a divided Christendom.

Whereas it was Newman's habit to make a virtue out of an inclination, one can begin to understand that his heart would naturally follow his intellectual pursuit for Truth. For both Newman and Pusey, the heart of Catholic faith and life lay in the Evangelical affirmation of the personal encounter between God and each human soul. Newman took this conviction with him to Rome. Only since the Second Vatican Council has it been possible to see the positive significance of Newman's conversion, an act which was not merely personal but which in a strange way brought the churches together by taking from one to the other a man who carried with him all that was best in the tradition in which he had developed and matured. Pusey could see this, and beyond his own sorrow of Newman's conversion, he understood the possibilities for reconciliation between Rome and the Church of England which would be brought about by Newman's obedience to his conscience and God's will.

Both men also recognized the necessity of the personal encounter between the sinfulness of man and a forgiving and loving God. Without that personal encounter the whole "catholic" system becomes lifeless and loses its principle motivation. This personal influence, not a doctrinal system, was Newman's *modus operandi*. He remained an Evangelical internally rather than a machine of the Magisterium after his conversion, and this is probably why he had such troubles with the Roman hierarchy. Cardinal Wiseman called him "more English than the English" and therefore more dangerous to Rome. The Roman hierarchy in England was jealous of Newman's influence and his liberal ideas; liberal according to Rome but a combination of evangelical and papist from the Church of England's point of view. They became particularly unnerved by Newman's interest in consulting the laity in matters of doctrine.

Even after Newman left the Anglican Church, Pusey quoted him often in his sermons and pressed for a spirit of unity rather than division from Rome. Being the mystic of the Oxford Movement, Pusey dealt with this subject in a manner which reflected his own spiritual convictions. In one sermon preached in 1845 shortly after Newman's conversion, Pusey spoke to the great need of the faithful to discuss their differences in the attitude of prayer with the communion of the saints rather than in the heat and rancor of partisan debate.

Following the course of the *via media* Pusey's moral conscience comes through clearly in his sermons and his book, *Eirenicon*, which means of course, "an instrument of peace". Pusey had no desire to place himself under the authority of the Roman Church, as

Newman did, yet he held out an unwavering hand in fellowship. In as much as the Anglican Church holds the Faith professed in the ancient creeds of the Ecumenical Counsels and played out in the practice of the sacraments, Pusey felt no division with Rome. To him both were the legitimate expressions of the One, Holy Catholic and Apostolic Church.

According to Newman, Anglicanism's strengths lay in her richness, having more than we know how to use. The problems Newman eventually discerned with Anglicanism, even in all her richness, ended up within the sphere of authority. Even though the Church of England possessed catholic truth, she represented no objective system, no authoritative structure. Therefore, according to Newman it was a "paper religion that has no structure except on paper".

John Mason Neale
1818 – 1866
KATAPHATIC
AFFECTIVE

Pusey and others held the opposite view and as such one of the results of the Oxford Movement was a revival of the ceremonial in public worship. Where the altars had been pulled down or turned into common tables, they now were returned to where they belonged, and services which had been shorn of their beauty regained the ornamentation befitting beautiful worship. One of the key figures in the revival of liturgical opulence was John Mason Neale.

Neale was a scholar from Cambridge rather than Oxford and with a friend founded the Cambridge Camden Society, which was for the promoting of the study of Christian art, architecture, symbolism, and hymnody and devoted much of its time and writing to these ecclesiological matters. Here, too, was a deliberate return to the rites and practices of the medieval church. Neale's great interest in church architecture lead him to promote the building or remodeling of churches which would exemplify the theology they housed. To him it was as important that the outward and visible fact of the church should speak to the sacramental principles of Catholicity as much as its interior life did. The fact that Neale balanced his spirituality with his theology can be recognized in his two loves of poetry/hymnody and architecture.

Neale was fascinated by the mystical element of Holy Scripture and was very well read in the mystics of the early and late medieval periods. Though many hymns were originally composed by Neale, just as many were translated by him from the Latin and Greek and would have been lost to our tradition had it not been for his diligence and foresight. He saw in these lovely works a way of reflecting God's majesty, of celebrating the glorious mystery of the eternal. Far from the stark Puritanism, Neale sought to enrich the externals of worship because they so directly influence the inner life.

Neale's propensity for the ceremonial display and transcendent spirituality did not pose an obstacle for the practical side of his nature. In 1855 he founded a religious sisterhood, the Society of St. Margaret, for the purpose of providing practical help for clergy and for ministering to those who needed nursing care. Following the pattern of St. Vincent de Paul's Sisters of Charity and drawing heavily from St. Francis de Sales' rule for the visitation Sisters, Neale formed a community which would figure prominently in the development of the nursing profession.

Another outlet for Neale's love of the beautiful and the profound was in his study of Eastern Orthodoxy. He wrote several volumes of history pertaining to the Russian and Greek expression of orthodoxy and was lauded by various diplomats and church officials for his efforts. This work perpetuated an important link between Anglicanism and the patristic church and fostered a continuing dialogue between Orthodoxy and the Anglican Communion.

However, not all was laudatory in Neale's life, particularly within his own Anglicanism. Because of the fear and suspicion toward the Roman Catholics in England,[79] anything remotely resembling the "papists" ways was suppressed and the offenders disciplined. As it was discovered that he made use of a Roman Breviary and a Latin translation of the Bible, Neale was marked as an offender and forbidden to function as a priest outside of the college where he was chaplain. This ban remained in effect for several years and was lifted only three years before his death.

It must be remembered that the classical age of mysticism is over and the age of enlightenment and industry well-settled. The visionary gave way to the practical. Yet the Oxford Revival provided for the need for the transcendent by its elaborate ceremonial, by the beauty of its music, and by the encouragement of pious devotion.

ChaRles C. GRafton
1830 – 1912
Kataphatic
Affective

Charles Chapman Grafton brought these things to the American Episcopal Church. Drawn by the ideals of the

---

[79] both in a political and a religious sense

Religious Life and the vocation to the priesthood, after having graduated from Harvard Law School, Grafton forsook the law profession to pursue his dream. At the climax of the American Civil War, Grafton sailed for England, under his Bishop's guidance, to investigate the monastic way of life. There he met and lodged for a time with Edward Pusey, who was his first mentor in the "consecrated life". While there, Grafton was put to work caring for the cholera victims of the 1866 epidemic, with Priscilla Lydia Sellon, the foundress of the Society of the Holy Trinity.

In 1866, the year of both Keble's and Neale's deaths, Grafton met with like-minded men, Simeon O'Neil and Richard Muex Benson, and the Society of St. John the Evangelist was formed. As they formed this community at Benson's church in Cowley, they began to be called the "Cowley Fathers". The Society offered a Benedictine Rule with an active apostolate of evangelism. It was within this Society that Grafton learned the ways of the consecrated life and through it brought his ideals back to America. It did not take long, however, before a conflict arose concerning loyalty and obedience due his Superior in England and that due his Bishop in America. Grafton resolved the conflict by choosing to leave the Cowley Fathers. In leaving them he did not forsake his ideals of the Religious Life and indeed became the founder of the Sisterhood of the Holy Nativity.

Grafton was elected the second bishop of the diocese of Fond du Lac, in Wisconsin, in 1889. It was a difficult and poor diocese and Grafton spent much of his own fortune as well as donations from wealthy friends in the East to keep it going. The population of the diocese changed dramatically as many of the old parishes were founded by Church people from the East while Wisconsin was still, very much, a frontier; as those people moved on, they left the establishments to a new foreign element which began moving in.

The cause of Christ and the advancement of His Church as a means of salvation of souls was the greatest passion of Bishop Grafton's life. His dreams of missionary enterprise in the United States and particularly in his own diocese were all focused on the promotion of God's Kingdom as visibly manifested in the Church as well as hidden in faithful souls. All of his efforts and those of the Religious orders he founded had this central goal in mind.

Likened by his contemporaries to Francis de Sales, Grafton's bearing expressed all the restraint and reserve which were perhaps the deepest notes of the Oxford Movement yet with a spirit of exaltation and a love of beauty sympathetic with that of the great Genevan bishop. Never a mere ritualist, Grafton loved an elaborate service because he loved the fullest expression of the idea of worship. This love he instilled in his daughters of the Holy Nativity. In fact, his relationship with Mother Ruth Margaret and her Sisters of the Holy Nativity was very suggestive of that between de Sales, Jane Frances de Chantal, and the Sisters of the Visitation. As the founder and writer of their Rule, Bishop Grafton desired to lead his Sisters into a true spirit of sanctity, enlivened by a deep love for their Spouse and Savior and by a burning zeal for the salvation of others.

In his last years, with declining health and unable to travel about his diocese, Bishop Grafton devoted himself to the work of writing. His works take up eight volumes, consisting of an autobiography, council addresses, sermons, and several essays. In them a person can experience the heart of the man in all its dignity and gravity as well as the perpetuation of a distaste for the Roman Catholic tradition while being enamored with Eastern Orthodoxy. Through his teaching, preaching, writing, and many pastoral activities, the Episcopal Church in America found itself being led toward a catholicity of practice and an orthodoxy of belief which has stood firm until very recently.

Today it is taken rather for granted that the principle service on Sunday morning is the Eucharist and that many churches provide daily celebrations of the Eucharist for their congregations. But had it not been for the diligence and courage of Charles Chapman Grafton, these things would probably not have found their way into the common life of our church. Though Bishop Grafton is best remembered for the rich use of ceremonial, his greatest contribution to the Church lay in his perception of the incarnation and his encouragement of the pursuit for holiness. All external expression or adornment was done for the purpose of making a worthier shrine in which to reveal the Incarnate God, particularly as He is revealed in the Blessed Sacrament. The second bishop of Fond du Lac impressed all those who knew him as one of marvelous spiritual insight and deep evangelical piety, a bishop who loved his Savior and Redeemer with a direct and personal devotion.

Chapter 12
The Contemporary Period

To know a bit about the persons who most have influenced a great spiritual master is to know something of the inner character of a saint. Therefore, in order to discuss the spirituality and importance of two contemporary spiritual writers and pilgrims on the mystic journey, Baron Friedrich von Hügel and Charles de Foucauld, we must first look at the life of a simple yet profoundly holy priest, Abbe Henri Huvelin (1838–1910). It was he who provided spiritual direction to both of these men and who did much to mold their religious practice.

Henri Huvelin
1838 – 1910
KATAPHATIC
AFFECTIVE

This saintly man reflected the same humility of spirit and straightforward discernment which characterized the life and ministry of Jean-Baptiste-Marie Vianney (1786–1859),[80] who could also well have been a subject for this study. Abbe Huvelin quietly ministered to his parish of St. Augustine in Paris, focusing much of his efforts toward the youth; however, many adults also went to the church's crypt to hear his wisdom. The fact that books were published under his name leads us to assume that Huvelin desired a wider audience than the groups that

---

[80] popularly known as the *Cure d'Ars*

met for his instructions. Nevertheless, this is quite contrary to the truth. The books that have come down to us were compiled from notes by those who loyally sat at the Abbe's feet, which shows the heartfelt response toward his spiritual genius. Huvelin never intended the promotion of his work, but those who recognized his worth saw to it that his posterity would benefit future generations. *Addresses to Catholic Women*, *The Love of the Lord*, and *Some Seventeenth Century Spiritual Guides* all saw publication ten to fifteen years after the Abbe's death, yet they have the ability to portray his spiritual temperament as though he had personally penned each one.

Besides the simple yet erudite catechetical instructions and sermons, Huvelin's best known ministry was that of spiritual direction. Like the *Cure d'Ars*, the Abbe spent many hours in the confessional, spending as many as twelve to fourteen hours at a stretch. He also maintained a habit of receiving visitors each afternoon. It is here where von Hügel and de Foucauld first tasted his able spiritual expertise. As time went on, letters were the primary source of Huvelin's authority in their lives.

The Abbe exemplified the qualities of holy priesthood. He spoke often of his role and the demands of such a vocation, holding up above all the complete nature of self-sacrifice. To him, a priest was no longer his own person but one who would perpetually be in the service of others. That service may manifest itself in small or trifling acts of kindness, but always the ultimate purpose was to bring a soul closer to God.

Though he had a fairly sophisticated intellect, being a master of classical literature and patristic theologies, his preaching and teaching remained easily grasped by the young and uneducated. Never a matter of "talking down" to his students, the kind Abbe simply had the gift of knowing the current or wavelength that reached through the mind and down into the heart. His primary aim was to teach others how to yield themselves to the operation of the Holy Spirit in their lives and, of course, a central focus of his piety was the Eucharistic worship of the Church.

Though von Hügel unashamedly referred to Huvelin as his "saint", the Abbe's humility requested people to recognize him in his frailty, in his ability to fall into temptation. However, Huvelin also was aware that visits to his classes or to hear his sermons had become the fashion, and although he desired to put a stop to such popularity, still he gave himself ungrudgingly to those who sought his counsel.

In his teaching Huvelin was fond of pointing out the frequent changes in theological opinion caused by the continual advance in science. The Abbe urged his hearers to be true to their conscience and to pursue a perfecting in charity. For him, truth and love are indissolubly bound, and heresy remained the greatest of all falsehoods, for in heresy a person allows him or herself to lie to God. He offered a remedy for heresy in urging the pursuit of truth for its own sake rather than for some personal motive. He redefined orthodoxy as an intellectual honesty toward things divine.

Charles de Foucauld
1858 – 1916
APOPHATIC
AFFECTIVE

Such was the spiritual legacy Abbe Huvelin passed on to those who revered him. As has been mentioned, one of his spiritual disciples was Charles de Foucauld, whose relationship with the Abbe lasted from 1886 to the Abbe's death in 1910. Huvelin had been a family friend and the spiritual director of Charles' cousin, Marie. Marie was Charles' soul friend and it was she who introduced him to Huvelin. When one becomes more aware of influences that flow between people, such as Teresa of Avila and John of the Cross or Francis de Sales and Jane Frances de Chantal, it is easy to see that holiness begets holiness.

Charles de Foucauld began life in the spoiled and impetuous environment of a doting grandfather and an undisciplined air of the minor nobility.[81] As a young man, his time spent in the French military shows him to have been an unkempt and disobedient officer. His affairs with women were many and his taste for life overindulgent. There seems a similarity between Charles' life and that of the young Augustine of Hippo. This similarity extends to his conversion to Christianity. Neither did anything by half measure; rather, they lived to the extent of their means, both in decadence and in devotion.

Besides Holy Scripture, de Foucauld was most profoundly instructed by a careful and continuous reading of the works of St. Teresa of Avila and to a lesser degree by those of John of the Cross. In the early years of his vocation to the monastic life, de Foucauld kept a copy of Teresa's works always with him and he once claimed to have read her entire works through ten times in as many years. Having burned her thinking, her spirit, into his own heart, it is somewhat surprising that he did not follow the Carmelite style of monasticism but initially was drawn to the Trappist (Cistercian) form.

---

[81] having lost his parents by the age of six

Brother Charles had a restless spirit all his life, which is manifested in the fact that he could not settle in one place for very long nor could he leave a Rule unchallenged. His earnest desire to follow the life of Jesus of Nazareth literally moved him from France to Nazareth, from the Trappist order to an independent eremitical lifestyle. One scheme in which he tried to coax Abbe Huvelin's permission was the purchase of the Mount of Beatitudes, there to establish a hermitage. Huvelin refused that permission, though Charles had already begun to collect the necessary funds. The good Abbe tried persistently to get de Foucauld to create a Nazareth in his heart, mind, and spirit. Even when Charles eventually moved to the Sahara desert, among the native peoples, he was still restless, always looking for the will of God in the next journey. He settled in a village called Tamanrasset, located in the wilderness of Algeria, and there de Foucauld spent many hours in devotion and many hours serving the people, particularly translating the Gospels into the native language of Tuareg.

Charles spent the majority of his pilgrim life working on a Rule for a brotherhood which never developed into the community he hoped would come to birth. No one ever came to join him in his eremitical journey. It was only after his death that some heard the call of the Religious Life and adopted the Rule of Life designed for "The Little Brothers of Jesus" and the "Little Sisters of Jesus". This Rule was grounded in his yearning for solitude and severe poverty coupled with a zeal for souls. The basis of love, for this holy hermit, is in imitation. To imitate the life of Jesus is the highest virtue and to this Charles gave himself entirely. Imitation was de Foucauld's key to successful Christian living. Of the men who did eventually take up the arduous Rule, we are probably most familiar with the splendid author Carlo Caretto, whose writings are still best-sellers in current spiritual reading.

Spending fifteen to sixteen hours a day before the tabernacle, in the deep prayer of contemplation, Charles leaves no doubt as to the focus of his piety. Although he had to go without receiving the Eucharist, sometimes for months, still he treasured his intimacy with the Lord in the Blessed Sacrament. His desire was to emulate the hidden life of Jesus in humility, poverty, prayer, and in mortifications. De Foucauld was not excessively encumbered by doctrinal structures, preferring instead a devotion to God based on a continual meditation of the Gospels. Besides contemplative prayer, he viewed his ministry as intercessory, praying continually for those he loved.

Only recently have Brother Charles' writings become available to the wider audience. His *Letters* and Meditations are short yet with a dynamism that propel the reader forward and into a sense of the desert spirituality, where all pretense is dropped and a soul stands exposed to the holy and mysterious other.

Baron Friedrich von Hügel
1852 – 1925
KATAPHATIC
AFFECTIVE

Another disciple of the Abbe Huvelin, whose vocation was extremely different from that of de Foucauld, was Baron Friedrich von Hügel. Von Hügel was born in Florence, Italy, of an Austrian father and Scottish mother. However, he spent the majority of his life in England. It has been said of the Baron that no other religious thinker has wielded more influence in England during his own lifetime, with the exception of Cardinal John Henry Newman, with whom he was also acquainted. In fact, Cardinal Newman influenced the Baron concerning insights into the Church and concerning the laity toward ecclesiastical authority.

Von Hügel had no formal university training, instead receiving his instruction from many private tutors. Still, his keen intelligence and articulate manner betrayed the fact that he was as well or better read than many an Oxford scholar. He possessed a deep philosophical insight which added power to his abilities in theology. Yet von Hügel described himself as mystical and positive rather than scholastic or theoretical.

Under Huvelin's direction, the Baron was taught how to attract souls to the Gospel of Jesus Christ. He was urged not to use any shortcuts or to minimize the Christian doctrine but instead to present it whole and complete. By that it would retain its integrity and its beauty and therefore draw even the most skeptical. Huvelin also encouraged von Hügel not to reduce the defense of Catholicism to mere syllogistic terms. By doing so, he would weaken his argument, since the syllogism takes a major and a minor premise with their known truths and uses them to assume a third or concluding truth.[82]

Baron von Hügel wrote decisively on the subject of mysticism. His major work, *The Mystical Element of Religion as studied in Saint Catherine of Genoa and her friends* provides us with his own definition of mysticism; namely that it is an experience of God as distinctly and independently other. He viewed the mystical ele-

---

[82] Example: snow is white and sugar is white, therefore snow and sugar must in some way be related.

ment of life as what humanity is in its essence and that which animates humanity to function as it does. Based upon the assumption that our humanity in itself represents a pilgrimage, both personal and historical, into the eternal truth, von Hügel avowed that mysticism is the vehicle of that pilgrimage. The three major elements abiding in religion von Hügel therefore interpreted as historical, intellectual and experimental, or in other words, institutional, intellectual, and mystical.

Around the turn of the 20th Century von Hügel became identified with a theological movement known as Modernism. He was an important link between the Modernists of France and those of England. Formally condemned by Pope Pius X in 1907, Modernism is the belief that the teachings and practices of the Roman Catholic Church should relate more closely with the modern points of view in philosophy and the sciences rather than ancient tradition. Here was urged a more critical analysis of Holy Scripture, an acceptance of Christian principles as based in the experience of life rather than on intellectual systems or creeds. With a "teleological" view of history,[83] the Modernists minimized the importance of the actual bodily reality of Jesus in favor of the development of the institution which came from the process of salvation history. Although condemned as heresy, it has become a rather prevalent mode of thinking in our present time. While many of the proponents of Modernism were excommunicated from the Roman Catholic Church, the Baron was not.

---

[83] that the importance of something lies in the process rather than a specific event

The Baron passed on his understanding of the mystical life and the legacy he had received from Huvelin to an Anglican laywoman who sought him out for spiritual direction: Evelyn Underhill. Not only was von Hügel an intellectual guide for Evelyn, but he also helped to foster her sense of interiority. From him she gained the understanding that the heart of the Christian desire to worship is that it is primarily a response to a God who has already initiated the relationship. Evelyn's maturity in the spiritual life comes through in her later writings as the years of study, devotion, and practice were synthesized into a homogeneous canticle of praise. Indeed, the heart of the Baron's teaching and Evelyn's response declared that the essence of religion is adoration.

Underhill was born in 1875, the daughter of Sir Arthur Underhill and Lucy Iremonger. Sir Arthur was a successful barrister and so was able to provide his daughter with the academic and cultural education not available to most English women of this period. Her subsequent marriage to another successful lawyer, Hubert Stuart Moore, when Evelyn was thirty-two years old, preserved her status among the privileged class.

One of the aspects that makes Underhill an interesting mentor for people pursuing their own search for holiness is that she was a laywoman and only made a firm commitment to the institutional church when she was forty years old. This fact makes her credibility more appealing than had she been a religious, vowed from her youth to a life unattainable by most. Rather than developing the literary style of the recluse or cloistered religious, Evelyn grappled with her spiritual quest and wrote her many manuscripts in the midst of a full and active life in society. Her schedule, even with the advantages of having several servants and no children to care for, was arduous as she juggled external engagements with the regimen of regular times for prayer, corporate worship, gardening, works of charity, research, and writing.

A characteristic of Anglicanism which has been a factor since the English Reformation is the function of the laity within the theological circles of the Church. This fact was promoted by Cardinal Newman in his move from the Anglican Church to the Roman Catholic Church and was met with strong resistance from the Roman hierarchy. Still the Anglican Church has encouraged and supported lay participation in its governmental structure and its theological development. Baron von Hügel himself was influenced by this fact and therefore promoted Evelyn's work and encouraged her desire for inquiry and analysis.

This Mrs. H. Stuart Moore becomes of particular interest to us because she was a modern woman and keenly aware of the forces which shape our contemporary world. She appreciated the power and achievement of modern science and technology yet always with an awareness of the ineffable holiness which pervades all of life.

Underhill's legacy to the Church of England in particular and the mystic tradition in general abounds in the volumes of her works. She is undoubtedly the most prolific spiritual writer in the English language in the 20th Century. Her mark on the Church was made long before the "women's liberation movement" by the fact that she was the first woman to lecture at Oxford

University and was the first woman (lay or religious) to lead retreats for clergy and laity within Anglicanism. To her credit are over three hundred essays, books, lectures, and book reviews as well as hundreds of letters of spiritual direction.

A strong point in her writing, specifically the more technical, is that Evelyn stressed the necessity of theology. She was adamant that doctrine is foundational to one's spiritual life and that faith is built upon creed and not the other way round. She claimed that keeping to the facts of the matter would lead one to true humility because they stretch one beyond any narcissistic individualism or sentimental impressions. However, Mrs. Moore's writings are not sterile or static, as some might suppose theological inquiry to be, and this can be particularly seen in her books *Worship* and *Practical Mysticism*. Her writings are full of rich, romantic imagery and the passion which accompanies a soul in love with the divine. In fact, Evelyn's definition of the mystic is most engaging, namely someone who has fallen deeply in love with God.

Underhill's later works tend more to the devotional partly because she began to move more and more toward the leading of retreats and functioning as a spiritual director for those who sought out her expertise. Several of her retreat addresses were compiled into book form and continue to be republished under such titles as *The House of Prayer* and *Fruits of the Spirit*.

In contrast to her religious work, Evelyn maintained a firm grasp on the concerns of society's ills and the needs of the present moment. In this she mirrors the quality of the true mystic as her piety did not negate her socio-political involvement. During World War I Underhill worked in the Naval Intelligence department, translating and preparing guidebooks. In terms of the early 21st-Century perspective, Evelyn personifies a prime specimen of the cosmopolitan, erudite, and compassionate woman. Yet perhaps the most appealing aspect of her character was her pragmatism.

In religious terms, Evelyn's pragmatic compassion and her profound insights speak boldly through her writings of a firm commitment to the Incarnational perspective. For her, the only authentic expression of holiness—and for Evelyn holiness was an all encompassing pursuit—was that which had its feet firmly planted in the matter of this world and its concerns. Spirituality became a dead issue if it did not connect intimately with an effort to serve others.

Thérèse of Lisieux
1873 – 1897
KATAPHATIC
AFFECTIVE

This concern for souls so characteristic of mystical piety, the coupling of the ineffable joys of union with God and the practicalities of gospeling the world, shows up with intensity in a young Carmelite from France, Thérèse of Lisieux. From an extremely early age to an extremely premature death, Thérèse showed herself to be a determined lover of the Lord as well as a profound lover of people. Although her Religious Life kept her in the cloister, her actions and prayers were done with a missionary spirit.

Thérèse lost her mother to breast cancer when Thérèse was very young and her eldest sister, who had taken over the responsibility for mothering her, entered the Carmelite convent not many years after their mother's death. Both losses left indelible scars on

Thérèse's emotional integrity. Yet this young saint had the amazing ability to turn her adversity into opportunity.

In reading her life, either the account from her own autobiography, *A Story of a Soul*, or one of the many biographies written about her, one might be tempted to categorize her by current standards as a victim of a dysfunctional family. Thérèse's father, Louis Martin, took a very early retirement and her mother, Zélie, would possibly have worked herself into an early grave had not the ravages of cancer taken her first. The family bound themselves together by an austere piety promoted by Jansenism.[84]

By the time Thérèse had turned fifteen, she had already made several stubborn attempts to be accepted into the same Carmelite convent in Lisieux, where two of her sisters had already entered. Because of her youth, permission was denied, even after repeatedly begging the local bishop to intercede on her behalf to the convent's superior. Thérèse was not one to accept a negative response from people when she believed God's will to be different, so in desire to advance her cause she literally threw herself at the feet of the Pope, with markedly improved results.

On the surface, one can easily pass off such overzealousness and impudence as a matter of Thérèse's indulgent upbringing and her psychological need to follow those who had nurtured her. But there is something deeper and more penetrating than either of these.

---

[84] That Calvinistic form of Catholicism which leaves its adherents with fears and doubts as to their own salvation. From such piety grew a rigorous pursuit of morality and devotion, doing all in one's power to try to stay out of Hell and to gain Heaven.

Thérèse continually and with no hesitation declared her fundamental desire to love Jesus and to make him loved. From this she never wavered, holding it at the center of her sacred mission.

Still, many find this youthful saint either too insipid or too saccharine for their spiritual palates. However, if one is willing to step beyond her stylized writing and the commercial marketing of her "Little Way", looking to discover and accept her version of total abandonment to the Divine Will, there one will find the spirit of a tigress and an adventuress. The "Little Way" stretches to a much larger idea than its name implies. Its major insight and gift to us is that no matter how seemingly small or insignificant our lives may be, when offered to God wholly, we are led into the liberating fullness and demanding responsibility of the Gospel life.

Thérèse's entire life and identity were formed by her complete surrender to God and her love for Him. She accepted all as coming from God and used all, including her intense sufferings, as her contribution to the missionary effort of saving souls. The "Little Flower", as Thérèse referred to herself, taught that humanity's very smallness and weakness give us the boldness to offer ourselves completely to God. Since we are nothing and He is everything, we have nothing to lose and everything to gain. In this she broke out of the severity of Jansenistic piety, not wasting precious time on her flawed humanity. Rather, Thérèse entered passionately into the pursuit of holiness. Not in spite of but because of her perception of littleness, Thérèse inspires others also to pursue lives of holiness, encouraging others to find God hidden in the obscure and mundane aspects of one's life.

Because of the seemingly trivial sacrifices Thérèse made throughout her life, when the excruciating pain of tuberculosis began to ravage her body, she met the challenges with heroic acceptance and patience. What, for us, may seem unnatural—the type of discipline foreign to us and no longer admired—Thérèse willingly acknowledged as a vital element for her formative process. She used every available occurrence as a proving ground for her spiritual life.

In contrast to the focus on littleness, Thérèse also possessed a capacity for greatness. Her heart grew large with the spontaneous affection which she gave so willingly and unreservedly. A favorite and famous story of her early childhood captures the imagination of the dichotomy between Thérèse's sense of insignificance and her uninhibited assumption that everything belonged to her. When one of her older sisters set a basket of personal belongings before all her younger sisters, offering them the opportunity to chose something for themselves, little Thérèse simply stretched out her arms and declared, "I choose all!" Beyond a child's natural tendency toward greed lay the unself-conscious belief that God's promise of abundant life is literally true if one only has the desire to grasp it. No less than the basket of goodies, Thérèse never settled for a portion of the Gospel life. She desired to have it all: all the love and all the blessings. In her mind's eye, God simply stood by waiting for her to take possession of all that He offered her.

Elizabeth of the Trinity
1880 – 1906
KATAPHATIC
AFFECTIVE

The French Carmelites produced not one but two phenomenal mystics at the turn of the 20th Century. Born Elizabeth Catez, but in the Carmel of Dijon known as Elizabeth of the Trinity, another simple and devout soul set God as her number-one priority.

If there is any truth to the myth that each of us has a "twin" somewhere in the world, Elizabeth certainly can claim a likeness of spirits with her contemporary, Thérèse of Lisieux. The similarity goes beyond their choice of vocations in Carmel and the fact that they each died very young. The intense and total intimacy with the Lord, holding nothing back in their givenness to Him, shows them as mirror images of one another. Elizabeth, like Thérèse, practiced the spirituality of the "Little Way", though Elizabeth's contemplative nature projected itself more substantially. This simply may be due to the fact that Elizabeth had a slightly more formal education than did Thérèse, having spent time at the Dijon Conservatoire where she displayed talent as a pianist. Elizabeth also seems to have leaned toward a more speculative approach to religious practices.

Following in the well-established mystical tradition of Teresa of Avila and John of the Cross, Elizabeth had a solid foundation from which to discern and reflect upon her own spiritual experiences. Though she was young—twenty-one when she entered the convent—Elizabeth assimilated the monastic life as though she had been born to it. Indeed, her desire for that life began at age seven and at her fourteenth birthday she made a private vow of virginity. This shows a remarkable focus and strength of character seldom seen in the Church today.

What we know of Elizabeth's life comes not only from a memoir, written by her superior shortly after her death, but also through the over three hundred letters that survive her. These letters tell of Elizabeth's deep commitment to self-forgetfulness. A hint of the *via negativa* worked in her understanding of the ultimate union with God; however, that way of nothing characterized Elizabeth's way of substituting God for herself. She referred to herself as "God's little anchoress", promoting the idea that the further we sink into the abyss, emptying ourselves of all self-motivating principles, the more filled with God we can become.

That we are a capacity for God, the Divine, Elizabeth would avow as our only true purpose. The more we realize this capacity, the more "divinized" our nature. Her words also echo both John the Baptist, who proclaimed that he must decrease that Christ might increase, and St. Paul, who said, "It is no longer I, but Christ who lives in me."

Supremely devoted to the mystery of the Holy Trinity, she expressed her ultimate desire as "the praise of the glory of God". Every action, every thought, every prayer proceeded to that end. In Elizabeth's purview, to become a living witness to the praise of His glory was the destiny for which she was born. While the "Little Flower" focused her yearning for apostolic ministry toward those who were far from God's grace, Elizabeth felt her vocation to lie closer to home. This had the singular effect that she became an icon of God's glory. Obviously the number of letters she wrote betrays the fact that she, too, had hope of winning souls for Christ, but her primary purpose she saw as being a vessel through which the Divine Being could satisfy His need to communicate Himself to the world.

Elizabeth, like Thérèse, also knew suffering. Stomach cancer ravaged her body, making it difficult and sometimes impossible for her to fully participate in the community's life. Her pain did not in any way, however, lessen her focus on her heart's desire. Indeed, it seems to have enhanced it. If love for God meant allowing Him to freely pluck the strings of her heart, rendering a Heavenly composition in her soul, then the suffering she endured for His sake acted as a harmonious accompaniment to the love song. Having such an attitude, Elizabeth accepted her illness willingly and with joy. She knew that her impending death simply opened the door to larger life, and she was eager for it. Like Thérèse, she died at an age when most women are just entering their prime (26). However, who dares to be saddened by this when once realizing that in her few short years, Elizabeth attained to riches beyond comprehension and certainly beyond her years.

Pierre Teilhard de Chardin
1881 – 1955
KATAPHATIC
SPECULATIVE

The simple yet divine abandonment of the two young Carmelites contrasts with the pro-found intellect of another French mystic, Pierre Teilhard de Chardin. This complex man, both Jesuit priest and scientific scholar, came to the revelation of the ineffable God through the solid fact of created matter.

Speaking in contemporary terms, Teilhard has sometimes been misinterpreted and during his life was silenced by the authorities in the Roman Catholic

Church because of his radically different way of expressing the Christian faith. He directed his studies and his prayer toward a synthesis of the religious truths of Christianity with the ever-growing discoveries made in the world of science. Teilhard did not view science and mysticism as antithetical but felt that as they came together there would be brought forth a newer and higher order of reality. Therefore, much of his writing expresses theological truths in the language of the laboratory.

In a very real sense Teilhard was led forward in his search for God by going backwards in time through the study of Paleontology. His questions concerning how the earth was formed, how life developed, how humanity evolved, were all at the foundation of de Chardin's quest for the Divine. In his youth he felt a conflict between his love for the hard stuff of matter and his inner devotion to the Spirit of God. As he grew into his scientific understanding and in his religious faith, Teilhard began to realize that these two things were not actually in opposition. His true conversion came with the dawning awareness of Christ as the "imperishable" one, that all of matter gets its reality from Him who lives forever.

Teilhard's mystical writings, such as the *Hymn of the Universe* or the *Divine Milieu*, capture the imagination and lead the reader step-by-step through an analytical process of scientific speculation and into the mystic's consciousness of God's presence. Both of these works are less theological treatises than they are poetic summations of Teilhard's "Christo-cosmic" vision. He moved continually between an awe regarding the tangible elements of the universe to the sublime potentiality of Christ-centered existence.

Teilhard claimed that not only the physical universe functions as a process of evolutionary development but also does faith. All of life Teilhard perceived as a reaching outward toward a living unity; all that "IS" coming together in a continuous process and proceeding toward the ultimate "WILL BE". For him, this ultimate reality, the culmination within divine love, he called the "Omega Point".

As Teilhard began working these concepts out we see him as a blatant pantheist;[85] however, as his theological understanding became honed to a fine expertise and as he followed the teaching of St. Paul ever more closely, this scientist/priest rejected the notion that unity means absorption. Not as a drop of water unites with an ocean; rather, de Chardin advanced the notion of unity within diversity and diversity within unity. The Body of Christ into which we become incorporated at our baptism has not the single-cell look of an amoeba but the complex structure of a rich and vibrant tapestry.

Edith Stein
1891 – 1942
APOPHATIC
SPECULATIVE

From one keen intellect to another, and yet one more star in the Carmelite crown, we move from France to Germany. The Carmelite order has certainly no lack of spiritual giants and another of the 20th Century indicates the wealth of a seemingly severe discipline.[86] This Carmelite who demands our attention is Edith Stein. In almost every

---

[85] God is all and all is God
[86] This gives one pause when considering the lack of discipline in current society.

way Edith stands as an antithesis to Thérèse and Elizabeth.

Born of Jewish parentage in Breslau, Poland,[87] Edith grew up motivated toward the academic life. Her scholarship led her first into the field of experimental psychology and then into phenomenology.[88] Through the guidance of several well-known scholars who had converted from Judaism to Christianity, Edith flourished both academically and spiritually, making her own decision for Christ. At the age of thirty, Edith discovered the *Autobiography of St. Teresa of Avila* which proved to be the decisive factor in her conversion. Edith's mother, a devout Jew, was shocked by her daughter's religious turn and never became reconciled to the fact.

Edith began her Christian pilgrimage and its course led her toward entry into the Carmelite convent in Cologne only ten years after baptism. With the horror of persecution of the Jews by Hitler, it became obvious to Edith that her life in the academic world was closing rapidly. Even after her conversion it was difficult for her to find the sort of teaching position she trained for. Publishing her writings was out, so Edith decided that it was time to follow her heart. She received the habit of Carmel on April 15, 1934, taking the name Sister Teresa Benedicta a Cruce.[89]

A woman who taught, lectured, and wrote on the intellectual level of the university willingly gave it all up for the love of God. However, her intellect was never suppressed. During her novitiate, Edith received encouragement to continue her writing and upon taking

---

[87] at that time controlled by Germany

[88] the study of life as it happens

[89] "Teresa blessed by the Cross"

her vows found herself commissioned to complete a manuscript begun before she entered Carmel.

This German Carmelite followed closely the spirit of her patroness, the great Teresa. She, too, held that the inner life could not be separated from exterior action. Given to long hours of prayer, Edith never recoiled from her own mundane tasks nor ignored those who requested her help. Warm and ready to laugh, her personality drew others to her, just as the nun from Avila had. The strength of her convictions and the intensity of her devotion supported Edith even as she was led away from her convent by the Nazis. Ultimately both Edith and her sister, Rosa, were murdered in the gas chambers of Auschwitz, but witnesses who survived this atrocity spoke of Edith's untiring aid to those incarcerated with her.

The best place to begin a study of Edith Stein is by reading her autobiography, *Life in a Jewish Family: 1891–1916*. Here one observes the beginning of her search for Truth and for the purpose of life. From this perspective, the understanding of the process of conversion Edith went through begins to take shape.

Interiorly, Edith regarded her vocation as an act of being transformed into God, becoming a pure temple of His spirit. Echoing the earlier Carmelite mystics, she brought to her own prayer a maturity, both intellectually and ethically, proven in the fire of experience. The deep core of God's indwelling life in us comes to the surface and manifests itself through the liturgy of the Church. Edith never wearied of participation in that liturgy and indeed yearned for it. Equally strong was her desire for solitude and personal prayer. If activity and duty kept her occupied during the day, Edith thought nothing of spending the entire night in prayer.

Her death in no way resembled the deaths of the two young Carmelites who preceded her except that she, too, knew the suffering which preceded it. She, like they, understood that the glory of God can only be attained by accepting the pain of the Cross and through a transformation of defeat into victory. Christ's way of self-sacrifice Edith claimed for herself. Though she did not actively seek a martyr's death, still she embraced it when she knew it was inevitable.

C.S. Lewis
1898 – 1963
Kataphatic
Speculative

Contemporaneous with the two great intellects, Edith Stein and Pierre Teilhard de Chardin, yet of an extremely different milieu, was the Oxford don, Clive Staples Lewis. Born in Northern Ireland of Welsh ancestry, Lewis progressed through the stages of atheism and the occult before his quest for "Spirit" led him to accept the Christian faith. Through his intense intellectual journey, Lewis emerged as one of the 20th Century's most revered apologists.

Whereas de Chardin encountered the Truth of God in the bones and stones of prehistoric humanity, Lewis was confronted by that Truth in the myths and legends, stories and poetry of classical literature and Norse mythology. From his youth, Lewis enjoyed reading and in making up his own stories, even to having conceived of a world of talking animals. To witness the effect which imagination had on Lewis, we need only to look at the many references he made to it, particularly in his autobiography, *Surprised by Joy*. Of great significance to Lewis' character was the overarching image of the Divine reality—Joy.

While other spiritual trailblazers described the encounter with God as heat, light, fire, or mystical marriage, Lewis came to know Divinity by the attribute Joy. We are reminded of Thomas Traherne, that other Anglican of three centuries before, who spoke of God in terms of Felicity. As he explained his pursuit of his heart's desire and confessed to the various false paths he took to achieve it, Lewis came to the realization that Joy could not be found in erotic pleasures nor in occult machinations. Truly he discovered that Joy could not be artificially induced; rather, it must be received and reverenced as a gift from the Christian God of Love. Parenthetically, I believe that Lewis received a manifestation of this gift in the woman he married only a few short years before her death, Joy Davidman.

True to the era of psychological idealism, Lewis wrote of the relevance of Aristotelian virtue as well as the inherent truths of Christian morality. His words speak of a "bent" world, created out of the image of the Divine initiative. That image became twisted by the arrogance and pride of a fallen humanity. To reclaim the divine image Lewis saw as humanity's spiritual journey. The logic of the Christian message impressed him as the profound hope of recovering the heritage that had been lost.

The language Lewis used to express his mystical side was fantasy. His creative imagination played a large part in his intellectual and spiritual development, and we reap the benefit of the process through the enchanting stories of the *Chronicles of Narnia* and his space trilogy: *Out of the Silent Planet*, *Perelandra*, and *That Hideous Strength*. Profound and difficult concepts of sin, redemption, virtue, and life-after-death meet one in the delightful *Screwtape Letters* and *The Great Divorce*.

But Lewis' genius did not only demonstrate itself through magical worlds and allegories. C.S. Lewis ranks among the elite in scholarship and has given us considerable insight into Christian doctrine in such works as, *The Problem of Pain*, *The Four Loves*, and *Miracles*. His writings are numerous and diverse, lucid and rational. They can also be difficult for those of us whose mental processes are not as agile when considering complex truths. Lewis taught that humanity ever builds in character as it accumulates experience and knowledge. We do not simply pass through stages as a train passes through stations. What we were at ten years old we still hold within our character at forty. This may help us understand why his books of fantasy hold as much charm and veracity for adults as they do for children.

He wrote out of the context of a war-torn Europe, of the Blitz, of the horror of Nazi atrocities; yet these were not the topics of his literature. Rather, Lewis focused on the war which rages in the spirit of man, the war of good versus evil. Sometimes accused of escapism, the Oxford professor ignored the externals of war, preferring to direct his reader's attention to the perils that kill the soul, not just the body. He displayed unique wisdom about humanity and the practical application of Christian morality to the ills of society.

C.S. Lewis died on November 22, 1963; his passing went relatively unnoticed since it was the same day as the assassination of President John F. Kennedy. Yet fifty years later he remains one of the most widely read authors in the English language. His books, readily available to an interested public, continue to be published in a variety of editions. His memory, lovingly preserved by the C.S. Lewis Society, assures us that this layman of the Anglican Church has a place amidst the fellowship of the saints.

But what does a mystic look like, after all? Can we tell that something extraordinary has happened to a person who is captivated by God when we study their portraits? To a cosmetically conscious society like ours, seemingly these are important questions. The spiritual masters of this era have, for us, the added dimension of photographic imaging to add to their biographies. Does this aspect enhance the charism of spiritual prowess or does it detract? Depending on one's point of view, perhaps the saint has an ineffable quality, or maybe we are disappointed because he or she looks so ordinary or even dull. I believe that the mystics of the 20th Century show us in their physical attributes what Evelyn Underhill professed all along; that the mystic life is ordinary to the life of the Church, not extraordinary. They come in all shapes and sizes, educational backgrounds and social climates. Mysticism reverberates an extraordinary love through a very common humanity. That some of the saints were highly intellectual, exceptionally talented or extremely personable, should not turn our understanding from the equally relevant fact that these also were simply human beings who chose the "one thing needful". C.S. Lewis was such a man.

dietrich Bonhoeffer
1906 – 1945
KATAPHATIC
SPECULATIVE

Dietrich Bonhoeffer was another. A Lutheran pastor who challenged the immoral and unchristian regime of Adolf Hitler, left his mark on the tradition of total self-giving. He chose to stand with his people rather than flee. His commitment to Gospel-centered living gave example to all those under his influence while in Germany and to those who still read his works.

At age fourteen, Dietrich announced to his family his intention to become a theologian. To this end Bonhoeffer's intellectual pursuits found him submitting his doctoral dissertation by age twenty-one. By twenty-five, he had established himself as a lecturer of systematic theology and as a pastor. It is hardly amazing then to imagine that he was only thirty-nine when martyred. Yet even in the early days of theological study and his ministry, Bonhoeffer tells us that he was not a committed Christian. He discovered his true faith only as he began to grow into the life of the Church. The elements which drew him toward conversion were Community and Prayer. As he engaged in a systematic reflection on Holy Scripture, as he lived a daily round of prayer, Dietrich's formation as a political dissident led him toward total commitment to the "Confessing Church", that body of Lutherans who refused to follow the scheme of Hitler's restructuring of Germany. He eventually became the director of an underground seminary and even allied himself with a group which plotted to assassinate the Fuhrer.

So we find in Bonhoeffer another spiritual man who spent a significant period of his life in prison. This experience, which culminated in his death, caused him to rethink his entire understanding of Christianity. The environment out of which he asked the Church to reassess its theological formulae, in light of their relevance to the world's situation, was a six-by-nine-foot cell. He asked not that the Church discard but that it reinterpret her traditional terms and concepts. Here he pressed to himself and to others his most poignant question, "Who is Christ for us today—really?" Is this not a question we must continue to press upon the Church?

Because of distance it is easier for us to see the fight for Christian truth when the enemy is called by the name of some heretical group, such as the Albigensians whom Dominic stood against, or Donatists, the foes of Augustine. More difficult for us to see are the enemies of Christ who stand not as a part of distant history but who parade about in front of our faces. Bonhoeffer recognized the idolatry which captivated his nation. He spoke against the Nazi regime, demonstrated his opposition, preached, and wrote. Not unlike all those other valiant warriors of the Faith, Bonhoeffer stood with conviction and courage against Hitler's madness.

A widely read book, *Cost of Discipleship*, reflects Dietrich's fortitude. In it he speaks of "costly grace", and we are left with no illusions about the nature of faith, the nature of our purpose in the world, or the nature of the Christian claim. Bonhoeffer's critiques—his legacy of the world—deal with individual and corporate piety, theology, the Church, and political ethics. He remains one of the great inspirational leaders of the 20th Century.

Perhaps his most captivating work, *Letters and Papers from Prison*, began as personal communications to those he loved. They reveal a man of complexity and deep passion. No idle conversation, these letters expose the dynamism behind his serenity and the sincerity of his devotion. Using family and friends as his listening audience, Bonhoeffer preached, expounded, and proclaimed the fullness of life in Christ, the vital necessity of existing for others, and most importantly, to find God in the midst of our life. One of the poems, written during this time, "Who Am I?", gives us a self-portrait of the man for others, and in my estimation, this poem reveals Bonhoeffer as a mystic. If Benedict of Nursia felt the pinch of being a Christian in an unchristian world, Bonhoeffer, fourteen hundred years later, felt that same pinch. Though his response led him to self-sacrifice in a manner quite different from the founder of Western monasticism—Benedict compiled a Rule for the regulation of one's life in the world—Bonhoeffer wrote *Ethics*. While the monk urged people to flee the world, the pastor urged total involvement. Yet they desired the same end: complete obedience to Jesus Christ, Crucified, Risen, and Ascended.

Bonhoeffer's passion manifested itself as a literal aspiration to bear the burdens of others. He claimed that a Church which does not reach out in solidarity ceases to be the Church. The very same can be said of the individual Christian. For Dietrich, there would be no point to profess Christ if one remains unwilling to imitate Christ. In fact, his Christology defined his sense of being. In his book, *Creation and Fall*, Bonhoeffer pointed out that creation itself must be viewed only in the light of the life-offering of Christ. In a letter to his fiancé, he wrote of his fear that people who stand with only one leg on earth[90] would only stand on one leg in heaven. This is why we must not view his death at the hands of Hitler's henchmen as only a political consequence.

---

[90] not totally given to life

A mystic of similar commitment, yet extremely different circumstance, to Bonhoeffer was a French woman of Jewish decent, Simone Weil. Most mystics are known for their depth of religious belief and only later, upon study and consideration, we recognize their social convictions. With Simone, the reverse happens. During her lifetime, she made her mark as an intellectual, teacher, and social activist. Only after death did the world have the opportunity to be introduced to her profound spirituality.

Simone was the product of an upper middle-class family. Her father, a doctor, instilled in his two children, Simone and her brother Andre, a love for learning. Like Edith Stein, Simone pursued a career in philosophy as a teacher, though left-wing politics bordering on Marxism compelled her along a much different path. Her drive for solidarity with the poor and oppressed had none of the sense of compassion and awe that one finds in Bonhoeffer. Rather, more a tragic figure, Simone sought to share the sufferings of the common laborer.

Weil is the sort of mystic who might make us very uncomfortable. She has been called an "outsider" by some, a nonconformist by others. The fact that she chose to remain outside the Church, unbaptized, throughout her life gives us pause, making us wonder about her motives and her spiritual integrity. Could a Lover of the Beloved choose to remain apart from all that has traditionally been accepted as veritable? Simone contended that the world needs "saints with genius", an apropos conclusion for one who demonstrated genius. But she did not mean mere intellect. The world has had many great minds. The genius

Simone pointed to blows across our awareness as "those who know in order that they might love".

She saw Christianity as preeminently a religion of slaves. Simone distrusted anything which spoke of happiness, peace, or liberation as false religion. Her love of austerity reminds us of those monastics and ascetics who determined that God requires extreme discipline of the body in order to purify the soul. Dying a violent death for Christ's sake, Simone deemed an honor. However, she did allow herself the luxury of hope that even if her friends met such a fate, it would be with joy and without anguish.

In 1938, Weil spent Holy Week at Solemes, a French Benedictine monastery where, she related, the music brought her close to God. It spoke to her of living in divine love in the midst of affliction. While at the monastery, someone introduced her to the Metaphysical Poets of England. Her discovery of George Herbert transformed her spiritual life. His poem, "Love Bade Me Welcome", became for her a prayer, and during a time of using it, she had an intense mystical experience, a personal encounter with God. She described this as a presence more personal, certain, and real than any encounter with another human being.

Simone chose to remain outside the Church because the God about whom the Church teaches was too small, dwarfed in comparison with the One whom she had experienced. She believed that the doctrines of Redemption, Salvation, Incarnation, and Resurrection were shallow, stilted, and suspicious. This God, in Christ, is too small. Only His Passion and Crucifixion, his total victimization, held her transfixed. Her rejection of the Church also stemmed from a rejection of the image St. Paul used of the body, where each part makes up the whole. Her own perspective involved a sense of wholeness from the beginning, that each soul united to Christ bears His completeness in itself. To view ourselves as merely parts of a whole, in Weil's view, would destroy the integrity of Christ's union.

Probably the least orthodox of all the Christian mystics, Simone Weil nevertheless draws our attention, makes us sit up and take notice. The collection of her spiritual letters and essays, *Waiting for God*, published posthumously, communicates her coherent arguments and her reluctant mystical journey. Indeed, Simone assured her friends that God Himself initiated their relationship; all the while she was intent on focusing her concerns toward the social ramifications of industrialization and political materialism. If Catherine of Genoa was led to social action through her intimate encounters with God, Simone Weil came to God through her intimate encounters as a social activist.

thomas merton
1915 – 1968
KATAPHATIC
AFFECTIVE

One of the most vital and far-reaching spiritual writers of the 20th Century is a gifted and complex Cistercian monk, Thomas Merton. Despite his desire to live a simple life of silence, contemplation, and solitude, Merton literally spoke and wrote volumes of reflections, poems, and observations on a multitude of topics, all with a connection to the spiritual life. At various times during his 27 years at the Abbey of Gethsemani in Kentucky, his voice and his writings were both encouraged and silenced by his Religious superiors.

Born in Prades, France, in 1915, Thomas was the elder of two sons born to artist parents. His father was a New Zealand Anglican and his mother an American Quaker. Both of them died when Thomas and his brother were still boys. Throughout Thomas' formative years, he experienced his education in a variety of places, including a boarding school in England and then Clare College, Cambridge. Later he attended Columbia University in New York, where he received a degree in English and discovered, in a profound way, his Roman Catholic faith. It was here that Merton felt called to enter religious life.

After unsuccessfully trying his new vocation with the Franciscans in New York, Merton moved to the Cistercian Abbey of Gethsemani, one of the strictest monastic orders in the Church. He entered there on December 10, 1941, just days after the bombing of Pearl Harbor. It was there that Thomas was ordained to the priesthood and given the monastic name, Father Louis. Although Father Louis was certainly a priest, he was probably better known at the Abbey for being a novice master, hermit, spiritual guide, poet, religious author, and social justice advocate. One might call Merton a "Pied Piper" for generations of those seeking a deeper experience of the Divine in the ordinariness of everyday life.

That Merton was a complex man is best witnessed through his several autobiographical writings: *The Seven Storey Mountain*, *The Sign of Jonas*, and his *Asian Journals*. It was *The Seven Storey Mountain*, published in 1948, which established him as an author of popularity and of note and which served to draw young men coming back from the "War" to the monastic life. As a result of his powerful writings, the number of monks in residence at the Abbey grew from 80 when Merton entered in 1941 to more than 240 by the mid-1950s.

To his credit, Merton wrote over 60 books along with hundreds of poems, articles, and letters of correspondence. Merton's focus on contemplative prayer as the undergirding practice that inevitably leads one to advocate for peace, justice, nonviolence, and civil rights was prophetic and clearly evident in his best known and widely-read books, *Seeds of Contemplation* and *Conjectures of a Guilty Bystander*. From his perspective, contemplation and all mystical wisdom expands our understanding of the life we each have been given and thus illumines our sense of responsibility of each human being toward the others. This led him to appreciate the superiority of nonviolence as a transformative stance to the political sphere. His positions came not from relying simply on metaphysical constructs but from an active awareness of the real threats of nuclear proliferation in the precarious political paradigm of the 1960s.

During his college years, Merton had become enamored with the spirituality of the Orient. However, a Hindu professor encouraged the academic to first read the foundational texts from his own Christian tradition before embarking on a study of Eastern sacred texts. While that wisdom actually led Merton toward his deep conversion to the Roman Catholic faith, ultimately the traditions of both the East and West strongly influenced his understanding of and trust in the abandonment of one's soul to God.

As Merton grew more deeply into his monastic vocation, he was led in two opposing directions. On the one hand, he was moved to ask his Abbot for permission to establish a hermitage on the grounds of the monastery. There he desired to experience the silence and solitude that was missing in his life in the monastery. He viewed contemplation as the highest expression of humanity's intellectual and spiritual life and yearned for the isolated physical surroundings which would help him achieve that goal. On the other hand, it was in the hermitage where he met with those many people who came seeking his advice and counsel and where he spent hours in correspondence with both ordinary people and world leaders and in writing his many articles and books. Merton the Christian hermit was becoming Merton the Christian Zen Master and Merton the Civil Crusader.

The legacy of this dynamic man lay not only in the stability of monastic life or the single-mindedness of his passion for peace and justice. Rather, Merton's legacy to the world was at least threefold: the Art of Contemplation; the Pursuit of Peace; and the Melding of Eastern and Western Mysticism. Although many of his writings were directed to a monastic audience, especially the novices he trained, a goodly number of his writings appealed to the lay-folk, the non-Catholic, even the non-churched.

The eclectic nature of this complex man that continues to attract followers comes from Merton's various early religious experiences. Prior to his college career, he encountered an expression of Christology through the exquisite Byzantine mosaics in the various Italian basilicas he visited. His interest in cultural anthropology was derived from the writings of Jacques Maritain and other Thomistic theologians. And his mystical and poetic leanings came from his admiration for the Jesuit poet, Gerard Manley Hopkins.

This cloistered monk felt keenly the urgency and turmoil of the 1960s, with a call to end the war in Southeast Asia and the tumultuous strife of the civil rights movement. At one point in Merton's literary career, his writings on racial equality and the danger of nuclear proliferation caused his Abbot to demand Merton's silence. Out of obedience, he did stop writing articles and books critical of these issues but turned to the medium of personal correspondence with friends and like-minded activists. Henri Nouwen called Merton "The Contemplative Critic".[91]

In 1968, the call of the East and a yearning to explore the truths of Ecumenism beckoned Merton to leave his beloved hermitage to participate in a conference of Catholic and Buddhist monks in Bangkok, Thailand. On December 10th, after delivering his talk to the group, Merton retired to his room for a rest and died from an electric shock after stepping out of the shower and touching an ungrounded fan. His death occurred on the 27th anniversary of his entering the Monastery at Gethsemani. One great irony was that his body was returned to his monastery via the same military aircraft that also carried the bodies of servicemen who had died in the ongoing Vietnam War, which he so strongly opposed. One wonders what Merton would have thought of these two quirks of fate; the anniversary date and his transportation home.

More than 20 books by Merton have been published since his death. Many of the works that he wrote while being silenced by his superiors have since been released, and his popularity is still vibrant and his ideas still as relevant as ever. Monastics and non-monastics

---

[91] Nouwen published a book about Merton by that very title

alike continue to benefit from the wisdom and the challenge that Merton brings to those who desire to live an authentic spirituality in a world that is hostile and greedy.

Chapter 13
A Look to the Future

That mysticism connects with activism should now be obvious to the reader. That the central themes of the mystical experience are the love of God and solidarity with creation ought no longer to come as a surprise. Yet we are left with a nagging question: Who are today's mystics? Who are the spiritual trailblazers, forging paths of holiness through their intimate experiences with divinity? Who is making a difference in the world by means of love and self-forgetfulness? We have seen that through the centuries that mystics have become known by their acts of redemptive love, be that in the passivity of prayer or by standing firm in apostolic action. Dare we name those who walk among us? The following men and women I have chosen may or may not possess all the "qualifications" for sainthood, but they are demonstrating through their lives and through their writings that the journey toward God is of vital importance in their lives.

I have little doubt that anyone would object to classifying **Mother Teresa of Calcutta** (1910–1997) as in the ranks of the spiritual giants. Her selfless love has been displayed for several decades. Her concern for the welfare of others equals that of any saint, so defined. That this diminutive nun puts Jesus in the center of every moment, who would question? One woman with a vision, with an immense love, leaves her mark in an ailing world. Who would have thought that the simple act of picking up the dying and the outcast from the gutters of India would have started such a movement of compassion? Yet the growth of the Community which she founded bears testimony to the global influence one person can have on others who are looking for a way to heal humanity. So yes, Mother Teresa is an obvious choice.

Her life and her work have been tested in the crucible of time. A market glutted with spiritual writings makes the head spin. How do we know which of them will lead us a step closer along the mystic way? Who among these current authors has the authenticity and integrity of life, as Mother Teresa demonstrated? Has the holiness of which they speak spilled over from their lives and into their books? It appears that we can only judge the answers to these questions superficially now. They must be seasoned by time and by discerning hearts.

Authors who currently grace the market with their insights and talents help us to realize the pitfalls and the victories common to our own milieu. **Henri J.M. Nouwen**'s (1932–1996) journals and books on the spiritual life, for example, introduce us to a man who acknowledged his continued search. He allows his readers to witness his vulnerability, his own questions and fears. Widely read and widely loved, this Dutch priest often described the process of sanctification as a movement from one state of being to another, from vice to virtue, from brokenness to health. He, too, speaks from the experience of having been on the pilgrimage where he has encountered failures, disappointments, and loneliness amid the glories and successes. Nouwen, a well-regarded theology professor, moved out of the world of academia and into the marginalized society of the handicapped. His own contemplative prayer, his own theological musings, nudged him into yet another arena for apostolic action.

The mystic way has touched the life and writing of an American, a Quaker, named **Richard J. Foster** (b. 1942). His books reflect the solid tradition of orthodox teaching while he points out the difficulties which confront those who are on the Christian journey. One of these difficulties he defines as "philosophic materialism", which sees the inner journey as merely fun or a frivolous pastime and not part of the real world.

Foster brings classical spirituality to the Protestant mind in a very gentle and non-threatening way, while all the time working toward a renewal of the Church in all its multifaceted expressions. He quotes liberally from both Roman Catholic and Anglican sources, and by so doing lends objectivity to intensely subjective topics which ease the suspicion of those from non-liturgical and non-sacramental denominations. But no matter what denomination one calls home, Foster helps us all reflect upon our own Christian behavior.

Creation-centered spirituality describes **Matthew Fox**'s (b. 1940) mystical perspective. His theological bent pushes him sometimes towards a heterodoxy which makes many traditional Christians leery. His own Religious community, The Order of Preachers (Dominican), ceased to support his views, so he left the Roman Catholic Church and continues to lecture, write, and teach. He endeavors in his work primarily to answer the question, "What is the relationship, if any, between mysticism and social justice?" Those who have placed themselves at his feet to learn from him have been encouraged to nourish and expand their mystical, social, and environmental awareness. He is another for whom an encounter with God prompts a call to action, for whom Awe calls forth indignation over the exploitation and destruction of the world's peoples and resources.

Because Fox makes use of Eastern religions and Native American spirituality,[92] he has become a champion for those Christians who have no use for theological boundaries. However, for this same reason, he has become anathema for those who hold firmly to orthodox Christian traditions. It has been said that the Church only likes "dead" mystics, those whose teaching has been studied and found within acceptable theological perimeters. At greater risk, we expose ourselves to thinking that is new, fresh, and unproven. Therefore it is of utmost importance to be thoroughly grounded in traditional Christian theology so as to have a solid base from which to discern truth and error.

Children's author and novelist **Madeleine L'Engle** (1918–2007) wrote as a lay-theologian. She gave us another glimpse of the divine through creative imagination, similar to the genius of C.S. Lewis. Her stories, though full of fancy, rang the bell of truth in their tales. They hinted of the divine spark which lies at the heart of humanity. That spark, a virginal response to the elemental caprices of the soul, comes through exceptionally well in the characters of her stories, especially as they interact with nature and super-nature: dolphins cavorting, starfish regenerating, and virtual unicorns.

Recurring themes throughout L'Engle's fiction are the conflict of good and evil and the difficulty in distinguishing one from the other. Often her themes

---

[92] as well as feminism and witchcraft

concern the nature of God and the danger of conforming to the status quo. Her works are characterized by their spirit, optimism, and divine grace hidden deep within life.

Would Madeleine herself embrace or be repelled by being classed among the mystics? Would she simply claim that she is a writer who also happens to be a deeply committed Christian? Saints or sinners, mystics or misfits, these deeply committed Christians radiate the life of God in their chosen professions, in the products which flow from their talents. L'Engle's trilogy of science fiction, *A Wrinkle in Time*, *A Wind in the Door*, and *A Swiftly Tilting Planet*, combine moral responsibility with redemption through love. They are complex and rich in mystical insight, mixing classical theology with contemporary family life.

If international, interdenominational recognition were criterion for characterizing someone among the ranks of the mystic domain, then certainly **Desmond Tutu** (b. 1931), the Anglican Archbishop Emeritus of Cape Town, South Africa, could not be left out. He who received the Nobel Prize for Peace in 1984 stood as one of the world's foremost critics of South Africa's apartheid government. He has spent long, agonizing years working to realize its abolition; another spiritual leader whose love for God is expressed in social action.

Early in his ministry, as a black priest in a society governed by a white minority, Tutu became convinced that the only thing that really matters is love. As a bishop, then as archbishop, he determined that his people and his clergy must know that they are loved. He bases his understanding of love on a total adherence to incarnational theology. Because God entered the world in Jesus, Tutu maintains that our encounter with

God also launches us into the world, to work together with our Creator to establish His Kingdom.

His politics therefore spring directly from that theology of love. Tutu would promote the notion that one must always judge political systems by the light of the Gospel. Nothing less will suffice. In this the Archbishop echoes Bonhoeffer, and one can surmise that if he were not such a global hero, Tutu would have met a fate similar to Bonhoeffer's long ago. When society gives wholesale assent to unchristian behavior and policies, those who put the Gospel of Christ first tend to reap the martyr's reward. Courage and conviction operate together to witness to the Spirit of Truth, the Spirit of Justice, but most importantly, to the Spirit of Mercy. Desmond Tutu reflects Gospel living in both word and deed.

Though there has been a dramatic decline in monasticism in the later part of the 20th Century, several authors of prominence still issue from those roots, and their writings currently grace the bookstalls with their mastery of the mystical life. Five who come to mind are **William Johnston** (1925–2010) and **George Maloney** (1924–2005) (Jesuit), **William McNamara** (b. 1926) (Carmelite), **Basil Pennington** (1931–2005) (Cistercian), and **Richard Rohr** (b. 1943) (Franciscan). Each of these men brings to the study of mysticism an experience steeped in the monastic traditions in which they were formed; yet they also speak with fresh voices which can only come from a personal encounter with the Lord of Love. McNamara expresses this experience as earthy or passionate mysticism, while Pennington focuses primarily upon the centering aspect of one's prayer life. Fathers Maloney and Johnston combine an interest in oriental religious practices with their traditional Catholicism. All of them, in their own manner, emphasize the personal nature of one's prayer as the means of establishing and maintaining a love affair with the Divine. They urge their readers to acquire the contemplative attitude toward life as a way of loving, as a way of building the future, to assimilate the grace of God in such a way as to more completely become the persons intended in our creation.

The mystics have taught us that faith acts as a point of convergence for light and darkness, for reason and emotion, for image and void. Through the centuries their threads of faith have woven a spectacular tapestry of religious conviction, moral virtue, and holy passion. The rough sketches made here barely scratch the surface of the vast arena of the Christian mystical tradition, but hopefully they have opened heart and mind to the multiple possibilities for spiritual guidance. I hope I have whetted some appetites for further reading, further study, and for a personal desire to experience a deeper spiritual life.

We must also bear in mind that there were and are many mystics who have gone and will continue to go unrecognized because they either have not left some vestige of their love affair with God or because any remembrance has been lost. There are mystics in our own parishes and in our own neighborhoods, but these often remain unknown to us. I am thankful for the opportunity and privilege to have met a few of these lovers of the Beloved, to have been blessed by the love which spills over into conversations and actions. Therefore with deep appreciation and awe this book is dedicated to such a one, in whom I have witnessed that grace which transforms nature and in whom I have often met the risen Christ. From this point on, I leave it to those who have caught the mystic spirit to discover their own mentors, their own spiritual guides, as they progress along the pilgrim trail.

APPENDIX A

Their Environment	The Mystics & Scholars

c. 33 A.D.

The Crucifixion & Resurrection
of Our Lord Jesus Christ

34–99 A.D.

Their Environment	The Mystics & Scholars
Fall of Jerusalem (70) Eruption of Mt. Vesuvius (79)	The Apostles (c. 34) Ignatius of Antioch (35–107) St. Paul (c. 65)

100–199 A.D.

Their Environment	The Mystics & Scholars
Establishment of the Church	Irenaeus (130–200) Clement of Alexandria (150–215) Tertullian (160–220) Origen (185–254)

200–299 A.D.

Their Environment	The Mystics & Scholars
Persecutions under Septimus Severus (202)	Decius (250) Anthony of Egypt (251–356) Valerian (257–260) Eusebius (260–340) Pachomius (290–346) Anthanasius (296–373)

300–399 A.D.

Their Environment	The Mystics & Scholars
Edict of Milan, Legalization of Christianity (313) First Ecumenical Council (325) Second Ecumenical Council (381)	Macarius (c. 300) Cyril of Jerusalem (315–386) Gregory of Naziansus (329–389) Basil the Great (330–379) Gregory of Nyssa (330–395) Ambrose of Milan (339–397)

Their Environment	The Mystics & Scholars
	Jerome (342–420)
	Augustine (345–430)
	Evagrius Ponticus (346–399)
	John Chrysostom (347–407)
	John Cassian (360–435)

400–499 A.D.

Their Environment	The Mystics & Scholars
Fall of Rome (410)	Leo the Great (–461)
Third Ecumenical Council (431)	Benedict of Nursia (480–550)
Fourth Ecumenical Council (451)	

500–599 A.D.

Their Environment	The Mystics & Scholars
Fifth Ecumenical Council (553)	Dionysius the Areopagite (c. 500)
	Columba of Iona (521–597)
	Gregory the Great (540–604)
	John Climacus (570–649)
	Maximus the Confessor (580–662)

600–699 A.D.

Their Environment	The Mystics & Scholars
Birth of Islam (610)	John of Damascus (675–749)
Sixth Ecumenical Council (681)	Boniface (680–754)

700–799 A.D.

Their Environment	The Mystics & Scholars
Last Ecumenical Council (787)	
Coronation of Charlemagne (800)	
Beginning of Holy Roman Empire	

800–899 A.D.

Their Environment	The Mystics & Scholars
	John Scotus Erigena (810–877)

Their Environment	The Mystics & Scholars

900–999 A.D.

	Simeon the New Theologian (949–1022) Romauld (950–1027) John of Fecamp (990–1054)

1000–1099 A.D.

The Great Schism (1054) The Norman Conquest of England (1066) The First Crusade (1097)	Peter Damian (1007–1072) William of St. Thierry (1085–1148) Bernard of Clairvaux (1090–1153) The Victorines: Adam, Hugh, & Richard (1096–1173) Hildegard of Bingen (1098–1179)

1100–1199 A.D.

Ghengis Khan (1162–1227) Building of Notre Dame (1163)	Aelred of Rivaulx (1110–1167) Joachim of Fiore (1132–1202) Peter of Celle (1145–1183) Dominic (1170–1221) Francis of Assisi (1181–1226)

1200–1299 A.D.

Magna Carta (1215) Kublai Khan (1216–1294) Marco Polo (1254–1300) Order of Teutonic Knights (1266)	John of Parma (1209–1289) Mechtilde of Magdeburg (1210–1280) Bonaventure (1221–1274) Thomas Aquinas (1225–1274) Jacopone da Todi (1230–1306) Ramon Lull (1235–1315) Mechtilde of Hackborn (1240–1310) Gertrude the Great (1256–1302) Meister Eckhart (1260–1327)

Their Environment	The Mystics & Scholars
	Dante Alighieri (1265-1321)
	John van Ruysbroeck (1293-1381)
	Henri Suso (1295-1366)
	Richard Rolle (1295-1349)

1300-1399 A.D.

Their Environment	The Mystics & Scholars
Avignon Popes (1305-1377) "Babylonian Captivity" Hundred Years War (1337-1453) "Black Death" Plague (1348-1349) Geoffrey Chaucer (c. 1343-1400) Reign of the House of de Medici (1389-1464)	Johannes Tauler (1300-1361) Bridget of Sweden (1303-1373) Gerard Groote (1340-1384) The "Cloud" Author (c. 1340-1396) Julian of Norwich (1342-1413) Catherine of Siena (1347-1380) John Gerson (1363-1429) Margery Kempe (1373-1433) Bernardine of Siena (1380-1444) Thomas à Kempis (1380-1471) Walter Hilton (c. 1396)

1400-1499 A.D.

Their Environment	The Mystics & Scholars
Leonardo da Vinci (1452-1510) Fall of Constantinople (1453) Printing press invented (1454) Magellan (1470-1521) Michaelangelo (1475-1564) War of the Roses (1485) Oliver Cromwell (1485-1540) Henry VIII (1491-1547) Columbus discovers America; Jews and Moslems expelled from Spain (1492)	Nicholas of Cusa (1400-1464) Henry Herp (c. 1400) Denis the Carthusian (1402-1471) Joan of Arc (1412-1431) Catherine of Genoa (1447-1510) Catherine of Bologna (1453) Garcia de Cisneros (c. 1492) Ignatius of Loyola (1495-1556) Peter of Alcantera (1499-1562)

Their Environment	The Mystics & Scholars

1500–1599 A.D.

Protestant Revolution (1515–1555)	Luis of Granada (1505–1588)
Elizabeth of England (1533–1603)	Teresa of Avila (1515–1582)
Counter Revolution (1540–1563)	Catherine de Ricci (1522–1590)
Sir Francis Drake (1540–1596)	Jacob Boehme (1525–1624)
First *Book of Common Prayer* (1549)	John of the Cross (1542–1591)
Sir Walter Raleigh (1552–1618)	Jane Frances de Chantal (1552–1614)
William Shakespeare (1564–1616)	Lancelot Andrewes (1555–1626)
Defeat of the Spanish Armada (1572)	Frances de Sales (1567–1662)
Cardinal Richilieu (1585–1642)	John Donne (1571–1631)
	William Laud (1573–1645)
	Dom Augustine Baker (1575–1641)
	Rose of Lima (1586–1617)
	Nicholas Ferrar (1592–1637)
	George Herbert (1593–1633)

1600–1699 A.D.

Founding of Jamestown (1607)	Jeremy Taylor (1613–1667)
First Settlement of Manhattan Island (1609)	Blaise Pascal (1623–1662)
Thirty Years' War (1618–1648)	Angelus Silesius (1624–1666)
Voyage of the Mayflower (1620)	Jacques Bossuet (1627–1666)
Peter the Great (1672–1725)	John Bunyan (1628–1688)
Johann Sebastian Bach (1685–1750)	Madame Guyon (1648–1717)
Voltaire (1694–1778)	François Fénelon (1651–1715)
	Jean Pierre de Caussade (1675–1751)
	William Law (1686–1761)

1700–1799 A.D.

Jean Nicholas Grou (1731–1803)	

Their Environment	The Mystics & Scholars
Wolfgang Amadeus Mozart (1756–1791)	
William Blake (1757–1827)	
Industrial Revolution (1768)	
Napoleon (1769–1821)	
Boston Tea Party (1773)	
Declaration of Independence (1776)	
The *Cure d'Ars* (1786–1859)	

1800–1899 A.D.

Their Environment	The Mystics & Scholars
Frederic Chopin (1809–1849)	Edward Pusey (1800–1882)
California Gold Rush (1849)	John Henry Newman (1801–1890)
American Civil War (1863)	Francis Libermann (1802–1852)
Opening of Suez Canal (1869)	Søren Kierkegaard (1813–1855)
Custer's Last Stand (1876)	John Mason Neale (1818–1866)
Discovery of the X-Ray (1896)	Charles Chapman Grafton (1830–1912)
	Charles de Foucauld (1858–1916)
	Evelyn Underhill (1875–1941)
	Elizabeth of the Trinity (1880–1906)
	Pierre Teilhard de Chardin (1881–1995)
	Edith Stein (1891–1942)
	C.S. Lewis (1898–1963)

1900–1999 A.D.

Their Environment	The Mystics & Scholars
Boxer Rebellion (1900)	Dag Hammarskjold (1905–1961)
Boer War (1900)	Dietrich Bonhoeffer (1906–1945)
First Automobile (1902)	Abraham Heschel (1907–1972)
World War I (1914)	Simone Weil (1909–1943)
Russian Revolution (1917)	
World War II (1939)	

Their Environment	The Mystics & Scholars
First Atomic bomb drop (1945)	Mother Teresa of Calcutta (1910–1997)
	Thomas Merton (1915–1968)
	Madeleine L'Engle (1918–2007)
	George Maloney (1924–2005)
	William Johnston (1925–2010)
	William McNamara (1926–)
	Desmond Tutu (1931–)
	Basil Pennington (1931–2005)
	Henri J.M. Nouwen (1932–1996)
	Matthew Fox (1940–)
	Richard J. Foster (1942–)
	Richard Rohr (1943–)

APPENDIX B
Bibliography of the Mystics' Works

ST. PAUL (c. 65)
- The Epistles
- New Testament, any translation
    > Thirteen letters from this persecutor of the Church turned
    > Apostle, to early communities of Christian fellowship.

ORIGEN (185–254)
- Selected Writings
    > Greer, Rowan A. tr. & intro. Mahwah, Paulist Press (CWS),
    > 1979
    > > Represents the heart of his spiritual vision concerning the
    > > Christian life

GREGORY OF NYSSA (330–395)
- From Glory to Glory: Texts from Gregory of Nyssa's Mystical
  Writings
    > Danielou, Jean, sel. & intro. New York, Scribner, 1961
    > > A revealing look at this Cappadocian Father's spiritual
    > > contribution to mystical theology
- Life of Moses
    > Malherbe, Abraham J., tr. & intro. Mahwah, Paulist Press
    > (CWS), 1978
    > > Reflects Gregory's spiritual sense of the Scriptures and its
    > > capacity for elevating the soul to God.

EVAGRIUS PONTICUS (346–399)
- The Praktikos & Chapters on Prayer
    > Bamberger, John Eudes, O.S.C.O., tr. & intro. Michigan,
    > Cistercian Publications, 1978
    > > Deals with the ascetical life and the place prayer in the life
    > > of the serious Christian

PSEUDO-DIONYSIUS, AREOPAGITE (c. 500)
- Mystical Theology
    > Watts, Alan W., tr. West Park, Holy Cross Press, 1945
    > > Deals with Dionysius' second way of knowing God, namely
    > > that God is infinitely transcendent from the world.
    > > Contemplation is the only way to come to this knowledge.

- The Complete Works
    Luibheid, Colm, tr. Mahwah, Paulist Press (CWS), 1987
        Contains his formulation of a method of the *via negativa*
        that stresses our inability to penetrate the cloud of
        unknowing.

AUGUSTINE OF HIPPO (345–430)
- City Of God
    Dods, Marcus, tr. & Merton, Thomas, intro. New York,
    Modern Library, 1950
        Here he examines the inefficacy of Roman religion and of
        human civilization in general. Blending Platonism with
        Christianity, he created the first Christian theology of
        history—planning a city based not on the Roman
        pantheon but on Christian love.
- Confessions
    Wirt, Sherwood E. tr. New York, Harper & Row, 1971
        Autobiography of Augustine in modern language. Shows
        his painstaking search for God through astrology, esoteric
        religion philosophy, and finally through the Christian
        faith.
- Works of Saint Augustine: A Translation for the 21st Century
  (in several volumes)
    Rotelle, John E., ed. New York, New City Press, 1990
        Sermons and treatises of the man who has been called the
        Father of Western spirituality

MAXIMUS THE CONFESSOR (580–662)
- Selections
    Berthold, Rev. George C., tr. Mahwah, Paulist Press (CWS), 1985
        Some of the spiritual works of this early theologian which
        point particularly to his idea of the deification of
        humanity.
- The Ascetic Life
    Sherwood, Polycarp, tr. Westminster, Newman Press, 1955
        The four centuries on charity and the ascetic life as taught
        in the early period of Church history.

MACARIUS OF EGYPT (300–390)
- Intoxicated With God (50 Homilies)
    Maloney, George A., S.J. tr. & intro. New Jersey, Dimension
    Books, 1978
        One of the outstanding features of these homilies is that
        they show Macarius' mysticism of Divine light.

JOHN CASSIAN (360–435)

- Conferences
    Luibheid, Colm, tr. Mahwah, Paulist Press (CWS), 1985
    A study of the Egyptian ideal of the monastic life.

BENEDICT OF NURSIA (480–550)

- The Rule of St. Benedict
    Van Zeller, Dom Hubert, commentary. New York, Sheed & Ward, 1958
    A deductive, practical & empirical approach to the Rule upon which all of the Benedictine orders are based.

JOHN CLIMACUS (570–649)

- The Ladder of Divine Ascent
    Moore, Archimandrite Lazarus, tr. London, Faber & Faber, 1959
    A handbook on the ascetic life in the Greek Church portrayed as a ladder which the aspirant must climb, each step being a virtue to be acquired.

SIMEON THE NEW THEOLOGIAN (949–1022)

- The Discourses
    DeCantanzaro, C.J., tr. Mahwah, Paulist Press (CWS), 1980
    Homilies preached to his monks at the morning office of Matins, on the various aspects of Christian perfection.
- Hymns of Divine Love
    Maloney, George, S.J., tr. New York, New Dimensions, 1975
    Shows a more personal side of Simeon, with his concept of the existential aspect of the Eucharistic celebration.

BERNARD OF CLAIRVAUX (1090–1153)

- On the Song of Songs (2 vol.)
    Walsh, Kilian, tr. Kalamazoo, Cistercian Publications, 1976
    These sermons are among the most famous and most beautiful examples of medieval scriptural exegesis.
- On Loving God
    Martin, Hugh, tr. & ed. London, SCM Press Ltd., 1959
    Emphasis on the earthly life of Jesus & stresses the needs for humility & gratitude before God.

FRANCIS OF ASSISI (1181–1226)
- The Complete Works
    Armstrong, Regis & Brady, Ignatius, eds. Mahwah, Paulist
    Press (CWS), 1982
        The first English translation of the critical texts of the 13th-
        Century friars as they portray the heart of Francis'
        spirituality.

HILDEGARD OF BINGEN (1098–1179)
- Book of Divine Works
    Santa Fe, Bear & Co., 1987
        A visionary work which unites the religion, science, and
        art of the medieval period.
- Scivias
    Hart, Mother Columba, tr. New York, Paulist Press (CWS),
    1979
        Contains the 26 visions of Hildegard.

HADEWIJCH OF ANTWERP (c. mid-13th Century)
- The Complete Works
    Hart, Mother Columba, tr. New York, Paulist Press (CWS), 1980
        Her letters, poems, and visions offer the finest example of
        Love mysticism of the Medieval period.

MECHTHILD OF MAGDEBURG (1210–1280)
- Meditations with Mechthild
    Woodruff, Sue, sel. & tr. Santa Fe, Bear & Co., 1982
        Devotional pieces from her writings arranged in a format
        for use in meditation.
- Flowing Light of the Divinity
    Galvani, Christiane Mesch, tr. & Clark, Susan, ed. & intro.
    New York, Garland Publishing, 1991
        The private revelation and visions of Mechthild.

GERTRUDE THE GREAT (1256–1302)
- Exercises of St. Gertrude
    tr. & intro. by a Benedictine Nun of Regina Laudis.
    Westminster, The Newman Press, 1956
        Expresses the spirituality of this medieval Benedictine,
        with commentary by a modern Religious. These exercises
        are reminiscent of St. Ignatius.
- Life and Revelations of St. Gertrude
    Westminster, The Newman Press, 1949

These revelations show us the familiarity & frequency of the heavenly communications which Gertrude had with our Lord. Her life was one continuous and almost uninterrupted succession of the highest states of spiritual life.

MEISTER ECKHART (1260–1327)

- The Essential Sermons
  Colledge, Edmund, tr. Mahwah, Paulist Press (CWS), n.d.
  Designed to provide a general introduction to the integral aspects of Eckhart's thought & faith.
- Teacher and Preacher
  McGinn, Bernard, ad. Mahwah, Paulist Press (CWS), 1986
  This collection illustrates the diversity of one of the most enigmatic & influential mystics in Medieval times.

JOHANNES TAULER (1300–1361)

- Spiritual Conferences
  Colledge, Eric & Sister M. Jane, tr. St. Louis, Herder, 1961
  Translations of selected sermons.
- Book of the Poor in Spirit
  Kelley, C.F., tr. New York, Harper, 1954
  A compact treatise of the basic teachings which guided the mystic spirit of the 14th Century.

HENRY SUSO (1295–1366)

- The Little Book of Eternal Wisdom/Little Book of Truth
  Clark, James M., tr. & intro. New York, Harper & Brothers, n.d.
  Shows Suso as the poet, ascetic & contemplative following Christ on the sorrowful way of the cross.

JOHN VAN RUYSBROECK (1283–1381)

- Seven Steps of the Ladder of Spiritual Love
  Taylor, F. Sherwood, tr. Westminster, Dacre Press, 1944
  Deals with the process of spiritual perfection, acknowledging that the process is actually the fruit of grace given to the soul.
- Spiritual Espousels
  Wiseman, James A., tr. Mahwah, Paulist Press (CWS), 1985
  A synthesis of Greek spiritual thought with Augustinian introspection, ending in yet another aspect of the *via negativa*.

THOMAS À KEMPIS (1380–1471)

- Imitation of Christ
    Chicago, Moody Press, 1958
        The most widely read devotional book in Western
        Christianity. Stands in the midst of the transition from the
        medieval period to the modern. Seminal work of the
        "Devotio Moderna", the late medieval reform movement
        which returned to the original Apostolic zeal and
        simplicity.

HUGH OF ST. VICTOR (1096–1141)

- Selected Writings
    tr. by a Religious of C.S.M.V. Squire, Aelred, OP, intro. New
    York, Harper & Row,1962
        Sketches of Hugh's reflections and commentaries on a
        variety of subjects in the ascetical life.

RICHARD OF ST. VICTOR (died c. 1173)

- Book of the Patriarchs/ The Mystical Ark/ Book Three of the
  Trinity
    Zinne, Grover, tr. Mahwah, Paulist Press (CWS), 1979
        Gives a sense of the early medieval considerations of
        mystical theology and an attempt to give it a system.

AELRED OF RIEVAULX (1110–1167)

- Jesus At Twelve Year Old
    Webb, Geoffery & Walker, Adrian, trs. London, A.R. Mowbray
    & Co. Ltd., 1956
        A devotional treatise on the Biblical text concerning Jesus
        as a boy, teaching in the Temple.
- Mirror of Charity
    Webb, Geoffery & Walker, Adrian, trs. London, A.R. Mowbray
    & Co. Ltd., 1962
        Expresses the concept of love as that which binds all living
        things together and is God's right to expect love from
        humanity.
- Spiritual Friendship
    Laker, Mary Eugenia, SSND, tr. Kalamazoo, Cistercian
    Publications, 1977
        Reflections on the theories of friendship offered by the
        stoic philosopher Cicero.

RICHARD ROLLE (1295–1349)
- The Fire of Love and the Mending of Life
    del Mastro, M.L., tr. & intro. Garden City, Doubleday, 1981
        Part autobiography and part practical guide to the devout
        life; an intense document of this mystic's love of God.

JULIAN OF NORWICH (1342–1413)
- Revelations of Divine Love (sometimes called The Showings)
    Colledge, Edmund, tr. New York, Paulist Press (CWS), 1978
        The recorded reflections on 16 visions which Julian had as
        a young woman. They speak of the feminine aspect of God
        and represent a significant contribution to mystical
        literature.

MARGERY KEMPE (1373–1433)
- The Book of Margery Kempe
    Windett, B.A., tr. Middlesex, Penguin Books, 1985
        The autobiographical account of a most unusual medieval
        laywoman. Less a work of mysticism than a record of
        human faith.

THE "CLOUD" AUTHOR (c. 1349–1396)
- The Cloud of Unknowing and Book of Privy Counsel
    Garden City, Doubleday, 1973
        Represents the first expression in the English language of
        the soul's quest for God and explains the *via negativa* in a
        captivating way.

WALTER HILTON (c. 1340–1396)
- Scale of Perfection
    Clark, John P.H., & Dorward, Rosemary, trs. Mahwah, Paulist
    Press (CWS), n.d.
        A superb example of medieval mystical prose. It shows the
        14th-Century doctrine on the pursuit of spiritual salvation
        through religious contemplation.

BONAVENTURE (1217–1274)
- The Soul's Journey into God/ The Tree of Life/ The Life of St.
  Francis
    Cousins, Ewert, tr. & intro. New York, Paulist Press, 1978
        1. A speculative mystical treatise on the vision of St.
           Francis of the six-winged seraph
        2. A meditation on the life of Christ

3.   The official biography of the founder of the
     Franciscan Order, commissioned by the general
     chapter in 1260.

JACOPONE DA TODI (1230–1306)

* Lauds
    Hughes, Serge Elizabeth, trs. New York Paulist Press (CWS),
    1982
    A fresh and readable rendition of this "Spiritual"
    Franciscan monk's poetry.

ANGELA DE FOLIGNO (1248–1309)

* The Complete Works
    New York, Paulist Press, 1993
    Her visions as dictated to her confessor and her
    instructions to her disciples, this is the dramatic story of
    Angela's passionate love affair with the "suffering God-
    man".

DANTE ALIGHIERI (1265–1321)

* The Divine Comedy
    New York, Penguin Classics, 1957
    A classic poem in three volumes of the soul's journey from
    worldly life to the beatific vision.
* La Vita Nuova
    New York, Penguin Classics, 1969
    Intended as a treatise for poets, it consists of a sequence of
    love poems to Beatrice, whom Dante later immortalizes as
    the symbol of Divine Love.

CATHERINE OF SIENA (1347–1380)

* The Dialogue
    Noffke, Suzanne, tr. New York, Paulist Press (CWS), 1980
    The aim of these dialogues was to instruct and to
    encourage those whose spiritual welfare was her concern.
* The Prayers of Catherine of Siena
    Noffke, Suzanne, ed. New York, Paulist Press, 1983
    Born of her intimate & loving communion with God, they
    represent a valuable model of authentic prayer.

CATHERINE OF GENOA (1447–1510)

* Purgation and Purgatory: The Spiritual Dialogue
    Hughes, Serge, tr. Mahwah, Paulist Press (CWS), 1979

These works are the works of her friends recounting of
what they heard from Catherine. They are truly her
teachings on the holy life.

RAMON LULL (1235–1315)

- Book of the Lover and the Beloved
    Peers, E. Allison, tr. New York, Macmillan Co., 1923
    A mystical romance of the dialogue between the Lover
    (Christ) and the Beloved (the human soul).

IGNATIUS OF LOYOLA (1495–1556)

- Spiritual Excercises
    Mottola, Anthony, tr. & Gleason, Robert, intro. Garden City,
    Doubleday, 1964
    A classic in spiritual direction and discernment by the
    founder the Jesuit order.
    Ganss, George, ed. Mahwah, Paulist Press (CWS), n.d.
    This edition contains his autobiography which tells of his
    mystical illuminations and gifts.

TERESA OF AVILA (1515–1582)

- Interior Castle
    Garden City, Doubleday, 1972
    Unequalled spiritual journey through the crystal globe (of
    seven mansions) to the soul's union with God.
- The Way of Perfection
    Garden City, Doubleday. 1964
    The inspiration of Carmelite piety, the instruction
    concerning constant prayer, as taught to her Sisters.
- The Autobiography of St. Teresa
    Peers, E. Allison, tr. Garden City, Doubleday, 1960
    Colloquial & matter of fact in her autobiographical
    narrative, Teresa shows us a clear and wonderful picture
    of herself.

JOHN OF THE CROSS (1542–1591)

- Ascent of Mount Carmel
    Peers, E. Allison, tr. & intro. Garden City, Doubleday, 1958
    Addresses informed Christians who desire union with
    God, concerning various experiences of the spiritual life.
    Describes the active part of the process of purification.
- Dark Night of the Soul
    Peers, E. Allison, tr. & intro. Garden City, Doubleday, 1959

Describes the passive process of purifications to attain union with God.

- Living Flame of Love
     Peers, E. Allison, tr. & intro. Garden City, Doubleday, 1962
          Delves into the Divine mysteries of the soul's response to God's love.

FRANCES DE SALES (1567–1622)

- Introduction to the Devout Life
     Ryan, John K., tr. & ed. Garden City, Doubleday, 1972
          Written for Christians in any walk of life, a handbook of spiritual reflection and inspiration.
- Letters of Spiritual Direction
     Wright, Wendy, tr. & ed. Mahwah, Paulist Press (CWS), 1988
          Treasures of lived Salesian piety which shows a daily attempt of laity, clergy, & religious to live in the spirit of Jesus.
- Treatise on the Love of God
     Ryan, John K., tr. & intro. New York, Doubleday, 1963
          A clear and simple account of the origin and development of supernatural love.

JANE FRANCES DE CHANTAL (1552–1641)

- The Spirit of Saint Jane Frances: As Shown In Her Letters
     Sister of the Visitation, tr. London, Longmans, Green, Co., 1922
          A portrait of this French saint as shown through her correspondence.

PIERRE DE BERULLE (1575–1629)

- Selected Writings
     Thompson, William M., ed. & intro. Mahwah, Paulist Press (CWS), 1989
          A comprehensive introduction to the spirituality of 17th-Century France. A blend of metaphysical speculation with flights of mystical love.

BROTHER LAWRENCE OF THE RESURRECTION (1605–1691)

- Practice of the Presence of God
     Delaney, John J., tr. & intro. New York, Doubleday, 1977
          A short spiritual classic by a lay Carmelite monk, at once homely yet provocative and profound in its discussion of the Christian life.

BLAISE PASCAL (1623–1662)

- Pensees
  - Krailsheimer, A.J., tr. New York, Penguin Classics, 1958
    - Showing the nature of the Augustinian influence of the time, here he explores the nature of religious truth and of humanity.
- The Provincial Letters
  - Krailsheimer, A.J., tr. New York, Penguin Classics, 1947
    - Nineteen letters written as a blistering satire of the irresponsibility of the Jesuit order in France.

FRANÇOIS FÉNELON (1651–1715)

- Letters to Men
  - London, Rivingtons, 1880
    - Shows his keen ability to direct souls in the way of Christian perfection.
- Letters to Women
  - London, Rivingtons, 1883
    - Archbishop Fénelon's spiritual guidance to women of the aristocracy of 17th-Century France.
- Christian Perfection
  - Stillman, Mildred W., tr. New York, Harper & Brothers, 1947
    - A book of devotion which reveals the spiritual wisdom, insights, and convictions of this man.

JEAN PIERRE DE CAUSSADE (1675–1751)

- Abandonment to Divine Providence
  - Beevers, John, tr. Garden City, Doubleday, 1975
    - Outlines the means to attain holiness through a simple surrender to God in all things. Here are revealed ways to conquer self-love and pride and points the way for experiencing each moment as a sacrament.
- On Prayer
  - Thorold, Algar, tr. Templegate, Springfield, 1960
    - Spiritual instructions on the various stages of prayer, according to the doctrine of Bossuet, Bishop of Meaux, France. It outlines a method of attaining that prayer of the simple presence of God.

LANCELOT ANDREWES (1555–1626)

- Private Devotions of Lancelot Andrewes
  - Martin, Hugh, ed. London, SMC Press, 1957

A book of prayers and devotions compiled from Greek and Hebrew texts which vividly portray his spirituality.

- Sermons
    Story, G.M., sel., ed. & intro. Oxford, Clarendon, 1967
    Shows the spirit of Anglican piety at its best.

JOHN DONNE (1571–1631)

- Poems of John Donne
    Shawcross, John T., ed. & intro. Garden City, Anchor Books, 1967
    Poetry which shows both the devotional and the practical side of Donne.
- Devotions upon Emergent Occasions
    Raspa, Anthony, ed. & comment. Montreal, McGill-Queen's Univ. Press, 1975
    Meditations and prayers of Donne.

GEORGE HERBERT (1593–1633)

- The English Poems of George Herbert
    Patrides, C.A., ed. London, Rowman and Littlefield, 1975
    Some of Herbert's best-known and best-loved works, which reveal his spirituality.
- The Country Parson & The Temple
    Wall, John N., ed. New York, Paulist Press (CWS), 1983
    Outlines a sober & well balanced ideal of the English clergyman, in simple and homely language.

JEREMY TAYLOR (1613–1667)

- The Rule and Exercises of Holy Living
    Harper & Row, New York, 1970
    A comprehensive and uncompromising aid for those who desire to lead the Christian life seriously. A substantial treatise, yet easily digestable.
- The Rule and Exercises of Holy Dying
    The World Publ., Cleveland, 1952
    A manual for those who desire a holy preparation for death, and for those who minister to the sick and dying.

THOMAS TRAHERNE (1636–1674)

- Centuries of Meditations
    Morehouse Publishing, Wilton, 1986
    A book devoted to expressing the joy of living. It is a mystical happiness because God is present in His creation and intimately involved in it.

WILLIAM LAW (1686–1761)

- A Serious Call to a Devout & Holy Life/ Spirit of Love
    Sanwood, Paul G., ed. New York, Paulist Press (CWS), 1978
        A simple yet vigorous teaching on the demands of
        Christian perfection. Likened to Francis de Sales'
        Introduction to the Devout Life
- Freedom From a Self-Centered Life
    Murray, Andrew, ed. Minneapolis, Dimension Books, 1977
        Discusses the means of achieving the Christian goal of
        being ruled by the Spirit of Love.

JOHN HENRY NEWMAN (1801–1890)

- Parochial and Plain Sermons
    Harrison, Ignatius Press, 1991
        Topics central to salvation and the Christian life.
- Prayers, Verses & Devotions
    Harrison, Ignatius Press, 1991
        Most profound of his devotional writings; also meditations
        on the Litany of Loreto and the Stations of the Cross.

EDWARD BOUVERIE PUSEY (1800–1882)

- An Eirenicon
    New York, D. Appleton & Co., 1866
        An "apology" in letter form to another founder of the
        Oxford Movement, John Keble. This sets forth Pusey's
        beliefs about the Faith and the Church that faith is based
        on.

JOHN MASON NEALE (1818–1866)

- Collected Sermons (several volumes)
    London, Joseph Masters, 1873
        Sermons preached in the Sackville College Chapel and in
        the convent of St. Margaret in East Grinsted, England.
- Commentary on the Psalms
    with Rev. R.F. Littledale, London, Joseph Masters & Co., 1874
        Exegetical and yet devotional commentary.

CHARLES CHAPMAN GRAFTON (1830–1912)

- A Journey Godward
    New York, Longmans, Green & Co., 1914
        The autobiography of this Episcopal bishop, who was one
        of the prime movers of the catholic revival in America at
        the turn of the 20th Century.

HENRI HUVELIN (1838–1910)

- Some Seventeenth Century Spiritual Guides
  Leonard, Joseph, tr. London, Burns, Oates & Washbourne
  Ltd., 1927
  > Adresses given to young people about the spiritual
  > masters of 17th-Century France.
- The Love of Our Lord
  Thorold, Algar, tr. London, Burns. Oates, & Washbourne Ltd.,
  1930
  > Reflections on the love of God as manifested particularly
  > in the Holy Eucharist.
- Adresses to Women
  Smith-Masters, Margaret, tr. London, Burns, Oates &
  Washbourne Ltd., 1936
  > Sponateous teachings of this simple, holy French priest, to
  > the women of his parish.

CHARLES DE FOUCAULD (1858–1916)

- Hope in the Gospels
  Marans, Nelly, tr. Brooklyn, New City, 1990
  > Meditations on the virtue of hope.
- Letters from the Desert
  Lucas, Barbara tr. London, Burns & Oates Ltd., 1977
  > Letters from his period of testing and trial of the ascetic life.

BARON FRIEDRICH VON HÜGEL (1852–1925)

- Letters From Baron von Hügel to a Niece
  Greene, Gwendolyn, ed. & intro. London, J.M. Dent & Sons
  Ltd., 1950
  > The spiritual direction of this great laytheologian to his
  > young niece. Valuable for those who prefer a more
  > personal touch.
- Mystical Element of Religion As Studied in Catherine of Genoa
  & Her Friends
  London, J.M. Dent & Sons, 1923
  > Combines the philosophy of religion with psychology,
  > history and textual criticism and their implications for the
  > spiritual life.
- Spiritual Counsel & Letters
  Steere, Douglas V., ed. & intro. New York, Harper & Row, 1964
  > Contains letters to his niece, as well as others to whom he
  > imparted his spiritual wisdom.

EVELYN UNDERHILL (1875–1941)

- Essentials of Mysticism
    New York, E.P. Dutton & Co., 1960
        An intensive discussion of special aspects of the theory
        and practice of mysticism.
- Mysticism
    New York. Doubleday, 1990
        A classic work in the scholarly approach to the mystic
        tradition. The study of the nature and development of
        man's spiritual consciousness.
- The Mystic Way
    Canal Winchester (OH), Ariel Press, 1991
        A psychological study in Christian origins, the object of
        which is to trace out that type of life which is called
        mystical.
- Practical Mysticism
    Canal Winchester (OH), Ariel Press, 1986
        To teach that the spiritual life is not a special calling but is
        part of the normal Christian life.
- School of Charity: Meditations on the Christian Creed
    Wilton, Morehouse, 1990
        Suggests to the modern Christian how close the
        connection is between the great doctrines of Christianity
        and the inner life.
- Spiritual Life
    Wilton, Morehouse, 1984
        The object of this book is to present some of the great
        truths concerning the spiritual life in simple language, as
        the heart of all real religion.
- Worship
    New York, Crossroad, 1982
        Her most comprehensive work on the phenomenon of
        worship and ritual within the Christian religion.

THÉRÈSE OF LISIEUX (1873–1897)

- The Story of a Soul
    Clarke, John OCD, tr. Washington, DC, ICS Publications, 1976
        Autobiography of a young Carmelite whose desire for God
        and for life was total.

ELIZABETH OF THE TRINITY (1880–1906)

- The Complete Works (vol. 1)
    ICS Publications, Washington, 1989

Letters, poems and reflections by this young Carmelite.
Follows in the footsteps of Little Thérèse of Lisieux.

PIERRE TEILHARD DE CHARDIN (1881–1955)
- The Divine Mileau
    New York, Harper Collins, 1975
        A meditation on the cooperation between our free will
        and God's. Shows that man's spiritual life can become a
        participation in the destiny of the universe.
- Hymn of the Universe
    New York, HarperCollins, 1976
        An intimate communication of Chardin's experience of
        God, intensely mystical and in the form of prose poems.
- Phenomenon of Man
    New York, HarperCollins, 1974
        A profound vision of humanity's role in the cosmic drama.

EDITH STEIN (1891–1942)
- Self Portrait in Letters
    ICS Publications, Washington, 1992
        Blessed Teresa Benedicta, OCD, becomes known to the
        English-speaking world through her letters to loved ones
        from World War I until her death at the hands of the Nazis
        in World War II.
- Life in a Jewish Family
    ICS Publications, Washington, 1987
        This autobiographical account tells of a young Jewish
        woman, who became a Carmelite nun during the era of the
        Holocaust.

C.S. LEWIS (1898–1963)
- The Narnia Chronicles (7 vol.)
    New York, Macmillan Child Group, 1970
        A set of children's books which sets the theology of
        Christianity in a mythical land of Narnia, with the Christ
        figure as Aslan, a lion.
- Mere Christianity
    New York, Macmillan, 1986
        Spells out what Lewis see as the essentials of the Christian
        life.
- Screwtape Letters
    New York, Macmillan, 1982

Fictional letters of a devil and his nephew which discuss the weaknesses of a man who is attempting to live the Christian life, and their attempts to thwart his attempt.

- Great Divorce
    New York, Macmillan, 1978
    The fantasy of taking a bus ride from Hell to the outskirts of Heaven.

DIETRICH BONHOEFFER (1906–1945)

- Cost of Discipleship
    New York, Macmillan, 1963; Magnolia, Peter Smith, 1983
    Explains each sentence of the Sermon on the Mount and exactly what it means to be a disciple in modern times.
- Letters and Papers from Prison
    New York, Macmillan, 1972
    Shows Bonhoeffer's theological reflections as well as the very personal sphere of his life during his imprisonment at the hands of the Nazis in World War II.

SIMONE WEIL (1909–1943)

- Waiting on God
    New York, HarperCollins, 1973
    Consists of letters to her friend & spiritual mentor Fr. Perin OP, as well as essays and reflections on human suffering and the love of God.

THOMAS MERTON (1915–1968)

- Assent to Truth
    San Diego, HBJ, 1981
    The function of this book is to define the nature of the contemplative experience by sketching the out the mystical life in general and looking at some mystics in particular.
- Life and Holiness
    New York, Doubleday, 1969
    A simple, powerful and beautiful exposition of the principles of the spiritual life.
- New Seeds of Contemplation
    New York, New Directions, 1972
    Thoughts and meditations which seek to awaken the dormant inner depths of the spirit.
- No Man is an Island
    San Diego, Harcourt Brace Javonovich, 1978

Develops the theme that through God's love no one is
entirely alone.
* Wisdom of the Desert
New York, New Directions, 1970
Sayings of the Desert Fathers; translated by Merton,
portraying a charming informality and spontaneity of the
originals.

MOTHER TERESA OF CALCUTTA (1910–1997)
* A Gift for God: Prayers & Meditations
San Francisco, Harper, 1975
The only book actually written by Mother Teresa, allows
the reader a glimpse into the heart of this remarkable
woman.
* Love: A Fruit Always in Season: Daily Meditations from the
Words of Mother Teresa of Calcutta
Harrison, Ignatius Press, 1987
Meditations arranged to coincide with the seasons of the
liturgical year.
* One Heart Full of Love
Gonzalez-Balado, Jose Luis, ed. Ann Arbor, Servant Books,
1984
Gathers together stirring addresses and interviews given
by Mother Teresa.

HENRI J.M. NOUWEN (1932–1996)
* Compassion: A Reflection on the Christian Life
authored with McNeill, Donald & Morrison, Douglas. New
York, Doubleday, 1982
A challenging call to make God's compassion manifest
through the disciplines of prayer and action.
* Genesee Diary: Report from a Trappist Monastery
New York, Doubleday, 1981
Reflections on a seven-month stay in the Cistercian
monastery of Genesee, in New York.
* Gracias!
San Francisco, Harper, 1990
A Latin American journal which explores faith and justice
in a poor, volatile, yet spiritually rich culture.
* Lifesigns: Intimacy, Fecundity, & Ecstasy in Christian
Perspective
New York, Doubleday, 1989

Examines three diverse and vital aspects of Christian
spirituality.
- Making All Things New
    San Francisco, Harper, 1981
        An invitation to life in the Spirit. It examines what it
        means to live a spiritual life.
- Road to Daybreak: A Spiritual Journey
    New York, Doubleday. 1988
        A day-by-day account of Nouwen's first year at L'Arche, a
        community for handicap persons in France.
- Way of the Heart: Desert Spirituality & Contemplative Ministry
    San Francisco, Harper, 1985
        Teaching spiritual survival through finding our home in
        solitude, silence, and prayer

RICHARD J. FOSTER (b. 1942)

- Celebration of Discipline
    San Francisco, Harper & Row, 1978
        Outlines the history and potential of the spiritual
        disciplines of meditation, prayer, fasting, study, simplicity,
        solitude, submission, service, confession, worship,
        guidance, and celebration and shows how to practice
        them in daily life.
- Freedom of Simplicity
    San Francisco, Harper & Row, 1981
        Offers guidelines for the individual, corporate, and
        ecclesiastical disciplines of simplicity in daily life.

MATTHEW FOX (b. 1940)

- Original Blessing
    Santa Fe, Bear & Co., 1983
        A primer in creation-centered spirituality. Here Fox
        reminds us that before there was original sin, there was
        the original blessing.
- Western Spirituality: Historical Roots, Ecumenical Roots
    Santa Fe, Bear & Co., 1981
        An anthology of essays concerning spiritual traditions,
        primarily Western, but also includes Russian, Hindu and
        Native American spiritualities.

MADELEINE L'ENGLE (1918–2007)

- A Wrinkle in Time
    New York, Dell Publishing, 1962

First of a trilogy of Christian mystical fantasy for children. These stories involve a family whose parents are scientists and whose children are inquisitive, intuitive, and open to life beyond the physical senses.

- A Wind in the Door
  New York, Dell Publishing, 1973
  Second in the trilogy of Christian mystical fantasy.
- A Swiftly Tilting Planet
  New York, Dell Publishing, 1978
  Third in the trilogy of Christian mystical fantasy

WILLIAM JOHNSTON, S.J. (1925–2010)

- Christian Mysticism Today
  San Francisco, Harper, 1984
  An illuminating portrait of mystical prayer, it redefines mysticism in light of the 20th Century's most pressing issues.
- Mysticism of the Cloud of Unknowing
  California, Source Books, 1987
  This work places the author of *The Cloud* in his historical context and offers a key to the timeless classic of medieval mysticism.
- The Wounded Stag (older title: Silent Music)
  San Francisco, Harper, 1986
  About meditation and mysticism. which he considers the deepest form of meditation.
- Inner Eyes of Love
  San Francisco, Harper, 1978
  Offers a contemporary theology of mysticism that locates it at the very center of authentic religious experience, and a practical guide for meditation.

GEORGE A. MALONEY, S.J. (1924–2005)

- Singers of a New Song
  Notre Dame, Ave Maria Press, 1985
  A mystical interpretation of the Song of Songs in which he blends the scripture with church teaching about God's love as revealed in Jesus.
- The Everlasting Now
  Notre Dame, Ave Maria Press, 1980
  Meditations on the mysteries of life and death as they touch us in our daily choices.

WILLIAM McNAMARA, OCD (b. 1926)

- Christian Mysticism: The Art of the Inner Way
  Rockport, Element Inc., 1981
  > This book attempts to answer the essential questions about mysticism, contemplation, and the mystical experience.
- Mystical Passion: The Art of Christian Loving
  Rockport, Element Inc., 1977
  > The author shows how authentic passion has its roots in the passion of God and explores the spirituality of Christian love.

BASIL PENNINGTON, O.S.C.O. (1931–2005)

- Call to the Center: The Gospel's Invitation to Deeper Prayer
  New York, Doubleday, 1990
  > This devotional book contains 30 excerpts from Matthew's Gospel with corresponding meditational essays that invite prayerful reflection.
- Centering Prayer: Renewing an Ancient Christian Prayer Form
  New York, Doubleday, 1982
  > Combines the best of Eastern Christian spiritual exercises (like the Jesus Prayer) with a spirituality for today's world.
- Daily We Touch Him: Practical Religious Experiences
  New York, Doubleday, 1990
  > Offers a few practical exercises to help us encounter God in the intimacy of prayer and the practice of God's presence.

APPENDIX C
Bibliography

ALLCHIN, A.M. *Participation in God*. Wilton, Morehouse Barlow, 1988

ANCELET-HUSTACHE, Jeanne. *Meister Eckart and the Rhineland Mystics*. New York, Harper and Row, Torch Books, n.d.

BAILEY, Raymond. *Thomas Merton on Mysticism*. Garden City, Doubleday and Co., 1974

BAINTON, Roland H. *Women of the Reformation in France and England*. Boston, Beacon Press, 1975

BEDOUELLE, Guy, O.P. *Saint Dominic: The Grace of the Word*. San Francisco, Ignatius Press, 1987

BERRIGAN, Daniel. *The Disciple of the Mountain: Dante's* Purgatorio *in a Nuclear World*. New York, Seabury Press, 1979

BLAKNEY, Raymond B. *Meister Eckart*. New York, Harper and Row, 1941

BOUYER, Louis, *Women Mystics*. San Francisco, Ignatius Press, 1993

BREMOND, Henri. *A Literary History of Religious Thought in France* (3 vol.). New York, Macmillan Co., 1930

BURROWS, Ruth. *Ascent to Love: The Spiritual Teaching of St. John of the Cross*. Garden City, Dimension Books, 1987

BURROWS, Ruth. *Interior Castle Explored: St. Teresa's Teaching on the Life of Deep Union With God*. New York, Sheed & Ward, 1981

CABAUD, Jacques. *Simone Weil: A Fellowship in Love*. New York, Channel Press, 1964

CAPPS, Walter H. & WRIGHT, Wendy M. *Silent Fire: An Invitation to Western Mysticism*. New York, Harper & Row, 1978

CHAUCHARD, Paul. *Tielhard de Chardin on Love and Suffering*. Mahwah, Paulist Press, 1966

CLARK, Anne L. *Elisabeth of Schonau: A Twelfth Century Visionary*. Philadelphia, University of Pennsylvania Press, 1992

CLISSOLD, Stephen. *The Wisdom of the Spanish Mystics*. Fair Oaks (CA), A New Directions Book, 1977

COLLEDGE, Eric. *Medieval Mystics of England*. New York, Charles Scribner's Sons, 1961

COLLIS, Louise. *Memoirs of a Medieval Woman: The Life and Times of Margery Kempe*. New York, Harper and Row, 1964

COPLESTON, Frederick. *A History of Philosophy* (vol. 2). New York, Image Books, 1962
CRAGG, Gerald R. *The Church in the Age of Reason*. New York, Penguin Books, 1976

CROPPER, Margaret. *Flame Touches Flame*. New York, Longmans, Green and Co., 1951

CUNNIGHAM, Lawrence S. *Thomas Merton and the Monastic Vision*. Liguori (MO), Triumph Books, 1999

DANIEL-ROPS, Henri. *The Protestant Reformation* (vol. 1). New York, Image Books, 1963

DAVIDSON, Hugh M. *The Origins of Certainty: Means and Meaning in Pascal's* Pensees. Chicago, University of Chicago Press, 1979

DE LA VIERGE, R.P. Victor. *Spiritual Realism of Saint Thérèse of Lisieux*. Milwaukee, Bruce Publishing Co., 1961

DE WAAL, Esther. *Seeking God: The Way of St. Benedict*. Collegeville, Liturgical Press, 1984

DORGAN, Margaret. "Prayer for Wandering Minds: Guidance from St. Teresa of Avila". *Spiritual Life*, Vol. 24, No. 2, Summer 1988

DOWELL, Graham. *Enjoying the World: The Rediscovery of Thomas Traherne*. Harrisburg, Morehouse Publishing, 1990

DREYER, Elizabeth. *Passionate Women:vTwo Medieval Mystics*. Mahwah, Paulist Press, 1989

DUBAY, Thomas. *Fire Within*. San Francisco, Ignatius Press, 1989

DUPRE, Louis & WISEMAN, James A. *Light from Light: An Anthology of Christian Mysticism*. Mahwah, Paulist Press, 1988

EGAN, Harvey D. *Christian Mysticism: The Future of a Tradition*. Santa Fe, Pueblo Publishing Co., 1984

EPINEY-BURGARD, Georgette & ZUM-BRUNN, Emilie. *Women Mystics in Medieval Europe*. New York, Paragon House, 1989

EWER, Mary Anita. *A Survey of Mystical Symbolism*. London, S.P.C.K., 1933

FOX, Matthew. *Western Spirituality: Historical Roots, Ecumenical Routes*. Notre Dame, Fides/Claretian, 1979

FREMANTLE, Anne. *A Treasury of Early Christianity*. New York, The New American Library, 1953

FURLONG, Monica. *Merton: A Biography*. San Francisco, Harper & Row, 1980

GANNON, Thomas M. & TRAUB, George W. *The Desert and the City*. New York, The Macmillan Co., New York, 1969

GATTA, Julia. *Three Spiritual Directors for Our Time*. Cambridge, Cowley Press, 1986

GREEN, Deirdre. *Gold in the Crucible: Teresa of Avila*. Longmead, London, Element Books, 1989

GUTHRIE, Barbara A. "The Spiritual Quest and Health and C.S. Lewis". Doctoral Dissertation for University of North Texas, Denton (TX), 1988

HARDY, Richard P. *Search for Nothing: The Life of John of the Cross*. New York, Crossroad Publications, 1982

HART, Br. Patrick. *Thomas Merton/Monk: A Monastic Tribute*. New York, Sheed & Ward, 1874

HEALEY, Charles J. *Modern Spiritual Writers: Their Legacies of Prayer*. Canfield, Alba House, 1989

HERBSTRITH, Waltraud. *Edith Stein: A Biography*. San Francisco, Harper & Row, 1983

HERRERA, Robert. *Lamps of Fire: Studies in Christian Mysticism*. Petersham (MA), St. Bede's Publications, 1986

HIGGINS, John J. *Merton's Theology of Prayer*. Spencer (MA), Cistercian Publications, 1971

HIGGINS, Michael. **The Unquiet Monk*. Maryknoll (NY), Orbis Books, 2015

HOLMES, Urban T. *A History of Christian Spirituality*. New York, Seabury Press, 1980

HUIZINGA, J. *The Waning of the Middle Ages*. Garden City, Doubleday & Co., 1956

HUVELIN, Abbe. *Some Spiritual Guides of the Seventeenth Century*. London, Burns, Oates & Washburne Ltd., 1927

JEREMY, Sister Mary, OP. *Scholars and Mystics*. Chicago, Henry Regnery Co., 1962

JOHNSTON, William. *The Mysticism of the Cloud of Unknowing*. New York, Desclee Company, 1967

VAN KAAM, Father Adrian & MUTO, Susan. *Studies in Formative Spirituality: Spiritual Formation and Mysticism* (Vol. V, No. 1). February, 1984

KATZ, Steven T. *Mysticism and Religious Traditions*. New York, Oxford University Press, 1983

KELLEY, C.F. *The Spirit of Love*. (Based on the teachings of St. Frances de Sales). New York, Harper & Brothers, 1951

KEMPE, Margery. *The Book of Margery Kempe*. New York, Penguin Classics, 1985. Translated by B.A. Windeatt with an introduction

KRAILSHEIMER, Alban. *Pascal*. New York, Hill and Wang, 1980

LACHMAN, Barbara. *The Journal of Hildegard of Bingen*. New York, Bell Tower, 1993

LECLERQ, Dom Jean. *The Spirituality of the Middle Ages*. New York, Seabury Press, 1968

MACNUTT, F.B. *Classics of the Inner Life*. New York, Hodder & Stoughton, n.d.

MACQUARRIE, John. *In Search of Deity*. New York, Crossroad Publishing, 1985

MARCEAU, William C. *Optimism in the Works of St. Frances de Sales*. Lewiston, The Edwin Mellon Press, 1989

McCANN, Justin. *Saint Benedict*. New York, Sheed & Ward, 1937

McCARTY, Doran. *Teilhard de Chardin*. Waco, Word Books, 1976

McGINN, Bernard. *Foundations of Mysticism* (vol. 1). New York, Crossroad, 1991

McMANNERS, John. *The French Revolution and the Church*. New York, Harper & Row, 1969

MENZIES, Lucy. *Mirrors of the Holy: Ten Studies in Sanctity*. London, A.R. Mowbray & Co. Ltd., 1928

MILLER, E.C., Jr. *Toward a Fuller Vision: Orthodoxy and the Anglican Experience*. Wilton, Morehouse-Barlow Publishers, 1984

MOLTMANN, Jurgen. *Two Studies in the Theology of Bonhoeffer*. New York, Charles Scribner's Sons, 1967

MOORMAN, John R.H. *A History of the Church in England*. Wilton, Morehouse-Barlow Co., 1963

MUTO, Susan. *John of the Cross for Today: The Ascent*. Notre Dame, Ave Maria Press, 1991

MUTO, Susan & VAN KAAM, Father Adrian. *Studies in Formative Spirituality: Spiritual Formation and Mysticism* (Vol. V, No. 1). February, 1984

NICHOLS, John A. *Distant Echoes: Medieval Religious Women.* Kalamazoo, Cistercian Publications, 1984

NOUWEN, Henri J.M. *Pray to Live: Thomas Merton, Contemplative Critic.* Notre Dame, Fides, 1972

NOUWEN, Henri J.M. *Thomas Merton: Contemplative Critic.* Liguori (MO), Triumph Books, 1991

PAYNE, Robert. *The Holy Fire.* Crestwood (NY), St. Vladimir's Seminary Library, 1980

PEERS, E. Allison. *Behind That Wall: An Introduction to Some Classics of the Interior Life.* New York, Morehouse-Gorham Co., 1948

PEERS, E. Allison. *The Mystics of Spain.* London, George Allen & Unwin Ltd., 1951

PEERS, E. Allison. *Studies of the Spanish Mystics* (3 vols.). London, S.P.C.K., 1960

PELIKAN, Jaroslav. *Spirit Versus Structure.* San Francisco, Harper & Row, 1968

PETRY, Ray C. *Late Medieval Mysticism.* Louisville (KY), Westminster Press, 1957

PIEPER, Josef. *Scholasticism.* New York, McGraw-Hill Book Co., 1964

POPE, Father Hugh. *The Teaching of St. Augustine on Prayer.* New York, Burns, Oates and Washbourne, Ltd., 1935

POURRAT, Rev. Pierre. *Christian Spirituality* (4 vols.). Westminster (MD), The Newman Press, 1953

POWERS, John D. *Holy & Human: Mystics for Our Time.* Mystic (CT), Twenty Third Publications, 1989

REIDY, Maurice F., S.J. *Bishop Lancelot Andrewes: Jacobean Court Preacher.* Chicago, Loyola University Press, 1955

REX, Walter E. *Pascal's Provincial Letters: An Introduction.* New York, Holmes & Meier Publishers, 1977

ROBERTSON, Edwin. *The Shame and the Sacrifice: Life & Martyrdom of Dietrich Bonhoeffer*. New York, Macmillan Publishing, 1988

SAYERS, Dorothy L. *Introductory Papers on Dante*. New York, Harper & Brothers, 1954

SAYERS, Dorothy L. *Further Papers on Dante*. New York, Harper & Brothers, 1957

SCHMUCKI, Octavian O.F.M. Cap. "The Mysticism of St. Francis in Light of His Writings". *Greyfriars Review*, Vol. 3, No. 3, December 1989 (pp. 241–66)

SEARLE, G.W. *The Counter-Reformation*. London, Rowman & Littlefield, 1973

SICARI, Antonio. "Teresa of Avila: Mystical Experience in Defense of Dogma". *Communio: International Catholic Review*, Spring, 1989

SITWELL, Gerard, O.S.B. *Spiritual Writers of the Middle Ages*. Hawthorn Books, 1961

SMITH, Cyprian, O.S.B. *The Way of Paradox: The Spiritual Life as Taught by Meister Eckhart*. London, Darton, Longman, & Todd, 1987

SMITH, Margaret. *An Introduction to Mysticism*. New York, Oxford University Press, 1977

SPITZ, Lewis W. *The Protestant Reformation: 1517–1559*. New York, Harper & Row, 1985

SPRINGSTED, Eric O. *Simone Weil and the Suffering of Love*. Cambridge, Cowley, 1986

SYKES, Stephen (with John Booty). *The Study of Anglicanism*. London, S.P.C.K., 1988

TOLLEMARCHE, Marguerite. *Spanish Mystics*. New York, Kegan, Paul, Trench & Co., 1886

TRAUB, George W. & GANNON, Thomas M. *The Desert and the City*. New York, The Macmillan Co., 1969

UNDERHILL, Evelyn. *Mysticism*. New York, E.P. Dutton & Co., 1961

UNDERHILL, Evelyn. *The Mystics of the Church*. Harrisburg, Morehouse, 1985

VOILLAUME, Rene. *Seeds of the Desert* (2 vols.). Notre Dame, Fides Publishers, Inc., 1966

WAKEFIELD, Gordon. *Westminster Dictionary of Christian Spirituality*. Louisville (KY), Westminster Press, 1983

WELLS, Albert N. *Pascal's Recovery of Man's Whoelness*. Louisville (KY), John Knox Press, 1965

WILLIAMS, Charles. *The Figure of Beatrice: A Study in Dante*. London, Faber & Faber Ltd., 1953

WISEMAN, James A. & DUPRE, Louis. *Light from Light: An Anthology of Christian Mysticism*. Mahwah, Paulist Press, 1988

WRIGHT, A.D. *The Counter-Reformation*. New York, St. Martin's Press, 1982

WRIGHT, Wendy M. *Bond of Perfection: Jeanne de Chantal and Francis de Sales*. New York, Paulist Press, 1985

WRIGHT, Wendy M. & CAPPS, Walter H. *Silent Fire: An Invitation to Western Mysticism*. New York, Harper & Row, 1978

WYON, Olive. *Desire for God: A Study of Three Spiritual Classics*. London, Fontana Books, 1966

ZUM-BRUNN, Emilie & EPINEY-BURGARD, Georgette. *Women Mystics in Medieval Europe*. New York, Paragon House, 1989

Appendix D
Glossary of Terms Concerning Mysticism

Affective—mystical knowing through the emotions (heart).

Anchorite/ess—from the Greek "to withdraw"; a person who lives a hermit type of lifestyle, usually walled up next to a church or place of pilgrimage.

Anchorhold—the residence of an Anchorite or Anchoress.

Apatheia—without passion; passive acceptance, calming of disoriented passions.

Apophatic—mysticism which is empty or void of images; knowing by not knowing.

Asceticism—the renunciation of social life and its comforts for the sake of religious devotion.

Cenobitic—pertaining to the communal, monastic lifestyle.

Contemplation—the art of keeping the eye or mind fixed upon some object or subject; focused on a single point.

Ecstasy—a state in which the mind is freed from or raised above the body or bodily senses.

Eremitic—pertaining to the hermit, or solitary lifestyle rather than the communal.

Kataphatic—mysticism which is full of images and associative; knowing by means of allegory, images, or analogies.

Meditation—turning a thought over in the mind; looking at a matter from different perspectives; active thinking upon a religious matter.

Quietism—a doctrine which developed in the 18th Century, particularly in France, that spiritual exaltation is attained by withdrawing the soul from outward activities; waiting upon the Holy Spirit to initiate the relationship.

Rationalism—reliance on reason alone (very much pursued in the Scholastic period as well as during the Enlightenment); rejects the authority of supernatural revelation.

Speculative—mystical knowing through the intellectual process.

Index

Alphabetical by first name with page and Appx B number (if any)

39418120R00168

Made in the USA
Middletown, DE
14 January 2017